Unit Operations

Unit Operations

An Approach to Videogame Criticism

Ian Bogost

The MIT Press
Cambridge, Massachusetts
London, England

MIT Press books may be purchased at special quantity discounts for business or sales
promotional use. For information, please email special_sales@mitpress.mit.edu or write
to Special Sales Department, The MIT Press, 55 Hayward Street, Cambridge, MA
02142.

This book was set in Bell Gothic and Garamond 3 by Graphic Composition, Inc., Athens,
Georgia, and was printed and bound in the United States of America.

Library of Congress Cataloging-in-Publication Data

Bogost, Ian.
Unit operations : an approach to videogame criticism / Ian Bogost.
    p.   cm.
Includes bibliographical references and index.
ISBN 0-262-02599-X (hc : alk. paper)
1. Computer games—Design. 2. Computer games—Philosophy. 3. Computer games—
Sociological aspects. I. Title.
QA76.76.C672B65   2006
794.8—dc22

                                                                2005056105

10 9 8 7 6 5 4 3 2 1

Contents

IV From Design to Configuration

Acknowledgments

This book represents the result of a long process of reconciliation of two areas of equal interest and expertise: literary theory and philosophy on the one hand, software technology and videogame design on the other. Certainly these fields are not immediately obvious bedfellows, and coercing them to abide if not enjoy one another's company has been a ten-year project of both personal and professional development. Many people shared their help and expertise in the writing of this book.

First of all, I owe a great debt to those critics and thinkers who guided and influenced my training as a comparatist: Peter Starr, Peggy Kamuf, Vincent Farenga, Dallas Willard, James Kincaid, Greg Thalmann, Jonathan Culler, and Samuel Weber. I am grateful to Emily Apter for her help during the conceptual stages of this project, and especially for her support and encouragement in helping me see its viability and importance. And I am especially indebted to Kenneth Reinhard, Katherine Hayles, Ross Shideler, and Kathleen Komar for their unwavering support and guidance.

Second, I owe an equal debt to my professional mentors and colleagues, with whom I shared many long nights and weekends building software. I am especially grateful to Ian McCarthy and Paul Fairchild for their rare and unique ability to discuss both philosophy and business. I am likewise thankful to the videogame development community, and especially the participants in the annual Game Developers Conference (GDC). They earn neither money nor fame for sharing their insights in that venue, and they do it nevertheless.

Third, I want to thank my peers in the international game studies community. I'm particularly grateful to my colleagues at The Georgia Institute of

Technology for their support and feedback during the completion of this project. Particular thanks go to Ken Knoespel, Janet Murray, Michael Mateas, and Michael Nitsche for their ongoing and collegial support. Portions of the argument presented in chapter 12 appeared in the *International Digital Media and Arts Association Journal* 2:1, in an article coauthored with the latter three. A different version of chapter 4 appeared in *Games & Culture* 1:1. An earlier version of the first half of chapter 5 appeared in *Doom: Giocare in prima persona;* I thank Matteo Bittani for his feedback on that and other portions of this book. Likewise I thank my friend and collaborator Gonzalo Frasca, whose ongoing feedback remains invaluable, and Noah Wardrip-Fruin for his invaluable feedback.

Finally, and most of all, I thank my family for supporting this project and all the others that led me to it. My parents David and Sheila offered both emotional and material support as well as a bottomless measure of eagerness. My son Tristan and my daughter Flannery have provided inspiration and much-needed perspective, especially during the last year of this project. Most of all, my wife Abbey patiently endured my many cycles of overzealous work, and her support was and remains invaluable and wholly incalculable. I dedicate this book to her.

Introduction

This book is an attempt to explore the nature of relationships between computation, literature, and philosophy. In it I will argue that similar principles underlie both contemporary literary analysis and computation. I will use this commonality to analyze a field of discursive production that has yet to find authoritative place in either world—videogames. My analysis will oscillate between theoretical and literary registers, leveraging a general literary-technology theory to motivate an analysis of particular videogames. This technique is not only applicable to software in general and videogames in particular, but also is useful in the analysis of traditional expressive artifacts such as poetry, literature, cinema, and art. My approach throughout this book is thus fundamentally a comparative one, and I have included examples from all of these fields as evidence for the usefulness and importance of a comparative procedural criticism. In particular, I will suggest that any medium—poetic, literary, cinematic, computational—can be read as a configurative system, an arrangement of discrete, interlocking units of expressive meaning. I call these general instances of procedural expression *unit operations*.

A practical marriage of literary theory and computation would not only give each field proper respect and attention from its counterpart, but also create a useful framework for the interrogation of cultural artifacts that straddle these fields. The humanists who define intellectual approaches to such texts must get serious about technology. Likewise, technologists ought to understand the precedents in critical theory, philosophy, and literature that trace, accompany, and inform the development of software technology. This book provides a toolkit for both domains to bridge the chasm between them, and to serve as a model for future collaborative encounters, both analytical and practical.

Videogames rely on a foundation in the industrial arts. The hardware and software tools that underwrite the production of these and other works of digital art and software remain rooted in the moil of the marketplace. While most of the advances in information technology, from ENIAC to the Internet, were sparked in one way or another by government interests (and most frequently by the military), innumerable technical advances have taken place in the past forty years at the hands of industry.

The two advances of greatest interest to the present work are the introduction and adoption of *object technology* (OT) in software engineering, and the advent of complex adaptive systems theory in the natural, information, and computer sciences. OT provides a framework for developers to create units of programmatic meaning that can be reused in different ways and for different applications without requiring recompilation of the source elements. OT was first popularized as the SmallTalk programming language by Alan Kay at Xerox PARC's Learning Research Group some thirty-five years ago.[1] Since then, the entire software industry has adopted its core principles. Complex network theory proponents like Stephen Wolfram argue that the kinds of object- and relational-effects OT fabricates for software are built into natural systems like human society and the brain. These approaches to a wide variety of social and biological systems underscore the configurative aspects of a whole range of human processes.

I can think of few other fields with more varied demands on the qualifications of their practitioners than the humanities and informatics. And when I speak of these two fields, I do not mean just their seats of origin in the university. Rather, I reflect on these fields in all their varieties both inside and outside the academy. The humanities include film and theater, literature and art, music and dance, philosophy and criticism. Informatics touches computer science, biology and medicine, chemistry and ecology, cognitive science and psychology.

Each of these fields are overwhelmingly esoteric. They require a considerable amount of abstruse knowledge and experience to practice effectively. However, the humanities and informatics are afflicted not only by intellectual obscurity but also by professional mystery, perhaps because they are so deeply rooted in our daily lives. Anyone who has ever tried to write a screenplay or a Windows application can bear witness to how esotericism haunts the production of works in either field. Likewise, anyone who has not grown up playing videogames or spent time in an academic department of the humanities can attest to the equal difficulty of orienting oneself in such specialized contexts.

Part of this difficulty has to do with the fields' propensity for jargon. Jonathan Culler, for example, says of literary theory: "A theory . . . can't be obvious."[2] For better or worse, this axiom has led to a wealth of highly specified, often obfuscated ways of talking about, creating, and critiquing human activity and production. In this way, the humanities are more like the industrial applications of informatics than they might think—or even wish—to be. Jargon and obfuscation is a way of laying groundwork for novel production. This was especially true in the twentieth century, which witnessed the transition from industrial capital to intellectual capital. Apart from aesthetes and professors, few readers of literature, viewers of film, or lovers of art could (or would want to) explain the aesthetic unity of New Criticism, or how the concepts of *aporia* or *pharmakon* help Deconstruction expose conflicting textual forces. At the same time, few Microsoft Word users could (or would want to) explain how the principles of polymorphism and inheritance make it possible for them to draw a chart with real-time data in a word processing document. If the move from real to intellectual property is what fueled the burgeoning technology industry of the past thirty years, then jargon is the raw material that helped industry forge that intellectual property.

The move from real property in the industrial era to intellectual property in the information era has much in common with the move from master–disciple institutionalized pedagogy to distributed pedagogy. Contemporary critical theory is much more like intellectual property, served with a zero-charge license for the production of criticism, than it is like doctrine handed down for repetition and mastery. For this reason, creators of literary theory or information technology approach their work with a different lilt; we create cogs rather than machines, bricks rather than houses, tacks rather than furniture. Works of literary criticism or technology are potential user guides, possible tools to incorporate into one's own critical and material products.

Videogames have their own jargon, as do videogame studies. I recognize that the reader may not be familiar with videogames, from either a popular or a critical perspective. *Ludology* is one way to address this need to explain what games are and how they work. From the Latin *ludus,* meaning game or sport, ludology addresses "games in general, and videogames in particular."[3] Ludological approaches often take up theories of play and the history of games throughout human culture, including the work of Roger Callois, Johan Huizinga, Brian

Sutton-Smith, and Stewart Culin.[4] Some critics have expanded the tenor of ludology, taking it to entail game studies in any sense of the word—including technical and cultural study. For the sake of precision, I will use the term in the narrower sense of the anthropological and especially formal study of games.

Ludology is an important part of videogame studies, and indeed situating videogames within the history of games and play is a worthwhile task. As a general practice, I am suspicious of the zeal with which the burgeoning field has relied on formalist approaches to its object of study, especially its approaches to ontology, typology, and classification. I discuss the state of the field in chapters 4, 5, and 12, but for now I wish primarily to encourage the use of criticism as a tool for understanding how videogames function as cultural artifacts, and how they do so along with other modes of human expression. I am specifically interested in the intersection between criticism and computation; in particular, I am concerned with videogames as a type of configurative or procedural artifact, one built up from units of tightly encapsulated meaning. As such, the present study does not try to situate itself generally within the history of games or the history of play. For this reason, I will avoid referring to ludology or "game studies" in the general sense, except to refer to those specific efforts to study games in the cultural context just described.

Despite my general concern for formalism, I do want to make one ontological clarification that I have found increasingly necessary, especially among humanists: the study of videogames is not necessarily a subfield of game theory, although the two are obliquely related.

Game theory is a field of mathematics used to study decision making in situations of conflict. Examples of game theory can be found in works as old as the Talmud and Sun Tzu's *The Art of War,* but John von Neumann (whose contributions to computational theory I will cover in some detail) is generally agreed to have developed modern game theory in the 1940s. While theorizing the act of bluffing in poker, von Neumann began to recognize the profound implications of game theory for economics. He teamed up with economist Oskar Morgenstern to write *Theory of Games and Economic Behavior.*[5] Initially, game theory concerned itself with the outcomes of strategic problems, like those in poker, war, and economics. Perhaps the best-known subject of game theory is the *prisoner's dilemma,* a game in which two prisoners in isolation decide the fate of the other. According to the logic of the game, both prisoners benefit if they both cooperate, but if only one cooperates, only the other one benefits. The mathematician John Nash, now well known thanks to the 2001 film about his life, added a set of influential approaches to cooperative games, including an approach known as *Nash equilibrium* that predicts outcomes based on each participant's preferences. Thus, the formal origin of game theory is as an analysis of parlor games like poker, and the "games" of game theory refer to abstract strategic structures.

When I speak of videogames, I refer to all the varieties of digital artifacts created and played on arcade machines, personal computers, and home consoles. Although videogames follow in the long tradition of parlor games, table games, pub games, and the many varieties of board games evolving from classic games like chess and Go, their necessary relation ends at this bit of common history. I am not concerned with a hard and fast definition of games in general. Instead, I would rather leave the work of building ontologies and typologies to the many capable theorists who are already undertaking such projects.[6] When I speak of videogames, I am generally content to let the reader understand the term in its "loose and popular sense" (*pace* Chisholm).[7]

About This Book

This book is divided into four parts, corresponding to the areas of focus common to both literary theory and informatics over the last several decades. Each of these parts will introduce a major theme of videogame studies and perform videogame analysis using the tools forged in the theoretical analysis. Within each of these I will discuss a variety of works from philosophy, psychoanalysis, literature, film, software, and videogames.

In the first part, "From Systems to Units," I introduce the concept of *unit operations,* a general conceptual frame for discrete, compressed elements of fungible meaning. I advance a practice of criticism underwritten by unit operations, which I call *unit analysis.* Beginning with classical antiquity and working toward the microcomputer, I discuss the conceptual antecedents for unit operations (Plato, Aristotle, Leibniz, Spinoza, Badiou). I then trace the increasing compression of representation that has occurred in structuralism and poststructuralism, relating this compression to advances in computation such as John von Neumann's conditional control transfer. I examine the ontological strategies of major voices in psychoanalytic theory (Freud, Lacan, Žižek) and media theory (McLuhan, Kittler, Poster) as examples of unit operations that are constantly at risk of collapsing into systems. Then I introduce the history of software architecture, discussing object technology as a practical unit-operational model for business systems. I use the four core principles of object technology to critique many of the popular academic works on digital media (Lev Manovich, George Landow, Jay Bolter) and genetics (Darwin, the Human Genome Project, Dawkins).

In the second part, "Procedural Criticism," I argue for a comparative approach to videogame criticism that identifies and analyzes configurative expression in multiple media. I explore the software and narrative structures of game engines from *Pong* to *Half-Life,* showing how these texts function and interact through unit operations. Then I offer a perspective on current approaches to videogame studies, including a critique of the ongoing conflict between ludology and narratology (Aarseth, Frasca, Jenkins, Murray). I then offer a prolonged, comparative analysis of procedural expression in poetry, film, and games (Baudelaire, Bukowski, Jeunet, Wright).

In the third part, "Procedural Subjectivity," I explore complex adaptive systems and elementary cellular automata as unit operations that transition between the material and representational worlds (Wolfram, Conway, Wright). I then explore the interaction between embedded representation and subjectivity, arguing that meaning in unit-operational systems arises in a place of crisis between configurative representation and subjectivity. Next I survey the relationship between play and the social power of art (Benjamin, Huizinga, Gadamer); I use this perspective to explore criticism's ability to vault videogames toward a status higher than entertainment alone, focusing specifically on an analysis of *Star Wars Galaxies* as a social text. Finally, I discuss aspects of bias in games, offering a revised concept of simulation meant to facilitate future criticism (Turkle, Frasca, Crawford).

In the fourth part, "From Design to Configuration," I put forward a sustained analysis of the field of Schizoanalysis (Deleuze and Guattari) in relation to complex network theory (Erdős, Milgram, Granovetter). Through Alain Badiou's critique of Deleuze I explore the potential and limits of nomadism and complexity as expressions of unit operations. Working from these principles, I perform an extended analysis of freedom in large virtual spaces, including videogames and the modern novel (*Grand Theft Auto 3, The Legend of Zelda, Madame Bovary, Ulysses*). Finally, I offer a vision for the future of videogame criticism and research that models itself after the configurative approach to analysis I advance throughout.

Critical theory, informatics, and videogames are all highly specialized fields, whose practioners when they write seriously tend to do so for one another rather than for outsiders. My intention is to produce an approach to criticism for procedural artifacts like videogames that can be put to use by humanists and technologists alike. To this end, I have tried to offer adequate explanation in addition to analysis when introducing complex topics in either field, without enervating its experts. I am hopeful and sincere about the future of real, tangible collaboration between these fields.

I

From Systems to Units

1

Unit Operations

To unpack the relationships between criticism and computation, I will rely on the notion of *unit operations.* Unit operations are modes of meaning-making that privilege discrete, disconnected actions over deterministic, progressive systems. It is a term loosely amalgamated from several fields, including software technology, physics, and cybernetics, but it could be equally well at home in the world of literary theory. I contend that unit operations represent a shift away from *system operations,* although neither strategy is permanently detached from the other.

In literary theory, unit operations interpret networks of discrete readings; system operations interpret singular literary authority. In software technology, object technology exploits unit operations; structured programming exhibits system operations.[1] In human biology, DNA nucleotide bonding displays unit operations; the Darwinian idea of acquired characteristics illustrates system operations. In effect, the biological sciences offer an especially salient window into the development of unit operations. Over the last two hundred years, biology has revised its conception of natural life from the random wholeness of natural selection (Darwin) to the command-and-control directedness of genomics (Mendel, Crick and Watson) to the periodicity of punctuated equilibrium (Gould) to the complexity of autocatalysis (Kauffman). In the 1980s and 1990s, independent researchers associated widely disparate genetic deformations as "causes" of mental disorders like manic depression and schizophrenia.[2] As scientists learn more about the human genome, they increasingly realize that no skeleton keys exist for human pathology; the nature of life is not so simple as crafting maps of biological processes that organisms follow like molecular tourist guides. Since the successful decoding of the human genome in 2000, biology has entered a "postgenomic" phase, recognizing that knowledge about the genes themselves is not very useful. Instead, scientists seek to understand the functions between individual genes, and how the complex configurations of genetic functionality underlie complex behavior. The shift from genes as holistic regulatory systems to genes as functional actors in a larger intergenetic play marks a move away from system operations and toward unit operations. Unit operations are characteristically succinct, discrete, referential, and dynamic. System operations are characteristically protracted, dependent, sequential, and static. In general, unit operations privilege function over context, instances over longevity.

Yet the relationship between units and systems is not a binary opposition. A world of unit operations hardly means the end of systems. Systems seem to play an even more crucial role now than ever, but they are a new kind of system: the spontaneous and complex result of multitudes rather than singular and absolute holisms. Unit-operational structures might also reaffirm systematicity, even if they deploy the most discrete types of unit functions, a kind of growing pain that relocates holism even as it attempts to expand beyond it. We need the integrity of systems to identify physical, conceptual, or cultural phenomena. But these new types of systems are fluctuating assemblages of unit-operational components rather than overarching regulators. The difference between systems of units and systems as such is that the former derive meaning from the interrelations of their components, whereas the latter regulate meaning for their constituents. Postgenomic biology does not strip genes of all value; rather, it reconfigures the role of genes in the systems of organic life from one of causality to one of contribution. Genetics becomes a process of gene combination, rather than a circumstance of gene existence.

The shift in focus from systems to units can also be understood as a special form of complexity. For the last half century, complexity has moved slowly from the esoteric domain of pure mathematics into every field of the physical and natural sciences. The first form of complexity was conceived in the 1940s, as biologist Ludwig von Bertalanffy's systems theory. Systems theory focuses on the interrelation between parts of a system as the primary basis for understanding that system.[3] It informed the growing area of cybernetics in the middle of the century, and it generally informs areas of complexity theory and self-organization. The last decade has witnessed an explosion of interest in a specific kind of complexity theory, often called *complex systems theory* or *complex network theory*. Complexity is heavily tied to the logic of networks, and the contemporaneous popularity of computer networking and the Internet helped fuel the fire. Complexity is a metascience that understands the operation of stable systems as sets of organized but nonpredictive individuated functions.

To understand the shift and its specific importance for our discussion, it will help to formally define the notions of unit, system, and operation. I have chosen the term *unit* because it does not bear the burden of association with a specific field. In essence, a *unit* is a material element, a thing. It can be constitutive or contingent, like a building block that makes up a system, or it can be autonomous, like a system itself. Often, systems become units in other systems. Software classes are models for computational behavior that instantiate in multiple software frameworks, and software frameworks assemble into multiple software applications. The word *object* is a suitable generic analogue, one used by philosopher Graham Harman in his innovative and related concept of an *object-oriented philosophy.*[4] Harman interprets Heidegger's analysis of *Zuhandenheit,* or readiness-to-hand, as a quality available to entities other than *Dasein.* Shedding the Heideggerian jargon, Harman suggests that all objects in the world, not just humans, are fundamentally referential, or form from relationships that extend beyond their own limits.[5] This is the sort of claim that complex network theorists are exploring in biology, pathology, sociology, and economics.

I am avoiding the term *object* and especially the phrase *object-oriented* because, as I will discuss later, these concepts have special meaning in computer science. Nevertheless, understanding units as objects is useful because it underscores their status as *discrete, material things* in the world. The notion of the object also carries the timbre of a reference or relation to other things, as do grammatical predicates—a verb takes a *direct object,* on which it acts. Harman insists on inanimate objects as necessary subjects for philosophy; while I include in my understanding of units ordinary objects such as the ones Harman favors ("person, hammer, chandelier, insect, or otherwise"), I also claim that units encompass the material manifestations of complex, abstract, or conceptual structures such as jealousy, racial tension, and political advocacy.[6]

When thought of in this way, units not only define people, network routers, genes, and electrical appliances, but also emotions, cultural symbols, business processes, and subjective experiences. Aggregates of these units, such as works of literature, human conditions, anatomies, and economies can properly be called *systems,* but such systems are fundamentally different from the kind units have unseated in the many disciplines noted above. Moreover, such systems can be understood in turn as units themselves. In a famous example, autopoetic system theorists Francisco Valera and Humberto Maturana showed that the neurology of the frog operates as a system that regulates the organism's behavior.[7] But that system also exhibits the properties of units in the form of neurological directives, for example to respond to insects with a flick of the tongue. Within its environment, the frog exchanges information with other systems around it, creating "structural couplings" or feedback loops between the organism and its environment. Taken further, the neurological system itself can act as a unit, as in predator–prey relationships within swamp ecosystems. Sociologist Niklas Luhmann extends the same privilege to social systems, which he claims regulate themselves by "creating and maintaining a difference from their environment, and [using] their boundaries to regulate this difference."[8] In Luhmann's systems theory, communication is the basic unit of social systems.

System operations are thus totalizing structures that seek to explicate a phenomenon, behavior, or state in its entirety. Unlike complex networks, which thrive between order and chaos, systems seek to explain all things via an unalienable order. For centuries, systematicity was the fountainhead of the sciences. Natural selection explained the origin of life based on a few fundamental, universal rules. The Newtonian world operates under a similar system of static behavior. In the social and human sciences, structuralism expresses the most affinity toward systematicity. Mark C. Taylor characterizes the structuralists' obsession with systems as an attempt "to discover reason in history by uncovering forms and patterns that are permanent and universal rather than transient and arbitrary."[9] Stability, linearity, universalism, and permanence characterize system operations.

System operations pay the price of openness for certainty. Accordingly, they often depend on attitudes or values that inform the approaches that created the systems in the first place. More so, systems imply a fundamental or universal order that an agent might "discover," one that exists by natural, universal, or common law. These factors help differentiate totalizing systems from the complex systems in which individual units relate. Complex systems are typically autopoietic or at least arbitrary, and characterized by exploration or interpretation rather than discovery.

Heidegger called the grasp of totalizing systems *Gestell,* or Enframing. Enframing is the modern condition of ordering the potential of structures in the world only to conceal and hold onto their energy for potential future use. Heidegger gave the name *Bestand,* or "standing-reserve," to the output of "everything [that] is ordered to stand by."[10] For example, the availability of cut, packaged poultry undermines our relationship with the tilling of the land for feed and the tending of the flock. Packaged poultry is *Bestand,* or standing reserve. Agriculture becomes a practice of putting things away for later, and the energy of the earth is harnessed such that we might be able to ingest whatever appeals to us, whenever it appeals to us. Heidegger's eco-pastoral perspective notwithstanding, his thinking shows how *Gestell* forces us to see the world only in terms of its quantifiable energy content. Systematic scientific work seeks to quantify, measure, and control the world, drawing it further away from human experience.

The distinction between systems as totalizing structures and systems as assemblages of units is not exactly like Heidegger's distinction between Enframing and "bringing-forth," or poiesis. But his perspective on technology points to the struggle waged between totalizing structures and componentized structures. We cannot escape systems, but we can explore them, or understand ourselves as implicated in their exploration. Heidegger's essay on technology is structured as a haptic analysis, akin to a walk in the woods, by which the stroller happens upon matters of interest. He takes this casual encounter as a paradigm for resistance. Like Heidegger's logic of the promenade, unit operations meander, leaving opportunities open rather than closing them down. Rather than give in to Enframing, Heidegger suggests that the only way out of its dangerous grasp is through identifying possible reconfigurations of its elements, "through our catching sight of what comes to presence in technology, instead of merely staring at the technological."[11] For Heidegger, this is the realm of art, expressive units that reconfigure our relationship with technology in new ways. Unit-operational systems are only systems in the sense that they describe collections of units, structured in relation to one another. However, as Heidegger's suggestion advises, such operational structures must struggle to maintain their openness, to avoid collapsing into totalizing systems.

In systems analysis, an *operation* is a basic process that takes one or more inputs and performs a transformation on it. An operation is the means by which something executes some purposeful action. Mathematical operations offer fundamental examples, especially the function as outlined by Leonhard Euler. Other kinds of operations include decisions, transitions, and state changes. I use the term *operation* very generally, covering not only this traditional understanding but also many more. Brewing tea is an operation. Steering a car to avoid a pedestrian is an operation. Falling in love is an operation. Operations can be mechanical, such as adjusting the position of an airplane flap; they can be tactical, such as sending a regiment of troops into battle; or they can be discursive, such as interviewing for a job. A material and conceptual logic always rules operations. In their general form, the two logics that interest the present study are the logic of units and the logic of systems. In the language of Heidegger, unit operations are creative, whereas system operations are static. In the language of software engineering, unit operations are procedural, whereas system operations are structured.

Complex networks are open, adjudicated by the nonsimple interaction of a variety of constantly changing constituents. The Internet, the brain, human genetics, and social fads are examples of complex, unit-driven networks. The systems that unit operations transition away from are not these complex systems. The movement away from systems thinking is really a movement away from the simple, orderly, static categorization of things. The gesture of a system operation is one of definition and explication. System operations can redundantly affirm the principles of an organizing system, as do Levi-Strauss's interpretations of cultural myths, but they do so only to affirm the validity and completeness of the orchestrating system. Unit operations articulate connections between nodes in networks; they build relations. Rather than attempting to construct or affirm a universalizing principle, unit operations move according to a broad range of diverse logics, from maximizing profit to creating new functional capacity. Such a broad understanding of the *operation* is required to facilitate the common processes of the artistic and technological acts that are my subjects.

Two characters from the history of philosophy help clarify the origins of complexity and the mutual transitions between system and unit operations: Benedict de Spinoza and Gottfried Wilhem von Leibniz. Apart from his role as a fundamental influencer of Gilles Deleuze, to whom I will return in chapter 10, Spinoza's thought itself informs the traditions that culminate in the present interest in complexity.

Spinoza held that there is only one substance comprising the whole of the universe. This substance is God or Nature (*Deus sive Natura*), two acting as one for Spinoza. As a fundamental Spinozist principle, *Deus sive Natura* itself offers a prototypical paradigm for a unit operation. The two terms, God and Nature, are related via the complex disjunction *sive*. The strict semantic meaning of *sive* in Latin is *or*, as it is translated here. But the force of *sive* is one of alternative equality, *either this or that, it doesn't matter which*, or *on the one hand . . . on the other hand . . .* This is the or of "chicken or pasta," not the or of "Catholic or Protestant." Understood in this way, *Deus sive Natura* not only articulates Spinoza's unitary substance but also sets the two forms of substance in perpetual, open relation to each other, across the bridge of the unit operational *sive.* The one substance expresses itself in the form of attributes that appear to us in an infinity of different modes. Spinoza's radical holism offers a single framework, Being, for every gesture of agency. Or, in the words of Deleuze, "What is involved is no longer the affirmation of a single substance, but rather the laying out of a *common plane {plan} of immanence* on which all bodies, all minds, and all individuals are situated."[12]

From the purview of this common plane of immanence, Spinoza's philosophy opens up the manifold relations between substances unified under Nature. This remarkable principle of radical universality organizes the whole of the universe. The unified substance ebbs and flows among itself in modes, or "affectations of a substance."[13] Consider the following extract from Spinoza's *Ethics:* "The mind imagines a body because the human body is affected and disposed as it was affected when certain of its parts were struck by the external body itself."[14] And soon after: "From this we clearly understand what memory is. For it is nothing other than a certain connection of ideas involving the nature of things which are outside the human body."[15] Spinoza's worldview merges ontological and epistemological materiality. Rather than conceiving of fixed bodies that have epistemic interactions with other bodies, in the excerpt above memory becomes a transgressive, unbounded space. The human mind not so much encounters and controls the objects of its memory as it does memorize the objects that interweave with that mind.

Spinoza's philosophy sets up a network-like superstructure for almost any kind of material relation. Like a ball of twine bunched up so that every point touches every other, Spinoza's singular substance sets the stage for future forms of complex systems. The crucial seed that Spinoza plants is that of innumerably re-creatable relations between objects.[16] Such language looks forward to forms of material relation like Valera and Maturana's autopoiesis, as well as the dynamic structure of software information systems.

Spinoza's open universe of relations stands in subtle opposition to that of his contemporary, Leibniz. Leibniz conceives of a world constructed of units called monads. Leibniz holds that these monads are "windowless," meaning that they are completely self-contained from their beginning into eternity. The universe is constructed of an infinite number of monads in consecutive succession from "clearest" (God) to "cloudiest" (inorganic matter). Because monads are windowless, their essences are predefined from the beginning of existence. The interrelation between monads is not relational in the Spinozist sense, but entirely preconceived by God, who dictated the interactions between the monads. In spite of his conception of discrete atoms that may seem to have much in common with our units, Leibniz arrests the universe into a preordained set of compunctions. Unlike Spinoza's world of shifting attributes, which hosts discrete affects of Nature in flux between subjects, Leibniz's universe arrests systems that fall in line according to an elemental divine order. Even though binary calculation is among Leibniz's many inventions, Spinoza is the more digital thinker.

Perhaps the closest philosophical precedent for unit operations is contemporary philosopher Alain Badiou's application of set theory to ontology. Transfinite set theory, first devised by nineteenth-century German mathematician Georg Cantor, deals with the representation of infinity, a concept previously left only to contemplation. In philosophy and mathematics alike, infinity was largely correlated with religion (the infinite as the "immeasurable" or the "indefinite"). Cantor's solution was to combine the notion of the infinite with that of the set, a coherent totality.[17]

Cantor's key innovation is important. Since the infinite is not mathematically measurable, Cantor needed to devise a replacement for measurement. Instead of trying to compute the size of the infinite, Cantor focused on the numerical order of different infinities, representing them as sets: "By a set S we are to understand any collection into a whole of definite and separate objects m of our intuition or our thought."[18] Any set of elements that could be made to correspond to the natural numbers is denumerable, and any infinite denumerable set has the same size. Cantor represented the size of this set, which corresponds to the size of the set of all the natural numbers, as $\aleph_0$, read "aleph-null."

Set theory allows for "subsets," articulations of different possible arrangements of the elements in a set. For example, the set {a, b, c} has among its subsets {a, b} and {b, c}. Cantor observed that the number of possible subsets of an infinite set, while still infinite, is clearly larger than $\aleph_0$. Cantor called this second, larger infinite cardinal C. C would equal the total number of possible subsets of an infinite set of size $\aleph_0$. The number of possible subsets of a finite set of size n happens to be 2^n, and thus is referred to as the *power set* of a given set, making C equivalent to $2^{\aleph_0}$. Cantor's famous "continuum hypothesis" (referred to as simply CH in mathematics) supposed that the power set C might be the transfinite cardinal just larger than $\aleph_0$, and therefore might be called $\aleph_1$. CH plays a colorful role in the twentieth century and remains neither provable nor disprovable under mathematics' standard rubrics.

After Cantor, philosophy's interest in set theory mostly centered on structural applications. The most well known of these are assuredly those of Gottlob Frege and Bertrand Russell: the "intensional" conception of a set as a collection of objects held together by a common predicate.[19] In an intensional set like "the set of all red things," "redness" serves as the foundation of the set. Such sets require a coherent and clearly defined set of properties, and as such intensional sets are top-down affairs: system operations. An opposite, "extensional" conception understands a set only by the collection of objects that it contains. The extensional set is fundamentally constructed from the bottom up. As Peter Hallward describes it, "such a set is simply a result, the result of collecting together a certain bundle of elements."[20]

Badiou's philosophy offers a concept of multiplicity that simultaneously articulates coherent concepts and yet maintains the unitarity of their constituents. For Badiou, there is only "the multiple without any predicate other than its multiplicity."[21] For this reason, Badiou has little interest in intensional sets. A set for Badiou is a collection of elements selected from the infinite possible collections of elements. These elements in turn must be thought of as multiplicities, as sets themselves. This concept of membership, borrowed from set theory, forms the basis of Badiou's ontology: "To exist is to be an element *of.*"[22] The method of inclusion in a set is left entirely open; it does not rely on an intensional principle of selection and construction.

Like the mathematics that grounds it, Badiou's philosophy is rich and complex, covering ontology and ethics, art and politics, psychoanalysis and love. I have no fantasy of offering a complete treatment of his thinking in the present context, but two core principles will help relate unit operations to this thinker's emerging legacy, namely, what Badiou calls the "count as one" and the "situation."

Because a multiplicity comprises multiplicities in turn (for all sets are multiplicities), any given multiplicity must be articulated or "made singular." Somehow, every multiplicity must be instantiated; as Hallward puts it, "every presented multiplicity is presented as one-ified."[23] Badiou calls this process the "count as one" (*compte-pour-un*). As a process or a frame for *a* multiplicity, the count as one *produces* a *particular* set; it takes a multiplicity and treats it as a completed whole. Because each "one" is always a multiple for Badiou, the set itself can never properly be called a unity (or a unit). But the result or "output" of the count as one, at the risk of tautology, is considered to be one; it is taken as one. Because Badiou relies on the extensional definition of a set, every count as one is its own gesture, its own operation.

This leads us to Badiou's notion of the "situation," a special extension of set-theoretical belonging. A situation is Badiou's name for an infinite set; being is a matter of belonging to a situation.[24] The situation is itself a "structured presentation," a set of *specific* elements arranged in a certain way.[25] As a set, the situation can be counted as one, but the form of that counting is omitted from the operation. The count as one itself is never part of the set it assembles; it is expended in the very act of counting as one. To address this problem, Badiou argues that the structuring process itself can be counted as one independent of the selection of the elements in a situation. This metastructure is the philosophical equivalent of Cantor's power set; Badiou calls it the "state" of a situation.[26] Hallward reminds us that Badiou uses the term "state" to refer both to the political and ontological senses of the set: it is "what discerns, names, classifies, and orders the parts of a situation."[27] Just as the cardinality of the transfinite power set eludes certain definition within the mathematical laws of set theory, the metastructure holds in check a fundamental disruption of the structure of the set, an occurrence that always remains possible. Badiou notes that all multiplicities rely on this void; he inscribes the void onto the set-theoretical notion of the empty set ($\emptyset$), which is always present in every set. He articulates this disruption of the set as an *event,* a concept I will return to in chapters 8 and 9.

In the early twentieth century, a group of mathematicians (including von Neumann) grounded Cantor's theory in a set of axioms, known as the Zermelo-Fraenkel (ZF) system. ZF formalized contemporary set theory's dedication to the extensional approach to set definition. Badiou's philosophy simultaneously extends set theory into the sphere of philosophy and remedies analytical philosophy's previous cooption of set theory for the support of top-down structures of knowledge. Badiou makes several gestures that resonate with my goals, starting with his general support of the extensional over the intensional. More important, however, is Badiou's insistence on "unit" as the fundamental building block for ontology.

Unit Analysis

For Badiou the set *qua* unit is never actually unitary; it is always a multiplicity, and more precisely it is a multiplicity of multiplicities. This fundamental principle might seem to distance Badiou's philosophy from the critical approach I am calling unit operations, but in fact it underscores the fundamental properties of organization and reorganization intrinsic to structures of all kinds. Both set theory and Badiou's philosophical adaptation of it articulate strategies of *configuration.*

Badiou has his quarrels with Spinoza's thinking, especially the latter's exposure of the infinite to an intellectual mode, but the two both posit belonging at the center of being.[28] Configuration's role is already apparent in the conflict between Spinozist and Leibnizian thought, a conflict that parallels the future divergences between relational unit operations and universalizing system operations: Spinoza suggests that an almost infinitely interchangeable set of substances (units) stumbles on complex modes of relation (operations), whereas Leibnizian thought maintains that static structures organize the worlds.

Where Badiou moves far beyond Spinoza is precisely in his treatment of the process of configuration. Badiou offers a means of thinking about the process of configuring things of any kind—the multiples of sets—into units, namely the count as one. The count as one serves as a process for constructing a specific multiplicity, enacted by an agent, formal or abstract, conceptual or substantive. Badiou's reliance on the formal structure of mathematics offers a logical and historical conduit to computational representation. At the same time, his transformation of set theory into a philosophical discourse unifies mathematical representation with cultural representation, a core requirement of a comparative procedural criticism.

In *Hamlet on the Holodeck,* Janet Murray argues that digital environments share four essential properties: they are procedural, participatory, spatial, and encyclopedic.[29] The first and in my opinion the most important of these properties, procedurality, Murray defines as the computer's "defining ability to execute a series of rules."[30] More specifically, procedurality refers to the practice of encapsulating specific real-world behaviors into programmatic representations. Murray's favorite example of a procedural system is Joseph Weizenbaum's famous Eliza agent, a computational representation of a Rogerian psychologist. Eliza crafted appropriate responses, typically in the form of leading questions, based on a set of natural language transformation rules. For example, Eliza might respond to a statement such as "Perhaps I could learn to get along with my mother" into "Tell me more about your family."[31] Procedurality is a name for the computer's special efficiency for formalizing the configuration and behavior of various representative elements.

The figure of the count as one helps serve as a ligature between computational and traditional representation, creating a common groundwork for understanding texts of all kinds as configurative. The count as one is the closest extant philosophical concept to what I am calling unit operations: an understanding, largely arbitrary, certainly contingent, of a particular situation, compacted and taken as a whole.

At the same time, the count as one tells us scarcely little about the way that the configured elements of a set function: what they do, and how they do it. In this way, Badiou's ontology bears some similarity to what computer scientists typically mean when they refer to an "ontology." In computer science and especially in artificial intelligence, an ontology is just a "conceptual model of the domain," typically a hierarchical framework of entities and relations of belonging between those entities.[32] These ontologies serve as frameworks for subsequent computational systems designed around the particular domain concept. As such, ontologies in the computer sciences sense of the word enable, but do not specify, the functional relationship between their constituent parts. Unit operations, however, strive to articulate both the members of a particular situation *and* the specific functional relationship between them. In Badiou's philosophy, this would be equivalent to a situation and its state; in computer science, it would be equivalent to an ontology and its procedural implementation.

Unlike Espen Aarseth's notion of the cybertext, which relies on configuration as a formal property of the artifact itself, unit operations are located both at the textual and the critical level. Aarseth articulates a "traversal function" that assembles a particular string of readable signs (what he calls "scriptons") from a possible array of textual signs (what he calls "textons").[33] At first glance this gesture may seem quite similar to Badiou's count as one, or my unit operation, and indeed Aarseth is describing a configurative practice. However, Aarseth musters his understanding of configurative texts as an ontological, not a critical tool; a cybertext is a work, not an instance of a particular critical practice. Taken to an extreme, cybertextual analysis could even be seen as a system operation; it seeks to construct an ontological domain that includes and excludes certain works by virtue of their overall function.

By contrast, a unit operation may be observed in any artifact, or any portion of any artifact, rather arbitrarily. I insist on this broader understanding of unit operations to allow its logic to resonate across expressive forms, from literature to film to software to videogames. While different media certainly exhibit qualitative differences in configurability—a videogame is more configurable than a poem in the "scriptonic" sense—the process of criticism might very well expose fungible unit operations at work in any text. More important, there is no reason to believe that the degree of configurability of a text might be directly proportional to its expressive relevance in a particular situation. For this reason, analytical practice by means of unit operations need not limit itself to computer texts.

In her exposition of digital environments, Janet Murray draws an analogy between procedurality and T. S. Eliot's notion of the objective correlative, a kind of literary formula for the production of an emotion.[34] Murray calls for the development of "new narrative art" that applies the themes of literature to the digital. Instead of articulating a divide between the literary and the digital, I want to suggest that unit operations give us a lever for understanding any form of human production as potentially procedural. Moreover, I do not contend that unit operations are necessarily components of narrative production, a topic that has become a thorn in the side of game studies and to which I will return in chapter 5. I am not particularly concerned with identifying and classifying works through new ontologies. Nor am I willing to make the reductionist suggestion that all works are digital works *avant la lettre* because all can be read as configurative. Indeed, I am not interested in making general statements about media forms of any kind.

Unit analysis is the name I suggest for the general practice of criticism through the discovery and exposition of unit operations at work in one or many source texts. Unit analysis is especially useful in comparative criticism across legacy and computational media, and it should prove equally useful in criticism of literature, film, or other artistic works. Each medium carries particular expressive potential, but unit analysis can help the critic uncover the discrete meaning-making in texts of all kinds.

Consider Steven Spielberg's 2004 film *The Terminal*. Studio publicity and online movie Web sites characterize the film's story as relatively traditional and rather mediocre. Viktor Navorski (Tom Hanks) comes to New York City from a fictional Eastern European country called Krakozia to carry out his father's last wish—collecting the one missing signature in a comprehensive collection of album covers of American jazz greats. While Navorski is in transit across the Atlantic, a coup overthrows the Krakozian government. The United States responds by repudiating any diplomatic ties with the country's rebel government, thus voiding Navorski's passport. U.S. Immigration refuses to allow Navorski entry into the country, but they also cannot deport him. Authorities tell Navorski to remain in the airport's international arrivals lounge until his situation can be resolved. This premise was based on a real man, Merhan Karimi Nasseri, an Iranian refugee who has lived in the departure lounge of Paris's Charles de Gaulle airport since 1988. Nasseri was awarded refugee status and a resident permit in 1999, but he refused to leave the airport. He has kept diaries since his arrival, versions of which were adapted into an autobiography and a French film, *Tombés du ciel* (Lost in Transit).[35]

In Spielberg's high-visibility Hollywood treatment, Nasseri is but an inspiration. Despite the fact that Spielberg's DreamWorks studio reportedly paid Nasseri "several hundred thousand dollars"[36] for rights to his rather remarkable story, *The Terminal* garnered largely mixed reviews, with many critics pouring scorn on its trite, saccharin, comic optimism.[37] In *The Terminal,* Navorski remains in the airport for an unspecified duration, perhaps a year, which offers enough of a temporal canvas for the film to touch a great many characters and themes. The recombinations of time horizons in the airport terminal allow Spielberg to paint the medium-term struggles of many characters, the long-term struggles of a few, and the short-term struggles of the airport itself. As different characters interact along one or more of these time horizons, the film's unit operations become apparent, and *The Terminal* reveals itself not as a film about a man struggling against governments for his identity, but as one about various modes of *waiting.*

Most obviously, Viktor Navorsky is waiting to enter the country. In the context of the film's story, he waits for the United States to decide how to respond to the new government of the fictional state Krakozia. But in a more abstract sense, Viktor is waiting for bureaucracy of the general kind; he is caught up in the absurdity of large organizations' slow response to unusual change. In this case the organization is governmental, but the experience Viktor endures resonates with anyone who has been oppressed in the "good-faith error" of a bureaucracy—victims of identity theft come to mind just as easily as accidental refugees. Despite the absurd condition under which he is withheld, Viktor waits patiently, accepting—even embracing—the bureaucratic red tape by which he is detained. Each day he files the same paperwork with customs, and each day the same immigration agent (Torres, a key character in another of the film's units) red-stamps it. Viktor's absurdist acquiescence to the bureaucratic rules of immigration even disrupts the immigration office itself. Office chief Frank Dixon expects Navorsky to try to escape the terminal since only sliding doors stand between Viktor and the United States.

But Viktor is also waiting for news of his homeland and waiting to gain an adequate mastery of English to understand the cryptic reports on the CNN broadcasts scattered throughout the terminal. In this sense, Viktor awaits clarity in an entirely unclear situation, one whose impetus and resolution are out of his grasp. Viktor abides this uncertainty, never giving up hope that his homeland will return to some semblance of its former state. When Dixon presses Navorsky to apply for refugee status in America, the latter refuses, reminding the former, "Krakozia is home."

Both the bureaucratic figure of the wait without guaranteed end and the political figure of the wait without certain resolution underscore a more basic kind of waiting that we might call the "uncorroborated wait," a waiting despite any guaranteed resolution. This figure constitutes the fundamental unit operation at play in the film.

Indeed, Viktor's very reason for visiting the States is motivated by such an uncorroborated wait. Viktor keeps a peanut can with him, and midfilm its contents are finally revealed to us: his father was a jazz lover, and in his youth he sent requests to every American jazz great in Art Kane's famous 1958 *Esquire* magazine photo, asking for a signature from each.[38] Slowly, replies made their way back to Krakozia, and Viktor's father collected them in the can. Only one remains, hard-bop tenor saxophonist Benny Golson, and Viktor comes to New York for the sole purpose of retrieving this last autograph for his father's collection, nearly fifty years later.

The film iterates the unit of the uncorroborated wait in each of its minor characters as well. Two characters wait for love: Enrique the airline food-cart driver courts Dolores Torres, the customs agent who denies Viktor passage every day. Enrique first uses Viktor as a kind of lover's scout, then months later as a messenger of his marriage proposal and requited love. Amelia the flight attendant waits for love too, this time the unrequited love of a married man with whom she conducts a sporadic affair during her stopovers in the city. Amelia simultaneously suspends several different yet complementary kinds of uncorroborated wait. For one part she waits to arrive in a city where she can meet her lover, unsure where her work schedule will take her next. For another part she waits for her lover to leave his wife and take her in legitimately. And for a third part she waits for him to call it off, leaving her stranded as a spinster in her late-thirties with no hopes for legitimate companionship. Viktor gets caught up in Amelia's interpersonal drama, the latter attracted to Viktor's apparent schedule—he, like she, seems to be constantly in transit.

Navorsky poses a special problem for Dixon whose promotion review happens to coincide with Viktor's arrival. Dixon has few options for handling Viktor's unique situation; he can't legally authorize passage, nor can he arrest or otherwise detain Navorsky. At the same time, Viktor's rogue presence as an ad hoc resident of the airport threatens to draw undesirable attention during

Dixon's review. Just as Navorsky waits for the resolution of his ambiguous political situation, Dixon waits for the resolution of his ambiguous professional one. But unlike Viktor, Frank Dixon has a much harder time facing the unknowable status of his professional review. Desperate to be rid of Navorsky, he even encourages Viktor to escape the terminal so that another law enforcement body might pick him up: their problem, not Dixon's. The minor character Gupta Rajan, a grumpy janitor, shares Dixon's bilious attitude toward the airport's passengers. In an effective portrayal of black humor, Gupta is often shown sitting in the food court waiting for unsuspecting travelers to slip and fall on his carefully placed patches of newly washed floor. But as Dixon's vitriol toward problem travelers reveals his own intolerance for waiting through uncertainty, so Gupta is revealed to carry the burden of a similar situation. Gupta, wanted for a violent crime in his native India, has spent the last twenty-six years waiting to find out if he will be discovered. While certainly a less honorable kind of waiting than Navorsky's stoic lawfulness, the film reveals the bitter Gupta to carry more human empathy than Dixon, even though the stakes of the former are much higher.

As a story about Viktor Navorsky and Frank Dixon's struggle against one another within a bureaucratic system, *The Terminal* hangs together only by threads; its narrative structure confuses the passage of time, and each character's motivation remains undeveloped at best, trite and contrived at worst. But when the viewer stops regarding the film as a story about a man's quest, *The Terminal* becomes a much more subtle meditation on the unit operations for various kinds of uncorroborated waiting. For my part, I was inspired to see *The Terminal* in this light only when it was properly contextualized: I watched it a second time on a transatlantic flight. The function of the in-flight movie itself is a medium for waiting; it is provided to distract passengers as they wait for the next milestone in the flight. We wait for the food or drink cart (or we wait for it to move out of the way, so we can once again see the in-flight movie). We wait for the seatbelt light to stop illuminating so that we can get up and wait for the lavatory. We wait to disembark so that we can wait to be cleared at customs.

The in-flight movie is an especially appropriate means of dissemination for *The Terminal.* As a film, the work is linear, told in the form of a rather forgettable, admittedly trite story about Navorsky's quest to fulfill his father's last wish. But when steeped in the experience of the airline flight, the viewer's proximity to airport experiences invites him to engage the film differently: not as a specific narrative about key characters, but as a framework of general figures for waiting. This impetus serves as an invitation for the viewer to perform a unit analysis on the film, to understand it as a procedural system rather than a narrative one. As the film plays out the interwoven stories of Viktor, Dixon, and Amelia, it challenges the viewer to abstract the film's specific representations of waiting into general, individual units of meaning that the viewer naturally recombines with his or her own experience. This process of viewership and of criticism exposes *The Terminal* as inherently unit operational, in contrast to the film's mediocre narrative coherence.

Analyzing an artifact like *The Terminal* as a unit-operational film about themes of waiting rather than a system-operational film about the story of a handful of developed characters thus demands a novel critical framework. In my unit analysis of the film, the story serves as the glue for a configurative work about specific modes of uncorroborated waiting. This approach is quite different from the inverse, an analysis of the story of Viktor, Amelia, Dixon, and others with common touch points in the common theme of waiting. Such a distinction is core to the critical process of unit analysis, which privileges discrete components of meaning over global narrative progression. It is tempting to argue that *The Terminal,* when viewed as a set of unit operations, ceases to function as a traditional film and begins to resemble a piece of software or a videogame. But I want to avoid such a deterministic view and instead suggest that unit operations naturally occur across media, and it is the job of criticism to shed light on them.

Structuralism and Computation

Both computer technology and critical theory share a common will to create all-encompassing representational models. Semiotics universalizes literature and theory, attempting to generate a self-sufficient determinate structure of rules governing the production of meaning. Logic universalizes information technology, endeavoring to encode all forms of meaning production for abstract manipulation. In most cases, the universalizing logic of computation is correlated with the digital, and especially with digital computing. Since this work concerns itself with fields of literary theory and information technology, it will be useful to unpack how unit and system operations function within each.

The problem of universals is one of the oldest in philosophy. It asks whether abstract concepts (universals) that range over individual things (particulars) exist in some realm outside human understanding. Thinkers like Plato, who conceive a "form" (*eidos,* idea) of universals inaccessible to human thought, are known as realists. Realists believe that universals "really exist," as much as or more than objects of individual experience. On the other side of the issue are nominalists, who hold that universals are nothing more than names (*nomina*), and that only individual things actually exist. The utmost nominalist was the fourteenth-century thinker William Ockham, although Locke, Hume, and Berkeley also qualify in a less extreme form. As empiricists, these philosophers privilege human experience, all but rejecting the notion of abstract ideas in any form. For nominalists, universals simply don't exist; only individuals exist. Hume writes, "Let any man try to conceive a triangle in general, which is neither Isosceles nor Scalenum, nor has any particular length or proportion of sides;

and he will soon perceive the absurdity of all the scholastic notions with regard to abstraction and general ideas."[1]

Aristotle makes a decisive gesture in the philosophy of universals. Although a realist like Plato, Aristotle shifted the position of universals from without to within human experience. Objects participate in two kinds of modes: their universal modes, such as the redness or roundness of an apple, and their particular modes, consisting of any other possible properties the object might possess. Aristotelian formalism informs system and unit operations in two important ways.

First, Aristotle renders a dualistic world in which universals (forms) do exist, but only in *matter,* in the material world of experiences. Plato's forms are perfect universals that the world can copy only coarsely—they are transcendent, isolated from the world by a strict separation (the *khorismos*). The mechanism by which these forms impress themselves upon the world is, like the forms themselves, mysterious yet ideal. For Aristotle, matter and form are fundamentally tied; they depend on one another. The union of matter and form marks a movement from transcendentalism to stricter materialism. Aristotle conceives of a mental function that allows us to gain an understanding of the form in the matter, the universal in the particular. He calls this faculty *abstraction,* a concept fundamental to contemporary object technology, to which I will return in the next chapter. For Aristotle, even though the universal form is accessible only through thought, it is nevertheless accessible in the material world.

By breaking the boundary between objects and a transcendental sphere, Aristotle establishes one of the first conceptions of the unit. This may seem to be a counterintuitive claim at first glance, given that Aristotelian objects still subsume formalism. Nevertheless, the absence of the Platonic separation hurtles formalism into radical individuality. As Graham Harman says, "we can speak of the 'form' as always the form of some *concrete* thing."[2] Aristotle's understanding is different from Hume's outright rejection of formal categories, as the former preserves a relationship between the form and the object, mediated by mental faculty. Hume explicitly denies that the mind can conceive of abstract forms.

Second, Aristotle posits a specific notion of causality. Final causality is the natural procession of matter toward the realization of its form. In the classic example, an acorn seeks to realize itself in an oak tree. The oak tree may be cut down and crafted into furniture, realizing another form. The final cause is the purpose objects work toward as they develop and change. In this sense, Aristotle's world is deeply teleological; things seek a formal, ideal purpose. Such striving relies on a purposiveness that orders and regulates the universe; a system that directs the movements of objects toward a directed end. Aristotle attempts to systematize the presence of forms; forms are necessarily *shared* properties, and the simultaneous individuation and generalization of them effectively collapses the discreteness of Aristotelian units onto a universal plane that strives toward some preconceived end, even if it is not seated across the Platonic *khorismos*. Leibniz makes the same philosophical gesture when he returns control of all monads to the hands of God. Compare this strategy with that of Spinoza, who allows individuals to meander mystically through the world like the universals of the ancient realists, or that of Badiou, who provides for the unexpected reconfiguration of a situation's constituent objects.

The tension between Aristotelian dualism and final causality offers an instructive model for the tension between unit and system operations. This tension returns twenty-five-hundred years later, in much the same way as Aristotle left it, in the work of the semioticians and structuralists of our last century. Ferdinand Saussure advanced the idea that general linguistic signs work in chains of differences, not by positive values. For Saussure (and Lacan, Derrida, and others after him), signs bear the fruit of meaning only in a play of relations within a larger system. Semiotics grounds the evolution of both structuralist and poststructuralist modes of literary and social analysis as trends toward unit operations.

The two varieties of the general sciences of signs proposed individually by C. S. Peirce and Saussure in the late nineteenth and early twentieth centuries rely on formalized, structured relations between signs and objects in the world. For example, the icon, according to Peirce, is a class of sign that functions by resemblance. An example immediately familiar to today's reader is the computer icon, which uses a pictograph to represent a file or a physical disk.[3] Saussure develops a linguistic semiotics that influenced much of twentieth-century structuralist and poststructuralist analysis, from Lévi-Strauss to Barthes. He concentrates on the kind of sign Peirce calls a *symbol:* arbitrary signs that bear no necessary connection between the verbal utterance and the corporeal world.[4] For Saussure and his progeny, signs bear the fruit of meaning only in a play of oppositions within a larger system. Saussure differentiates the *parole,* a single utterance or single use of the sign, from the *langue,* or the general system underlying the use of any particular sign.

In semiotics, particular uses of signs (*parole*) are unit operations. The broader flows of signification (*langue*) are system operations. The ceremony and ritual that anthropologists before Lévi-Strauss would have placed inside a cultural tradition are system operations; they proffer a depiction of a coherent society that strives toward inner closure. When Lévi-Strauss analyzed myths as a structural rather than a cultural phenomenon, he began to abandon *systems* of cultural production in favor of *instances*[5] of unit-meanings.[6] Semiotics opened a world in which analysis strove to define rigorous, all-encompassing codes that rule meaning.

By the late 1960s, structuralism's foothold on critical analysis waned, thanks to the new critical viewpoint of poststructuralists like Derrida, Barthes, and Foucault. Poststructuralists attacked the idea of a stable structure that pulls the strings of the system while remaining outside it. Poststructuralism's reliance on reading, readers, and the universal "text" as the object of the analysis process furthered structuralism's destabilization of systems. Even more than was the case for structuralism, poststructuralist tactics like Derrida's differential play of meaning or Barthes's death of the author underscore the dynamic, referential functionalism of unit operations.[7]

Despite these definitive shifts toward units of discrete criticism, many poststructuralist approaches to open meaning became doctrinal, closed methods that threaten to collapse into system operations. One approach that has stood the test of time despite such problems is deconstruction. Deconstruction consists of a variety of neologistic tools (trace, *différance,* etc.) that the critic can deploy in almost any program. These tactics appear to be highly unit operational; deconstruction musters an approach to reading that seeks to expose the internal inconsistencies that cause apparently stable systems to break down. Derrida is obsessed with dismantling totalizing systems, an aim that won significant empathy, leading to vast application in a wide variety of fields, from literature to architecture. However, taken as a whole, deconstruction can also be said to exhibit remarkable systematicity. While Derrida succeeds in upsetting the hierarchies of binary systems, in so doing, the process of deconstruction itself threatens to become a closed, static system. The certainty that all subjects of analysis are bound to destabilize could be construed as a new, alternate system of eternal return, a return to fundamental instability. It can only stand in suspension as a problematic or a question. In Mark Taylor's words, "What Derrida cannot imagine is *a nontotalizing system or structure that nonetheless acts as a whole.*"[8] The stability of fixed, totalizing meaning risks replacement by the ironic stability of play. Likewise, deconstruction could be said to assume that any thinkable system must necessarily totalize. Alain Badiou suggests that deconstruction is fundamentally a negative philosophy, one oriented against totality and obsessed instead with instability. This instability, argues Badiou, marks the final victory of polyvalence over truth.[9] The tension between unit operations and system operations is not a hierarchical one; programs that deploy themselves via unit operations still must vigilantly encourage trespass over their borders.

As structuralism and poststructuralism gained popularity, the need for computer processing increased dramatically. Beginning in World War II, military and industrial need drove the development of computation for problem solving. Answering this necessity, engineers at the Moore School of Electrical Engineering at the University of Pennsylvania built a high-speed electronic computer capable of handling calculations for weaponry operation. The machine was called ENIAC (Electrical Numerical Integrator and Calculator). ENIAC was huge, using some 18,000 vacuum tubes and nearly 2,000 square feet of physical space.[10]

Among the first true high-speed electronic digital computers, ENIAC's main disadvantage was a considerable one: it contained programmatic instructions in separate segments of the machine. These segments needed to be properly plugged together to route information flow for any given task. Since the connections had to be realigned for each new computation, programming ENIAC required considerable physical effort and maintenance. Noting its limitations, in 1945 ENIAC engineer and renowned mathematician John von Neumann suggested that computers should have a simple physical structure and yet be able to perform any kind of computation through programmable control alone rather than physical alteration of the computer itself. While most of the history of computation has attributed the architectural advances based on this observation to von Neumann himself, more recent historians have suggested that von Neumann took unjust credit for the findings, eclipsing the contributions of his collaborators John Eckert, John Mauchley, and Herman Goldstine.[11] Despite this quarrel for proper credit, history would call the new approach to computer design the *von Neumann architecture,* or more generally the *stored-program technique.* Stored-programming makes units of each program reusable and executable based on programmatic need rather than physical arrangement. Von Neumann, Eckert, Mauchley, and Goldstine designed a control instruction called the *conditional control transfer* to achieve these goals. The conditional control transfer allowed programs to execute instructions in any order, not merely in the linear flow in which the program was written. Commonly used sets of instructions (subroutines) could be kept in libraries and loaded in multiple programs, greatly reducing the work of programming. Machines that employed the advances of stored programming, such as random access memory (RAM) designed to hold instructions for quick access when needed, included the un-realized EDVAC and the midcentury standby UNIVAC.

In general, the problems of ENIAC had to do with the structure of the machine. Von Neumann was a mathematician and logician, and concerned himself with the task of creating a new and generic logical structure for EDVAC (the conditional control transfer) that enabled the machine to retrieve instructions for execution. Of top priority was EDVAC's future as an all-purpose computer capable of general computation for any purpose.[12] The conditional control transfer allowed individual computational functions to be preserved across programs, just as the film camera allowed individual photographic functions like exposure to be preserved across images. The von Neumann architecture marked the beginning of computation's status as unit operational, rather than system operational.

The universal computer that would mimic the structure of the human brain was a vision of both von Neumann and Alan Turing, who separately developed his own computational architecture called ACE (automatic computing engine).[13] Both von Neumann and Turing obsessively equated their universal computation projects with attempts to model the human brain; the famous Turing test serves as an illustration of such a goal. It is important to note that, this is not the same as creating a replica of the brain. The von Neumann architecture, as the conditional control transfer design has become known, is the basis for all modern computing. The key to von Neumann's success was not the specifics of his solution so much as his approach to the problem of computation. Rather than treating universal computation as an engineering problem, he recognized it as a logical one, antecedent to any specific instantiation.[14]

For Turing and von Neumann, universal representation is a common idea from which both human cognition and digital computation derive. But the notion that computation might mimic a mode of representation on a higher plane than mental cognition does not suggest that Turing and von Neumann believed in transcendence akin to Platonic *eidos* or even Kantian reason. Their longing to create an antecedent for universal cognition is not just another example of Western metaphysics' obsession with totalized understanding, or what Derrida called pure presence. Rather, the two saw the brain as a tentative conceptual model that prefigures cognition and computation, without ranking them in a hierarchy: a hypothetical rather than a necessary model of universal representation. The consequence of this contribution is decisive: it places computation and cognition in a commensurate relationship, not a hierarchical one.

Taken together, structuralist and poststructuralist theory along with information technology drive a new charge toward the universalization of the material world. Most general notions of universalization suggest a collapse of referential meanings into a single, irrefutable source. The universalization that underlies the critical theory and information technology of the twentieth century uproots the notion that meaning-making serves a universal*izing* purpose. In its place, however, these fields posit another kind of universalism: that of an iterable, strategic process or praxis. This praxis, while applicable to a set of highly contingent circumstances, creates fields of relation reliant on structure and method rather than on content to generate meaning.

Although structuralism of the Lévi-Straussian sort may assume an unseen, ordering center—a system—access to this center begins to emerge through the units of individual meaning. Riddled with points of relation rather than points of influence, poststructuralism amplifies structuralism's move away from systems, favoring a more concentrated application of unit analysis and creativity across media, discipline, and culture. With the advent of the von Neumann architecture, the software of a computational system made a strategic break from the hardware, allowing engineers to focus more on atomizing small computational problems even within the most complex of systems. In both fields, universalization became an approach rather than an outcome, dispersing totalities of organization into less visible totalities of method. In this sense, the continuing endurance of surface effects and end products in the arts, humanities, and technology industries demands questioning.

It is worth taking inventory of the most commonly cited universalism of digital culture: the bit. Theorists of digital media often rely on the ability to render material of any kind—images, text, video—into bits as the preeminent paradigm shift of the medium. Such observations are legitimate and at times even useful. However, theorists like Lev Manovich and Friedrich Kittler spend a great deal of time discussing the impact of digitalization *itself,* rather than the strategies information technology uses to work with binary data. For example, Manovich portrays cinema and other media as the "origins" of the combinatorial facilities he ascribes to digital media, but spends little time exploring the software structures that underwrite digital manipulation.[15] I want to avoid these gestures of privilege, the traps of mistaking theory for an unseen transcendental signified. Rather, I am suggesting that the force and power of such media comes not only from their material structure, but also from an amalgam of their logical and functional structures—the fashion in which computational and cultural works are created and used. The difference between a unit-operational artifact and a system-operational artifact is far more important than the formal nature or cultural genre of the artifact.

In *The Language of New Media,* Lev Manovich claims that binary digital data signals a sea change in representation; digital computers manipulate content previously of different media forms (audio, video, text, image, etc.) and represent that content in unitary structures. Unlike analog media, computers commingle content as byte data, and thus offer what appears to be a universal mode of representation, the bit. Even though it is correct to oppose the digital to the analog when speaking of tools for computation, it is wrong to claim that digitalization introduced the notion of universalism to computation.

The main distinction between analog and digital calculation is that the former uses a physical surrogate (an analog) for the physical system to be measured. The work of analog computation was indeed universali*zing;* however, it was not *generally universal* as is digital computation in the von Neumann architecture. Mathematician Georges Ifrah makes this distinction clear in his remarkable history of computing. Says Ifrah, "no analogue device, no matter how complex or extended its structure may be, is capable of becoming sufficiently general to serve for the solution of arbitrary categories of problem. An analogue calculator is not 'universal.'"[16]

Universal they may not be, but analog computation systems do begin to universalize certain representations in the same way the conditional control transfer would later broaden. Analog systems fashion one-to-one representations of a phenomenon in the real world: for example, the film camera matches patterns of luminescence from a lens onto patterns on a chemical-treated film. These precise, iterable manifestations of natural phenomena make it possible to map the material world with little more than the squeeze of a shutter, an act requiring little or no specialized training or convention. Walter Benjamin observes a "decline in the aura" of mechanical reproduced artifacts, a dissolution of the bonds between artistic production and ritual.[17] In Benjamin's conception, when representative practice became possible anywhere, anytime, the ties between art and tradition unknotted, freeing the art for use in other contexts, such as protest and revolution. This too is a kind of universalization, a universal "serviceability" previously unavailable to art. Such too is the universalizing capacity of the stored-program technique, a universal serviceability for virtually any kind of computational expression. Individual computational expressions are unit operations that keep in the shadow of systemic computational expression.

N. Katherine Hayles's approach to cybernetics offers a useful alternative to both the digital and the theory-centrist obsessions. Hayles argues that cybernetic systems function within a dialectic of pattern and randomness.[18] In the immense world of binary data, meaning emerges where authors or users create or recognize patterns. Pattern creation or recognition systems, *pace* von Neumann, usually take the form of unit operations that perform one kind of action on data, resulting in some judgment about its worthiness as a *particular* pattern. One person's signal is another's noise.

But pattern recognition too can act either as a unit or a system operation. To take up a contemporary example, consider a data analysis system that attempts to profile airline patrons in order to determine which are likely to be terrorists. In this case, is pattern recognition unit or system operational? Hayles's approach relies on the dialectic as a one-way door through which pattern recognition as unit operation can escape into a new context, in which questions like these can be posed and contended with. The individual act of information processing that identifies patterns in a field of random data, for example, a software subsystem for determining airline passenger risk, is indeed a unit operation. Such a system might perform linguistic analysis on passenger names, or match them against a database of known terrorist sympathizers in order to determine an individual's worthiness for suspicion. As a discrete computational unit, such a data analysis system would indeed produce outputs for every input. But what kinds of conclusions can the system's operators draw from its output? These political, social, economic, and ethical issues are not so simply mapped to machine processes, although computer scientists continue to look for ways to model and encapsulate such computationally challenging phenomena.

One example is Bayesian filtering, which creates predictive models based on previous computer-mediated human decisions, offering outputs in the form of likelihoods rather than absolutes. Bayesian algorithms are used in anti-spam software, but they are less useful in terrorist-response systems. After all, the consequences of false negatives are much higher in terrorism than in spam. Who wants to decide whether passengers should be stopped and arrested at 60 or at 70 percent "terrorist likelihood"?

The United States' Homeland Security Advisory System also underscores the tension between unit operations and system operations. In 2002, the newly formed U.S. Department of Homeland Security (DOHS) released a system meant to standardize, formalize, and regulate the communication of terrorist threats to the American public. This system, dubbed the Homeland Security

Advisory System, articulates terrorist threat according to five discrete levels: low, guarded, elevated, high, and severe. The DOHS assigned a color code to each of the levels, from green for low to red for high. Since its establishment, the government has disseminated changes in the country's alert level through the general media.

After the events of September 11, the public has continually imagined a wide range of interpretations of the peril it genuinely feared. By standardizing the types of terrorist threats into unit operations deployable via extremely compact visual representations, the government hoped to communicate clearly and concisely its interpretation of the range of risks the country might be under at any given time. The DOHS and the White House presented the terror-threat levels as a stable continuum of possible danger. Since the system was announced, the government has made several adjustments in the terror alert level, moving up or down between elevated (yellow) and high (orange).

Although the DOHS has provided action plans for government and law-enforcement agencies, individual citizens have little historical or political context for regulating their responses to the system's states, save acknowledging the relative relation between the threat levels and general movement up or down on the scale. As time passes, the limitations of the Security Advisory System have become only clearer; even though it maps complex security threat conditions onto a finite set of representations, it is an entirely "extrospective" tool. The system seats terrorism and the fight against it from the sole vantage point of a stable and unblemished Homeland. It assumes that Americans can remain safe, gazing from inside our borders at the horrors of a harsh outside world. Of course, if we should learn anything from September 11, it is that we are very much implicated within that harsh world. As such, the unit operations of the DOHS are revealed to enforce a broader geopolitical system operation, one in which the United States of America is the only meaningful term. The promise of universal computation is precisely what the logic of unit operations must take care to exceed. If we have indeed begun to represent and understand the world via discrete, encapsulated logics that both include and exclude a variety of conditions, then we must understand how these unit operations work, where they attach to one another and to our understanding of the world, and how we should approach them as users, creators, and critics.

Humanism and Object Technology

Questions about objects are often ontological questions, questions about what exists or what form existing things take. Historically, ontological questions have been questions of depth and stasis: *what is existence?* or *how do I know if something exists or not?* Earlier, I discussed Aristotle's notion of abstraction, the mental function that allows us to gain understanding of the universal in the particular. For Aristotle, even though the universal form is accessible only through thought, it nevertheless *is* accessible in the material world. By breaking down the divide between objects and a transcendental sphere, Aristotle establishes one of the first conceptions of the unit. More recently, movements in structuralism and poststructuralism have shifted ontology from stasis to reference, from systematic toward differential ontology. Practices like deconstruction, which muster flexible tactics against a wide variety of subjects, also threaten to collapse analysis itself into a closed, static system from which nothing can escape.

The ontological claims of information technology and literary theory have much in common, especially critical and technological approaches in which ontological questions uncover temporary relationships between discrete units. Psychoanalysis in particular has a penchant for assembling theoretical arguments and clinical approaches from individual units of meaning.

As a clinical strategy, Freudian psychoanalysis relies almost exclusively on appeals to discrete structures. These structures not only provide tactile grips for the analyst, but also help abstract the functions of the unconscious. Much of the ontology of psychoanalysis is indebted to the use of jargon. Dreams, argues Freud, entail four forces: displacement, condensation, symbolization, and resistance.[1] Such forces are not constitutive of the dream (that's the job of the unconscious); instead they are common principles ready to hand during analysis. These principles are like the moves in a playbook, and the analyst is like a coach; he can only help the patient make progress in the process of analysis. A possible answer to the question, *what is psychoanalysis?* might be a catalog of these Freudian "plays." When assembled in appropriate configurations, they constitute the units of an approach to a curative process. Even though Foucault cites Freud among his famous "founders of discursivity," there is still a struggle in Freudian psychoanalysis between the discursive application of unit operations and a system operation of preordained conditions.[2] Freud's obsessions with sexual symbolism and hysteria offer testimony to this drive. Nevertheless, psychoanalysis required little compulsion to overcome Freud's personal idiosyncrasies, reducing this tension considerably.

Jacques Lacan extended Freud's strategy, but folded it in on itself. Fixated on the breaks between the operation of the conscious and the unconscious, Lacan designed his entire œuvre as a material performance of this very gap. Often he devised algebraic signs and "mathemes" that function as algorithmic units in his psychoanalytic concepts, further condensing the encapsulated representation of the psyche that Freud began.[3] There are many such units on which to dwell, so I will choose just one, the *objet a,* or the "little other."

Lacan holds that the gap (*béance*) of the unconscious is *preontological,* that is, it does not "exist" as such.[4] When the subject constitutes itself in consciousness, Lacan argues, it leaves a symbol of the gap as a chasm that can never be bridged. The *a* in the *objet a* is the "little" other (*autre*), as opposed to the big Other (*Autre*). The *Autre* is a radical alterity that cannot be assimilated into consciousness; the realm of language and the law. The *objet a* functions as the cause and aim of desire, as a "piece" of the *Autre* that incites the subject's desire. For Lacan, the subject's relationship to the *objet a* is an impossible one. To seek out the object of desire is not to achieve it, but only to readdress its function and position as a lack, as a preontological gap. Lacan encapsulates the function of fantasy in the matheme $\$\lozenge a,$ read as "the barred subject's relationship with the other."

In the futile repetition of Lacanian desire, there emerges a highly discrete, structured unit operation ($\$\lozenge a$) whose purpose is to return the system to an uncompromised state. The Freudian tension between unit operations and system operations is magnified in Lacan, both through the use of mathemes and the inherent return of the system to a state of predictable compunction. Worth noting here are the similarities and differences between Lacan's unit of fantasy and

Spinoza's one substance. Lacan compresses the two terms into their algebraic form, and he mediates them with the reflexive lozenge or *vel* (◊). This conjunctive disjunction has a similar etymological resonance as the *sive* in Spinoza's *Deus sive Natura*. The fundamental difference between Spinoza's and Lacan's unit-operational systems is that the former underwrites an open set of relations between materials in the world, whereas the latter always returns the relation to an impossible rift in consciousness itself.

While his rich, creative work certainly exceeds this simple characterization, Slavoj Žižek has made his name by invoking and using the discrete principles of Lacanian psychoanalysis as unit operations. Examples abound, but consider this characteristic reading of the Hitchcock classic *Rear Window*:

The rear window is essentially a fantasy window (the phantasmatic value of the window in painting has already been pointed out by Lacan): incapable of motivating himself to action, Jeff puts off indefinitely the (sexual) act, and what he sees through the window are precisely *fantasy figurations of what could happen to him and Grace Kelly.* They could become happy newlyweds; he could abandon Grace Kelly, who would then become an eccentric artist or lead a desperate, secluded life like Miss Lonely Hearts; they could spend their time together like the ordinary couple with a small dog, yielding to an everyday routine that barely conceals their underlying despair; or, finally, he could *kill* her. In short, the meaning of what the hero perceives beyond the window depends on his actual situation this side of the window: he has just to "look through the window" to see on display a multitude of imaginary solutions to his actual impasse.[5]

A reasonable question to ask of interpretations like this one is what part is the reflection on the glass, and what part is the view outside? An astute reader of the popular and accessible work that contains this citation, *Looking Awry: An Introduction to Jacques Lacan through Popular Culture,* made the following observation in an online book review:

This book is very interesting but I think it would have been better to call it "An Introduction to Popular Culture trhough [*sic*] Jacques Lacan." This would be a proper title because Žižek dedicates more space to tell us what some products of popular culture are about . . . than to explain, or even outline, the theories of Jacques Lacan. This in itself is not a critique, I just want to say that the title can be misleading. You will not find here an explanation or an introduction to Lacan, but rather a Lacanian reading or interpretation of some products of popular culture.[6]

On the surface, this may seem to be nothing more than a framing issue, but it poses an insightful question about the nature of criticism. Does the critic seek to illuminate the subject of criticism, or merely the act of criticism itself? Žižek might argue that the entire question begs redress to the gap between appearance and human fantasy, or the Lacanian Real, or the desire for the *objet a*—the search for insight into Lacanian psychoanalysis only postpones or prolongs the search. Žižek's analysis often relies on this retroactive causality, in which, to use Žižek's own words, "every context is always already retroactively constituted by a decision."[7] In other words, the very "objection" the reviewer poses is part and parcel of the functioning of the Lacanian subject. The tension that persists throughout Žižek's work could be construed as one of a strategic, realistic use of Lacanian unit operations through the disruption of the gap of desire, the Lacanian Real.

Graham Harman argues that the problem with Žižek's retroactive causality is not this tension itself, but Žižek's strict restriction of causality to human perception. Harman insists that "even inanimate objects display this sort of fantasy . . . . [R]etroactive causation is a global ontological structure, and not a narrowly psychoanalytic one. . . . [T]here is nothing ontologically special about human retroaction."[8] Peter Starr offers a similar but less radical critique, addressing Žižek's notion of the sublime body, or the manifestation of the Lacanian *objet a*. "Žižek's principal example of such a sublime body is Lenin's in its mausoleum . . . . however, I would argue that this model applies to nothing so much as to the sublime body of the Lacanian theorist, the primary function of which has been to conceal a vicious circularity endemic to the Lacanian system, and thus proper to the Lacanian law."[9]

Harman's and Starr's analyses help us see the subtle tipping point at which the strategy of unit operations collapses and returns control to a system. Despite such objections, I perceive Žižek's use of Lacanian units as a fundamental break from systematicity. While undergoing tension similar to that between the unit operations and system operations present in Freud and Lacan, by relating to problems outside the closed system of psychoanalysis, Žižek's Lacanian units remain (or become) subject to further reconfiguration. The reviewer's response to *Looking Awry* bears witness to this success. Žižek's critical faculty successfully leverages Lacanian tools without returning necessary control to the Lacanian project.

While mathemes serve as consolidated representations of Lacanian ideas, they are not fungible in any extant symbolic system, such as pure mathematics, language, or computer science. In this sense, Lacan's domain-specific use of unit operations influences Badiou's extension of mathematization to all domains. Given his application of mathematics to philosophy, it is not surprising that Alain Badiou finds great utility in Lacan's use of the matheme, extending the latter's use of mathematical transmission for key relationships between the symbolic and the real to the entirety of possible relationships in general. Unlike Lacan, Badiou believes that it is possible to alter situations by reconfiguring their structure; the structure, akin to the power law in set theory, enforces a fundamental reorganization in every multiplicity.

In Badiou's philosophy, the Lacanian real is most closely related to the void, the empty set ($\emptyset$). But where Lacan insists on a passive relationship with the real structured by a single unit operation (for example, the $\$\lozenge a$ of desire), for Badiou this structure is always potentially in flux; the void maintains the promise that a situation can be reconfigured. Badiou calls this restructuring of a situation an "event," although he uses the term in a rather unusual way. The event is not an ordinary happening, but an unprecedented and radical alteration of the situation's status quo.[10] The event is a structuring of a situation that heretofore has never existed. Peter Hallward offers a useful example:

The members of those situations structured as anti-Semitic, for instance, cannot meaningfully see *individual* Jews but can see only an indistinct gap in the normal social fabric, the living lack of all "positive" (Aryan) characteristics. . . . Likewise, gays are clearly an element of predominantly homophobic situations, but not—not in any really substantial sense—as particular men and women engaged in particular relationships.[11]

A restructuring of either of these situations would be capable of construing Jews or gays as individual persons, but such a structure is unthinkable in the current situation. Badiou's philosophy does not correlate directly with the broader project of psychoanalysis; he demonstrates how the psychoanalytic-development unit operation can itself be reconfigured to underwrite new representations of worldly things.[12]

Technology Objects

The same threats of a return to systematicity that characterizes the evolution of psychoanalysis also plague the evolution of media technology. From the perspective of ontology, few claims regarding media technology are better known than Marshall McLuhan's view that technologies are extensions of our bodies.

Even though McLuhan's ideas are usually thought of as phenomenological rather than ontological—he questions how our sensory and social perceptions are changed by the presence of technology—his thought has had a decidedly ontological influence; it redraws the boundaries of technology, implicating humanity within it. William Gibson's concept of cyberpunk is McLuhanian, with its reliance on physical connectors to supersensory apparatuses.

Media theorist Friedrich Kittler reads McLuhan from a strictly ontological perspective. Kittler reverses McLuhan's claim, arguing that we are in fact the product of the technologies we use, the would-be-rulers who turn out to be mere subjects. Kittler articulates a notion of "partially connected media systems" that emerge from the segregated, disembodied media machines of the turn of the twentieth century: the gramophone, film, and typewriter.[13] These do not yet realize the horrifying "fully connected media systems" of Kittler's imagination, digital storage and computation.[14] This is the realm of *The Matrix* instead of *Neuromancer.*

When dealing with such universally translatable systems, Kittler's tone is ambiguous. He focuses on transfer of human knowledge and experience into binary data for electronic storage. Dogmatic sociologist Neil Postman makes his opinion on such matters plainer: "People now commonly speak of 'programming' or 'deprogramming' themselves. They speak of their brains as a piece of 'hard wiring,' capable of 'retrieving data,' and it has become common to think about thinking as a mere matter of processing and decoding."[15] Postman steadfastly opposes technology for technology's sake, going so far as to say that the computer "subordinates the claims of our nature, our biology, our emotions, our spirituality. The computer claims sovereignty over the whole range of human experience, and supports its claim by showing that it 'thinks' better than we can."[16] Again we see an ontology that implicates humanity in technology's wake.

Postman is nostalgic for this lost humanism, while Kittler hopes to replace humanism with media theory. But both Kittler and Postman trace universal binarization to Turing, who first raised what Kittler editor and critic John Johnston neatly calls "the recurrent specter of a totally programmable world."[17] Postman reacts by ardently rejecting the claim that computation serves as a metaphor of any kind. Kittler's reaction is subtler. In several short essays that engage computer technology in admirable detail, Kittler tries to show that there are limits to how far software and hardware metaphors can be taken owing to inherent limitations in the nature of switchable machines. Kittler articulates a "price of programmability," in which hardware constraints limit the possible actions and effects software programs can perform.[18] No matter the talent or manipulation of the human programmer, human experience of the machine (which must always be mediated by software) is limited by the architecture of the hardware. In simpler terms, it is only possible to make a software program do things that the computer hardware allows. Because human relation, with the computer is software-based, we need to understand technology's own agency, and how hardware relates to particular software packages.[19] Kittler performs a detailed analysis of the Intel 80386 microchip architecture, demonstrating how software expression has become subordinated to the design decisions and limitations of the chip.[20] The common thread in analyses like those of Kittler and Postman is that even a word processing program limits the ways humans relate to the world in a radical way, almost to the point of constituting an ontological threat. Even though Kittler speaks elsewhere of computer programming and its potentially beneficial effect on our understanding of media, he reconciles information technology only indirectly with human understanding.[21]

In truth, the promise or threat of collapsing all human experience into digital or binary data storage and translation goes back much farther than Turing. Leibniz developed the first system of binary arithmetic, the basis of all digital technology. Since binary arithmetic uses only 1 and 0, Leibniz concluded that all reality is therefore constructed of extensions of this notion, Being (1) and Nothing (0). The philosophical residue of Leibniz's interpretation of binary arithmetic, namely the goal of turning human reasoning itself into pure mathematics, now seems like a naive aspiration. An alternate lesson from Leibniz and Turing suggests that technology affords and constrains human activity, the mechanization of programming offering a kind of authorship that is expressive in the same way as literature, art, and cinema.

Postman seeks to understand technology from the perspective of the monster: the system's inevitable control over its master. Kittler claims that software as human metaphor is viable only in relation to its hardware constraints. But such a claim has merit only if one wishes to construct or reconstruct human experience through software. Instead, we should consider software and programming as a possible mode of expression equivalent to any other, striving to meet, describe, and comment on human activities, needs, and relations. Binary data storage then becomes an accident of convenience, one undeniably relevant, but given the same status as was accorded manufactured ink to the book in the nineteenth century or monochromatics to the early cinema.

By the 1970s, industry had made considerable progress converting processes of human cognition to mechanical computation. This era of electrical engineering, known as *large-scale integration* (LSI), radically reduced the space required to house the many transistors required for computation. Minicomputers distributed with their own software packages soon became available. Continued integration (*very large-scale integration,* or VLSI) allowed digital computer circuits to reside on a single chip. By the late 1970s and 1980s, Apple, Radio Shack, and IBM were manufacturing microcomputers that individuals could afford to buy and to accommodate.

Before microcomputers, powerful and expensive minicomputers ran client–server applications. One big, powerful computer (the server) ran a huge application in its own memory space, and hundreds or thousands of dumb terminals (clients) accessed the mainframe. Benefits included good security, reliability, and control, as the mainframe was one machine in one location.

With the advent of microcomputing, disaggregation of program elements became highly desirable, allowing microcomputers to contain common instructional symbols. Among others, early microcomputer operating system authors like Microsoft and Apple devised successful ways to consolidate and protect their base of programmatic symbols and to allow software developers to do the same as long as they based their creations on the publisher's platform.[22] Before operating systems like Windows, entire programs would be loaded into and run from memory. The single-use strategy simplified distribution and, in the short term, development, but as the graphical user interface (GUI) emerged in the mid-1980s, programs required access to instructions, objects, or symbols that bridged all applications, making up the operating system as such.[23] To negotiate the conflicting demands of protecting proprietary symbolic code and leasing that code to thousands of independent developers, the notion of component objects was born. Compiled components enclose similar symbols in binary files that expose certain aspects of a discrete task. In the current incarnation of Microsoft's Windows operating system, these component objects generally reside in *dynamic link libraries,* or DLLs. DLLs contain object classes with instructions for constructing a window, populating a menu bar, or handling scrollbars.[24] The benefits of the system are clear to both the software publisher and its developers. On the one hand, the publisher can protect the integrity of its codebase and operating system while allowing vendors to author applications for it, in turn increasing the publisher's total market share. On the other hand, developers gain free access to the world's most popular computer operating systems, yielding a huge potential market for their product.

This method of encapsulating intellectual capital in human-machine accessible black boxes characterizes the software development practice known as *ob-*

ject technology (OT), also called *object-oriented programming* (OOP). OT has existed in various forms since the 1960s, but it is most frequently associated with SmallTalk created by Alan Kay at Xerox PARC in the early 70s. The popularization of object technology came with the market domination of Windows operating system in the late 1980s, Microsoft's C++ driven COM architecture in the early 1990s, and then with Sun's Java in the mid-'90s.[25] Object technology is a set of techniques for constructing software from reusable parts. It has enjoyed great success in the business world, where its similarities to Fordist manufacturing have not failed to go unnoticed. Object technology, says one executive guidebook, "when used correctly, enables you to leverage skills across the organization, reduce mid- and long-term software development costs, shorten system development time, and produce higher-quality, more reliable software systems."[26] There are many reasons that OT gained such acclaim, but the primary motivation descends directly from John von Neumann's dream of universal computation. If universal computers model the material world in the same way as the human brain, then it stands to reason that computer systems that manage information in the same way as human cognition would reduce the inefficiencies of translation and mechanization that plagued the systems of the 1940s and 1950s. Software systems model things, relations, and events in the material world. OT attempts to close the gap between human experience, its programmatic representation, and its computational execution. Computational systems thus strive to create more successful implementations of automated human needs.

Software must exhibit four properties to be considered object oriented: abstraction, encapsulation, polymorphism, and inheritance.[27] *Abstraction* is the programmatic representation of an object, disassociated from any specific instance; only modified or instantiated versions of an object model or *class* actually exist.[28] *Encapsulation* means that the content of the software object is hidden from other parts of the system. *Polymorphism* means that different *derived instances* of a class can have different behaviors.[29] And *inheritance* means that the class itself can be used to create other classes, which adopt or inherit the parent classes' structure, attributes, and behavior. Software objects are made up of algorithms and other embedded logics, but taken several steps further than casual discussions of computational representation allow.

In *The Language of New Media*, Lev Manovich introduces the concept of transcoding as one of the five principles of new media. According to Manovich, transcoding is new media's tendency to computerize aspects of nondigital organization, conflating their structures with the structure of the computer it-self.[30] As a result of the material necessity to store digital media, "the logic of a computer can be expected to significantly influence the traditional cultural logic of media; that is, we may expect that the computer layer will affect the cultural layer."[31] Manovich articulates a particular instance of transcoding in the logic he claims computer culture applies to human culture: "The world is reduced to two kinds of software objects that are complementary to each other—data structures and algorithms."[32]

Manovich uses the term *algorithm* to denote "A final sequence of simple operations that a computer can execute to accomplish a given task."[33] Historically, algorithms were methods of calculation that used Arabic numerals rather than operations of the abacus.[34] Over time, the term was generalized to indicate a "systematic procedure of calculation."[35] Manovich misuses the terms somewhat; algorithms are actually sets of operations of greatly varying complexity, an important correction for the purposes of understanding object technology. Software objects may contain algorithmic constructions as part of their internal or external interfaces, but the structure of objects is based on simplicity and concealment rather than complexity and exposition. The methods that compose software objects thus do not necessarily condense the complexities of the natural world via mathematical or symbolic reductions; rather, they encapsulate representations of the world into specific software structures.[36] Nevertheless, Manovich's observation is important: the logical structures of software design have begun to remap themselves back onto the material world they were invented to represent.

But object-orientation and remapping are much subtler than Kittler and Manovich would lead us to believe. Manovich is correct to observe that the material world must be compressed to be represented in software. But rather than thinking of this phenomenon as a mechanical overthrow of human culture (Kittler), or as a mere influencer of human culture (Manovich), I would suggest that these technologies serve as structures that frame our experiences of the material world, while offering representations that cause us to think critically about those experiences.[37] In other words, unit operations can help us expose and interrogate the ways we engage the world in general, not just the ways that computational systems structure or limit that experience.

To illustrate this point, I offer a simple example. In introductory computer programming, object technology is often introduced through a simple business scenario that everyone already understands, such as the relationship between a bank and its customers. Customers have one or more accounts, and accounts of different types have different properties, for example a savings account might yield interest while a checking account does not. Customers can perform operations on their accounts, such as making deposits, withdrawals, and transfers.[38]

The property of object technology that makes it possible to discuss abstract relations between entities in the material world and the computational world is *encapsulation.* Encapsulation hides the internal workings of a particular operation (called a *method* in OT jargon) for the purposes of reducing complexity and protecting the real or intellectual property of the operation. In the example above, the bank takes great interest in ensuring that deposits are handled the same way every time, and that customers themselves not know how the process of getting money into an account really works. Encapsulation is often tied to capital exchange, and, for better or worse, it founds the primary basis for the defensible intellectual property of software systems.[39]

By encapsulating the customer–account relationship, and by reinforcing the behavior of banking through software systems, the banking industry has succeeded in remapping the material reality of capital exchange with its objectified, encapsulated object equivalent. In other words, our relationships with banks have become unit operations. For example, the practice of accessing one's account and withdrawing funds often comes at a premium, especially if the procedure is performed via a foreign bank's computer system (the ATM surcharge). The policy associated with the ATM surcharge has been encapsulated into the withdrawal operation itself. This seemingly benign structure has numerous real-world consequences. On the one hand, we don't have to do much thinking about banking transactions, and we don't have to go to our home banks to interact with our money; we can reinvest that mental and physical energy into other aspects of our lives. On the other hand, we have come to accept the fact that access to the exchange value of one's own labor comes at a cost. This state of affairs itself was certainly conceivable before computers drove the business processes of banking, but object technology has framed this cost of exchange back into the material world by encapsulating the rules of its execution into the methods of personal commerce. In this case, the material world and the software world mutually inform one another, and the technology exposes the unit operations for basic commerce.

Can one construe the same unit operational strategy in literary and cultural artifacts? Critics have long observed archetypes and models in literature, from Homeric epithets to the picaresque novel. Poetry, from Apollinaire's calligrames to the imagism of the expressionists and high modernists, uses literary device to encapsulate meaning.[40] But the esoteric nature of literary criticism somewhat obfuscates the appearance of objectified, encapsulated property. Jay Bolter and Richard Grusin come close in their work *Remediation.* Presented as a technique for approaching works across media without historical prejudice, Bolter and Grusin claim that all media articulate or pay homage to previous media, thus "remediating" previous media forms. For example, the World Wide Web remediates print graphic design, video, and the printed book. Among other things, Bolter and Grusin observe the encapsulation of cultural products as an artifact of the process of remediation. The two offer the Batman franchise as an example: "the goal is to have a child watching a Batman video while wearing a Batman cape, eating a fast-food meal with a Batman promotional wrapper, and playing with a Batman toy."[41] Product licensing is not an information technology in the usual sense, but it does exhibit the same unit operation of legal right and instantiation as object technology. There are fortunes built around licensing. Since 1976, the Japanese company Sanrio has done nothing but license its popular Hello Kitty character for use in other forms of cultural capital, from shirts to plush toys to car interiors to sex toys. Licensing is an example of the fungible use of a unit operation in the cultural, commercial, and legal registers.

In his writings on hypertext, George Landow observes the surface effects of the unit model in literary theory. Drawing comparisons between the writings of Derrida and decentered textuality, Landow makes the following observation:

Derrida properly acknowledges (in advance, one might say) that a new, freer, richer form of text, one truer to our potential experience, perhaps to our actual if unrecognized experience, depends on discrete reading units. . . . The implication of . . . citability and separability appears in the fact, crucial to hypertext, that, as Derrida adds, "in so doing it can break with every given context, engendering an infinity of new contexts in a manner which is absolutely illimitable."[42]

The citation is from Derrida's influential early essay, "Signature Event Context." The content of Landow's analysis is indeed exciting; he is, even if implicitly, drawing a connection between the practice of literary theory and the method of a kind of technological production. Indeed in the right circles, one could probably pass off the Derrida passage as a quote from John von Neumann or Alan Kay, discussing the conditional control transfer or the software object. The crucial error Landow makes is to privilege the theory over the technology. Even if it is merely a casual aside, Landow claims that Derrida's work anticipates *in advance* the kind of discrete reading process he attributes to hypertexts. Rather, he should observe that the particular kind of poststructuralism Derrida advances seems to have the same properties as the particular kind of technological production offered by hypertexts. Some logical follow-up questions present themselves: What *is* this more general kind of discrete operation? How does it operate? And what does it tell us about how we live?

Discreteness is one of the principle properties of unit operations, and it relates to the property of encapsulation that characterizes object technology. Landow's appropriation of Derrida serves not a critical or cultural purpose, but an economical one. Perhaps the "illimitability" of citation makes the practice of deconstruction one that has, in the most literal sense, more return on investment than other modes of textual engagement. Bolter and Grusin's Batman example makes the same point, even if more directly (the relative return on investment of one Batman film with product licensing and sequels is greater than that of four individual films). Suddenly, literary production and technology production appear to operate in much the same fashion, provided their users use a specialized toolset. But information technologists have formalized their toolset much more than have literary critics, thanks in large part to the former's interest in creating and protecting a position in the marketplace.

Human Objects

It is not just symbolism and business processes that participate in the ontology of units. Since the evolutionary processes of genetics have been understood as functions of DNA, human life has been implicated in the logic of unit operations. In 2000, the Human Genome Project achieved its goal of mapping the gigantic structure of human DNA, publishing a tomelike map of what some consider the encyclopedia of humanity. The discovery has been called, among other things, "the most important scientific achievement in the history of mankind."[43]

The Human Genome Project assumes that sequences of the four base pairs of DNA provide enough information to proxy for the most developed of social relationships, from paternity to homicide. Although the reality of genetic engineering, selection, or social normalization is still far off, DNA fingerprints and typing have already provided forensic and legal evidence that has far-reaching and very real implications. The goal of these scientific efforts is to build an armature for humanity as such, a guidebook for diverse human applications from legislation to behavioral genetics to medicine and gene therapy.

The Human Genome Project is possibly the world's most audacious system ontology. Here are its goals as laid out by the Department of Energy (DOE):

- *identify* all the 100,000 genes in human DNA,
- *determine* the sequences of the three billion chemical base pairs that make up human DNA,
- *store* this information in databases,
- *develop* tools for data analysis,
- *transfer* related technologies to the private sector, and
- *address* the ethical, legal, and social issues (ELSI) that may arise from the project.[44]

The salient part of DNA (that is, the part that carries information about the organism or individual) is contained in the four kinds of nitrogenous bases arranged along a sugar-phosphate backbone. The type and order (sequence) of these bases composes the genetic "encoding" for the organism or individual. The project hopes to identify and "name" the units of human DNA, then understand the operational sequences each performs.

At its heart, the Human Genome Project is not interested in the complexity of human life, but its radical simplicity. The DOE's goal to "develop tools for data analysis" underscores the project's assumption that the identification and sequencing are the most difficult parts of the project. The project assumes from the beginning that the final datamap will prove overwhelmingly simple. The DOE even encapsulates the "ethical, legal, and social issues" into a jargon-rich unit, "ELSI," in a hopeful gesture that such issues will be as easily managed as the DNA sequences themselves. Despite its disposition toward symptomatic criteria for the calculation of human individuality, the Human Genome Project attempts to account for humanity as a holistic system operation rather than a complex, discursive set of unit relations. It serves as an example of a unit-operational model interpreted or forced into the framework of a system. Albert-László Barabasi puts it this way: "The behavior of living systems can seldom be reduced to their molecular components."[45]

Even if the Human Genome Project exposes itself as a search for systemic truth, more successful applications of the DNA model have appeared in the cultural adaptations of genetics in the study of human culture. Cyberneticist Murray Gell-Mann conceives of units of "cultural DNA" that "*encapsulate* the shared experience of many generations."[46] Unlike the DOE, Gell-Mann understands that there are no shortcuts to understanding culture and that the operation of units of cultural evolution is necessarily complex.

Perhaps the most well known proponent of units of cultural evolution is Richard Dawkins. In his now classic book *The Selfish Gene,* Dawkins articulates a unit of culture called the *meme.* Writes Dawkins, "Examples of memes are tunes, ideas, catch-phrases, clothes fashions, ways of making pots or of building arches. Just as genes propagate themselves in the gene pool by leaping from body to body via sperm or eggs, so memes propagate themselves in the meme pool by leaping from brain to brain. . . ."[47] Memes are units of culture. The network of these units and the processes by which they operate, the complex unit operations of the meme, Dawkins calls the *memeplex,* a kind of cultural unit cluster in which memes encapsulate themselves into the social systems we perceive and participate in.[48]

To understand the impact of theories like Dawkins's, it helps to look at the commercial adoption of his principles. With the traditional advertising market losing ground every year, marketers have adopted concepts like the meme as a way to affect and change the memeplex. In a recent book, self-proclaimed "futurists" Ryan Mathews and Watts Wacker devise a simple scale for understanding cultural unit operations.[49] Mathews and Wacker conceive of a memelike superentity they call the *devox,* which effects cultural change through the promulgation of deviance.[50] In a similar unit-operational strategy, Seattle-based marketing company Mimetic Systems offers a direct marketing adaptation of Dawkins's theories. In a recently popularized marketing practice called "viral marketing," Mimetic Systems tries to measure and inject key memes into the culture via conduits on the Internet.[51] Mimetic Systems has even deployed a software tool for measuring the effects of their culture-building efforts. This data extraction system, WebQL from QL2 Software, folds the process of cultural unit operations in on the unit-operational framework of object technology: a software unit operation to measure the success of a social unit operation.[52] Even though these strategies are coherent and inclusive, they all maintain the individual function of the unit, rather than collapsing into overarching system operations.

As I described earlier, to be object oriented, a software system like WebQL must meet four founding criteria: abstraction, encapsulation, polymorphism, and inheritance. I have already introduced in some detail the notion of encapsulation and shown how literary criticism shares this property without articulating it as such. Reviewing the definitions of the properties of OT, one can see a correlation between abstraction and the transcendental signified, or between polymorphism and intertextuality. Indeed, we already encountered abstraction in Aristotle's terminology, where it represents a faculty of reason that allows access to the universal in the particular. But it is not my wish to show how culture, philosophy, and critical theory can be made to "look like" object technology.

Janet Murray offers another way to look at the relationship between narrative and technology, what she calls *procedural authority:* "The most important element the new medium adds to our repertoire of representational powers," says Murray, "is its procedural nature, its ability to capture experience as systems of interrelated actions."[53] Critics and creators can use a common toolkit to approach art and cultural objects that have equal home in both the worlds of the literary and the technological; we can understand unit-operational systems both inside and outside technology. To take Murray's claim further, the new medium not only expresses systems of interrelated actions, but also teaches us to read both technology-based works and non-technology-based works from the single perspective of their shared procedurality. To exercise this point, I will now turn my attention to videogames.

Procedural Criticism

Comparative Videogame Criticism

In *The Savage Mind,* structuralist anthropologist Claude Lévi-Strauss character-izes two modes of thought, the mythical and the scientific. Mythical thought is grounded in observation of the sensible world, whereas scientific thought is grounded in the imperceptible. Lévi-Strauss draws an analogy between mythi-cal thought and *bricolage,* a French word with no precise English equivalent, but similar to our notion of tinkering, of dabbling. The *bricoleur* is a skillful handy-man, a jack-of-all-trades who uses convenient implements and ad hoc strategies to achieve his ends. Unlike the engineer, the scientific thinker who strives to construct holistic, totalizing systems from the top down, the bricoleur performs his tasks from spare parts, from odds and ends. The scientist strives to create events by means of structures, whereas the bricoleur seeks to create structures through events.[1]

In his critique of Lévi-Strauss's reliance on scientific thought as a production of universalism, Jacques Derrida shows that even the engineer is a bricoleur himself, a myth:

A subject who would supposedly be the absolute origin of his own discourse and would supposedly construct it "out of nothing," "out of whole cloth," would be the creator of the verbe, the verbe itself. The notion of the engineer who had supposedly broken with all forms of bricolage is therefore a theological idea; and since Lévi-Strauss tells us else-where that bricolage is mythopoetic, the odds are that the engineer is a myth produced by the bricoleur.[2]

As Derrida reminds us, Gerard Genette draws a direct correlation between bricolage and literary criticism; it is a process of borrowing concepts and putting them to use.[3] This metaphor of bricolage as analysis continues into the present; Norman Denzin and Yvonna Lincoln took it up as a metaphor for social scientific research in their influential 1994 collection *The Handbook of Qualitative Research.*[4] For Denzin and Lincoln, the contemporary researcher is a kind of bricoleur, a "flexible and responsive" agent willing "to deploy whatever research strategies, methods or empirical materials are at hand, to get the job done."[5] This *rechercheur bricolant* is also "technically curious" and "reflexive," his research an "interactive process shaped by . . . personal history."[6] I am sympathetic to such a "personalization" of analysis, yet I cannot help but see a more literal connection between the notions of criticism and bricolage.

On the one hand, my formal training is in comparative literature, a field of study known for exploring "the interactions between literature and other forms of human activity" through a wide variety of critical study.[7] This phrase "and other forms of human activity" comes from the mission statement of the American Comparative Literature Association (ACLA), and it stands as a great *et cetera* on the end of literature, implying a kind of bottomless pit of possible sources for further analysis.

On the other hand, my professional background is in Internet technology and videogames, domains known for their rapid and unconventional approaches to development. Although not always mated to sound business principles, ardent inventiveness characterized the technology industry in the 1990s. The creation of the World Wide Web was borne out of Tim Berners-Lee's determined dabbling on the NextStep development environment, itself widely regarded for its proclivity toward rapid software assembly.[8] Likewise, videogame developers typically push the computational boundaries of everyday devices, often working outside the safe boundaries of customary application programming interfaces (APIs).[9] This bricoleur is more *Macgyver* or *A-Team,* less mere handyman.

Together, comparative criticism and videogame software development entail the bricoleur, the deft handyman who assembles units of preexisting meaning to form new structures of meaning. An intersection of these two domains—a comparative videogame criticism—suggests a more intimate interrelation of two spaces of bricolage, that of criticism and that of production.

One way of articulating this intersection is through formal analysis. In such studies, criticism seeks to find the local expression of abstract principles that characterize the medium itself. Espen Aarseth's notion of cybertext has been called such a one, an approach to texts whose functional differences among the mechanical parts play a defining role in determining this aesthetic process."[10] Cybertexts are examples of what Aarseth calls "ergodic literature," works in which the user must perform "nontrivial effort."[11] Videogames and hypertexts are some of the artifacts Aarseth has in mind, but he carefully extends the notion of cybertext to include artifacts outside the realm of the digital, including configurative texts like the I Ching and Raymond Queneau's *Cent mille milliards de poèmes.*[12] Such an approach is clearly comparative, and perhaps it comes as no surprise that Aarseth's background is in comparative literature.

While Aarseth carefully argues that cybertext is an extension of current forms of literary studies and not a break from it, he is primarily concerned with the functional, rather than the "material or historical" aspects of such artifacts.[13] Says Aarseth,

My main effort is . . . to show what the functional differences and similarities among the various textual media imply about the theories and practices of literature. . . .

My final aim is to produce a framework for a theory of cybertext or ergodic literature and to identify key elements for this perspective.[14]

For Aarseth, videogames and related technologies offer a window onto a broader, perhaps unexplored functional tradition; they "should be studied for what they can tell us about the principles and evolution of human communication."[15] These principles rely principally on configuration—the arrangement of an I Ching hexagram or the arbitrary progression through a virtual space in *Zork*.

Despite Aarseth's ontogeny, and despite his entailment of several literatures in his articulation of cybertext, he makes a clear break from literary studies. "Especially," says Aarseth, "I wish to challenge the recurrent practice of applying the theories of literary criticism to a new empirical field, seemingly without any reassessment of the terms and concepts involved."[16] For Aarseth, such an obsession with the ideal of literature underscores an ideology at work in fields like comparative literature—for the ACLA, after all, the "other forms of human activity" seem subordinate to the primary object of study, literature. Aarseth is unequivocal about this problem, calling the use of terms like "interactive fiction" an "unfocused fantasy rather than a concept of any analytical substance."[17]

Since the industrial revolution, much literary criticism about technology has focused on the uncanny ligatures between humanity and machinery. The movements casually grouped under postmodernism provided special theoretical avenue into recombinant literary-technological texts, as postmodernism in general valued amalgamations of cultural objects such as pastiche and self-reflexivity.[18] When microcomputer technologies began to change the face of writing on a mass scale in the 1980s and 1990s, theorists like Bolter and Landow latched onto the potential for a computational praxis of contemporary critical theory, especially that of Derrida and Barthes.[19] These works advanced the assumption that software instantiations of theoretical methodologies uncovered a new way to read and write. Even today, projects in the "digital humanities" are almost entirely instrumental, providing instructional and research tools for traditional humanistic research;[20] part of Aarseth's unequivocal reaction against literary studies is fueled by these early theoretical missteps. Even as Aarseth draws a fundamental connection between videogames, hypertexts, poetry, and literature, he distances this new domain of cybertext from traditional forms of artistic expression, and especially from literature.

Today, just short of ten years after the first publication of *Cybertext,* the field of videogame studies reaps what it sowed—functionalist separatism. In 2004 the Digital Game Research Association (DiGRA),[21] videogames' international research organization, launched a column series called "Hard Core," "a forum within which academics are invited to debate what constitutes as central to digital games research."[22] While the epithet "hard core" is usually reserved for explicit pornography, it is also frequently used in the videogame industry and press to refer to its most active and committed audience. As the most devoted group of videogame consumers, "hard core gamers" are sometimes the most unrelentingly myopic of players as well, fulfilling the unfortunate stereotype of those who forgo all other cultural, social, or even hygienic activities in favor of videogames. This is an unfair reductionism, but it sets up an evocative comparison when transferred from videogame consumption to videogame studies: does the "hard core" comprise those researchers who forgo all other critical activities in favor of videogames?

Such an attitude is subtly different even from that of Aarseth, who privileges cybertextual functionalism, not media centrism. While the DiGRA Hard Core editorial board gives lip service to the potential openness of their brand of game studies ("core might not necessarily mean a centralized approach to digital games research"), its published articles tell a different story.[23] In one such column, DiGRA president Frans Mäyrä offers an especially unambiguous vision of "three theses" for game studies:

Thesis one: *There needs to be a dedicated academic discipline for the study of games.*

Thesis two: *This new discipline needs to have an active dialogue with, and be building on of existing ones, as well as having its own core identity.*

Thesis three: *Both the educational and research practices applied in game studies need to remain true to the core playful or ludic qualities of its subject matter.* [24]

The first thesis—one that "should be obvious" according to Mäyrä—erases all progress Aarseth made in attempting to connect games to other cultural forms. "Games," says Mäyrä, "have their own distinctive features and fundamental character or ontology, which are not shared as such by other cultural forms." [25] Mäyrä's second thesis appears to open the door to critical overlap, but his intentions are quickly revealed to focus not on comparatist approaches but on potential acquisitions for the dedicated discipline of thesis 1: "There are many ways in which games overlap with other areas, such as various forms of storytelling, audio-visual media and arts, science and the art of programming, or various fields in business and marketing. There is therefore no need to reinvent the wheel. . . . There is already some existing research to learn and profit from." [26] The third thesis acts as a kind of normative ethics for the first two; it is a pragmatic call to "coordinat[e] the research work and coursework in ways that will keep the qualitative core of games and playing visible." [27]

The field of "hard core" game studies is thus revealed to be essentialist and doctrinaire, its theorists hoping to reinvent a different kind of isolationist techno-textual criticism that privileges the ludic over the literary, culturing the virulent oppositions of a future whose media ecology we cannot foresee. For better or worse, this essentialism has its origin in Aarseth's functionalism, an approach that, even if "eclectic," still privileges the material at the cost of the expressive. [28]

I want to turn away from this kind of pure functionalism while still retaining Aarseth's otherwise useful analysis of games as configurative texts. Instead of focusing on how games work, I suggest that we turn to what they do—how they inform, change, or otherwise participate in human activity, to borrow the ACLA's words. Such a comparative videogame criticism would focus principally on the expressive capacity of games and, true to its grounding in the humanities, would seek to understand how videogames reveal what it means to be human.

Comparative literature in the traditional sense seeks to consolidate a coherent Western tradition; as first conceived in the nineteenth century, it sought principally to establish the overarching whole that united the various (European) languages and literatures. While such Eurocentric universalism has certainly waned, the comparatist's core commitment to multiple literary and cultural traditions has not. In a more contemporary model, the comparatist critic invokes a theoretical framework to construct a more specific critical analysis across several domains of human activity. Some works avoid a theoretical superstructure, directly applying close readings of one tradition to those of another. In many cases, the critic invokes an intervening third term, either literary or theoretical, to intervene between a stalemate of the other two terms.

Comparative videogame criticism would not turn its back on functionalist approaches, but rather would recognize the utility of functionalist approaches to games as a useful lever for explication. Such a criticism would focus on the aesthetic meaning revealed by a cybertext's parts. Functionalist questions about videogames—what they are, or how they function—are not invalid or even unwelcome. But equally, or dare I say more important questions exist: what do videogames do, what happens when players interact with them, and how do they relate to, participate in, extend, and revise the cultural expression at work in other kinds of artifacts?

In the figure of the bricoleur, the critic and the videogame share the same processes of selection and configuration. The ad hoc, even hackneyed process of comparative criticism should include those artifacts left out by Aarseth's cybertext: poetry, film, fiction, and television are media that are not obviously made configurative by the author may but may be made so by the critic.

Videogames and Expression

Videogames are complex software programs. As software, they take advantage of the componentization of object technology. In a game with a complete three-dimensional world, common elements like object physics or reflective luminance can be abstracted into object-based software components. But the game engine dramatically increases the scope of unit-based abstraction compared to other forms of cultural production. The first-person shooter (FPS) has played a fundamental role in founding the industry of game engines, assemblages of common software components and tools used to make other games. While some may question the cultural value of games like *Doom,* this genre ushers in a new mode of cultural production, of which the FPS will prove to be but a prehistoric artifact.

Common gameplay in works of the same genre makes it possible to develop new games based on the code written for existing games. Aarseth made this observation of early adventure games like *Zork:* "Creating a new version is mainly a matter of editing and then recompiling a program file; the end result can be as similar or different from the original as the programmer wants."[1] The notion of a common substructure for similar games grew into modern game engines, component-based software systems useful not only for rendering background effects like physics, but also for orchestrating the crucial functions of the gameplay itself. In modern games, recompilation is not even required; the engine is split up into software objects and frameworks accessible through developer-friendly APIs (application programming interfaces). Furthermore, developers often create tools to allow nonprogrammers to build game components that the engine in turn runs. Of these, the most common are plug-ins to import three-dimensional models and animations from popular three-dimensional programs like *3D Studio Max* and *Maya.* Taking this a step further, level editors allow non-programmers to lay out environments for use inside such games. Among the most popular level designers is Valve's *Hammer Editor,* the editor used to create levels for the popular FPS *Half-Life. Neverwinter Nights* (a role-playing game [RPG] rather than an FPS) ships with the *Aurora Editor,* a tool intended to allow players to capture the adventure scenario-building spirit of the pen-and-paper *Dungeons & Dragons* role-playing games.

Game engines move far beyond literary devices and genres. Unlike cultural categories like the modern novel or film noir, game engines regulate individual videogames' artistic, cultural, and narrative expression. Part of this divergence centers around the medium's status as an industrial art, a creative process that participates in the market economy. Of course, books also participate in the market economy: publishers choose titles based on historical and projected market responses. They also influence the material substance of written works, for example by limiting the length of the manuscripts they select for publication. Commissioned studio art and installation works are also commonplace, wherein organizations or individuals fund a specific artist to produce a work for a specific purpose. But the film industry remains the dominant example of an industrial art, where large teams of individuals with specific skills (both artistic and technical) produce a work often, but not always, funded by large corporate investors. Unlike most literature and studio art, videogames and films require sizable budgets and large, diverse teams of creators. Still, even the most lavish videogame budgets pale in comparison to Hollywood blockbuster films. While a mid-range game might require 5 to 10 million U.S. dollars to develop, films like the hit *Titanic* or even the bomb *Waterworld* run tabs well over 100 million U.S. dollars for production alone.[2]

Instead, the main difference of videogames, and especially the FPS games that rely most on game engines, is their particular use of intellectual property (IP). Like component software, game engines are IP. They exist in the material world in a way that genres, devices, and clichés do not. While the largest Hollywood studios do believe that the holy grail of film marketing comes in the form of intellectual property, their IP is of a different form: a franchise that can be spun into sequels, licensed products, and marketing partnerships, like Bolter and Grusin's *Batman.* The industry creates some of these properties from scratch; the *Indiana Jones* series is a good example. But nowadays studios more commonly license proven properties from other media; recent examples include *The Lord of the Rings* trilogy, the *Harry Potter* series, *Shrek, Spider-Man,* and *Charlie's Angels.* In these cases, it is the content, not the form of the film, that is subjected to IP licensing. *Shrek* is among the most formal examples of content-based licensing; the aspects of the original book that are preserved in the film are limited to the name of the title character and the fact that he is an ogre.[3] Of course, there are also examples of iterated formal models in popular cinema. Film studios often structure their films around proven models or formulas, such as the buddy cop movie, the coming-of-age movie, the romantic comedy. But they do not produce, own, and sell those models themselves. While one could imagine a film studio carping on a critic for slotting one of their releases into a genre formula, the studio could never go so far as to claim ownership of that genre, such that the critic's mention of it would violate the parameters of a studio's licensing arrangements.[4]

Game engines are no more transcendental than genres, in the sense that one cannot play a game engine but only a game that encompasses and integrates that engine to create a work. However, game engines do enjoy a different status with respect to authorship and criticism. The first-person shooter is clearly a genre of videogame and, for better or worse, perhaps the medium's most common genre. But first-person shooter game engines construe entire gameplay behaviors, facilitating functional interactions divorced from individual games. Genres structure a creative approach to narrative; they describe a kind of story. While one can imagine a conceptual description of any of the film genres just mentioned, it is much more difficult to imagine the unit-operational underpinnings of such a genre.[5] The buddy cop movie would have to contain driving, gun handling, foot chases, perhaps even embittered divorce disputes. The romantic comedy would require chance encounters, urban near-misses, frustrating misunderstandings, and touching resolution. Game engines differ from genres in that they abstract such material requirements as their primary—perhaps their only—formal constituent.

An early example of shared game code offers a quick case study. Atari founder Nolan Bushnell did not create the first computer table-tennis game, but he did popularize and commercialize *Pong* as the first success of the videogame industry.[6] After releasing the hugely popular ping-pong ur-game, Bushnell made a rather unusual strategic decision: he created a competitor. When distribution practices limited Atari's reach in the coin-op market, Bushnell recruited his neighbor, Joe Keenan, to start a new company with the goal of capturing more total market share. The new company was called Kee Games, and Atari founders Bushnell and Al Alcorn sat on its board. To fuel the clever deception, Bushnell had two of his top Atari men defect and join Kee.[7]

Among Kee's 1974 lineup were eighteen games, six of which were variants of *Pong*.[8] The most successful of these was *Tank,* a game in which each of two players (human or computer) maneuvered a tank through a maze. The players fired rounds from their tanks, which ricocheted off the walls of the maze. The goal was to disable the opponent's tank by striking it with one of these projectiles.

Although *Tank* and *Pong* did not share a game engine in the same way as contemporary games that are literally built on a technology framework like the *Unreal Engine,* their common gameplay properties relied entirely on the same codebase—the end result of Kee's acquisition of Atari's top developer, Steve Bristow. This was a time of low margins of error in game development; rather than APIs and components, Bristow brought his assembly code to Kee. Portions of *Tank* abstract *Pong*'s gameplay to its core: a unit operation for object vectors with collision effects. Taken as a unit of gameplay, *Tank* took the notion of vector geometry as a mediator of competition between two players. After Atari reincorporated Kee Games, *Tank* was ported to the Atari 2600 as *Combat,* one of the early console's most popular titles. *Combat* made use of the same fundamental units of gameplay, with small variants added to produce twenty-seven games on a single VCS console. *Tank, Pong,* and *Combat*'s relation to one another is far stronger than interpretive notions like intertextuality or new media concepts like remediation allow.

Game Engines

Following up on his unorthodox move to create a competitor to increase market share, Bushnell later founded the Chuck E. Cheese's pizza/arcade chain in 1977, after selling Atari to Warner Communications for nearly $30 million.[9] A true visionary, just as Bushnell understood the promise of transferring the material structure of one game to another, he also recognized the potential of transferring one play environment to another. Earlier games like *Pong* and *Tank* were installed initially in bars; the marketing materials for these mid-1970s titles typically depicted men in their twenties playing a stand-up arcade box with an attractive young lady linked to his arm, or a young man and young woman playing against one another at a sit-down, "cocktail table" style arcade box. Bushnell recognized that the social experience of arcade play constituted a unit operation that could be transferred from adult venue to family venue. Interestingly, this kind of social play was largely lost during the 1990s, until first-person shooters reintroduced multiparty gameplay in LAN and Internet-based arena matches.

Most important, the relational meaning between the two games *Pong* and *Tank,* for example, as person-to-person combat simulators, aggression-release devices, or pub traffic generators, is *materially* bound to the common logical structure of the works themselves. The early case of Steve Bristow may resemble individuated filmic or literary influence more than today's abstract, impersonalized software systems; but unlike filmic or literary techniques, this material form exists entirely independently of its creator; there is little precedence for such a total alignment between the intellectual proprietary, material, functional, and discursive modes of authorship.

In fact, the entire hardware architecture of the Atari 2600 (also called the Atari Video Computer System, or VCS) was crafted to accommodate *Pong*- and *Tank*-like games. The device's memory architecture and hardware register settings provide access to a playfield backdrop, two player sprites, two missiles, and one ball. The VCS is generally considered one of the most difficult platforms to program, and gameplay innovation on the platform required developers to work within its constraints. These constraints are not only physical (a paltry 128 bytes of RAM and 2 kilobytes of game data on the cartridge) but also conceptual: the hardware was designed for games like *Pong* and *Combat,* artifacts based on tennislike attributes. While ROM size 2600 carts eventually increased, new game concepts required VCS programmers to manipulate the hardware's affordances to create new play experiences. The VCS offers a striking example of how the structure of a technology platform exerts expressive pressure on the software created to run on it.

The truly componentized, unit-operational game engines of modern games only further accentuate this merger of functionalism and materialism. Ben Sawyer observes that "as a media form, games have perhaps the closest relationship between advancement of the medium and advancement of its underlying technology and production processes."[10] Perhaps the most common and commonly discussed game engines are those that power first-person shooter games like *Doom, Quake,* and *Unreal Tournament.* Epic Games's releases of Unreal Engine, the game engine behind their popular series of multiplayer FPSs, often garner more press and anticipation than the games themselves. The focus of this critical lens shows the importance of a hybrid material-functional analysis of the unit operations of game engines in game criticism.

Modern game engines were born with *Doom,* not the first FPS but perhaps the most influential. After *Doom*'s tremendous success in the early 1990s, two things became clear. First, there was tremendous market potential for FPS games—*Doom* sold over 600,000 copies in retail, and hundreds of thousands more were likely distributed via shareware licenses.[11] Second, there was tremendous market potential for *facilitating* the creation of FPS games. After the success of *Doom,* its developer iD Software recognized that they could capitalize not just on games they created, but also on helping other developers create similar and derivative games. The key to this opportunity was abstracting and extracting the game's core features, its most salient unit operations. iD turned that idea into the *Quake Engine,* which has become the basis for dozens of titles released since, including *HeXen 2* and *Half-Life.*

Game engines in the contemporary sense are far more complex than *Pong*'s and *Tank*'s reuse of vertex collision routines or the VCS's sprite and ball constraints. This complexity was born primarily because modern game engines manage three-dimensional worlds that demand incredible programmatic complexity. The engine's principal effort, rendering, has nothing to do with actual gameplay. Game engines also abstract routines for characters and objects in the world; manage physics routines to keep objects from falling out of the world and to dictate their interaction; and provide sound management, artificial intelligence (AI), network communications, scripting, and tools. The latter two are especially interesting traits, as they make the entire game engine accessible to other systems that might modify or add to it. In object technology terms, this makes the engine's software routines polymorphic.

Game engines are partly responsible for the massive growth of the game industry, and in principle there is no reason not to celebrate them: after all, they take much of the drudgery out of game development, which should allow developers to focus on innovation instead of mechanics. But even in the simple case of *Pong* and *Tank,* the links created by their common underlying technology are many: intellectual proprietary, material, functional, and discursive. It is worth asking how each of these relates to contemporary game engines, what they enable, and what they forgo of expression in videogames.

Pong and *Tank* shared their codified intellectual property not by license but by direct ownership. Kee and Atari were the same company; their separation served only as a ruse to satisfy regulators. In the case of the *Quake II* engine, released by iD Software under a paid licensing program, both the licensor and licensee benefit from the shared property. iD would receive a license fee, starting at $10,000 per title, and other developers won the opportunity cost savings of starting from an engine rather than from scratch. This relationship played out well for Valve Software, who released *Half-Life* in 1998, based on the *Quake II* engine. *Half-Life* in turn spawned a multiplayer edition called *Counter-Strike,* which remains among the most popular Internet/LAN games today. Both *Tank* and *Half-Life* demonstrate how formal intellectual property relationships between games and their developers or publishers encourage growth that benefits both.

At the same time, this legal relationship makes the two games very different from other creative artifacts. In literary studies, there is no legal body to regulate consensus about intertextuality and the influence of tradition. In his concept of the "anxiety of influence," Harold Bloom argues that all literary texts are misrepresentations of the texts that precede them.[12] "Strong" poets, such as Keats, are able to achieve a high "revisionary ratio" based on their internalization of writers like Milton and Wordsworth that vaults them out of obscurity and into the literary canon as original writers. There is a calculation in the anxiety of influence, and Bloom argues that the poet works against himself, and against the fear that he will be snuffed out and forgotten. Bloom psychologizes this struggle in relation to Freud's Oedipus complex. But Bloom's can only ever be a theoretical explanation, not a material one.

Although one could argue that *Half-Life* has anxiety of influence for *Quake* as a father figure, their relationship is more formal than even psychoanalysis can characterize accurately. *Half-Life* literally embodies core portions of *Quake,* the abstracted unit operations to which the engine provides access. Although the two games do relate to one another in a history, and perhaps even a hierarchical history of the FPS, their relationship is not one of Oedipal anxiety. In lieu of this anxiety, both games agree to mediate their commonalities through an external structure: intellectual property. Unlike psychoanalysis or literary theory, IP is a stable relationship regulated by governments and markets instead of critics. The rules of IP are flexible and may change, but its fundamental principle is legal, not literary. T. S. Eliot did not license rights to Homer and Dante in order to make their works fungible in his own.

IP as an external mediator also differs from Bolter and Grusin's idea of remediation. Remediation does describe a technique that may be at work in *Half-Life,* but the "borrowing" is mediated by outside forces, both legal and commercial. The game's very access to the unit operations it seeks to borrow from *Quake* are themselves redeemed through another unit operation: licensing. Licensing is a legal function, not a discursive one.

Literature and art have always had a volatile relationship with permissibility—censorship and book burning are nothing new. Recently, U.S. courts have entertained fair use violation cases related to audio sampling in hip-hop music. But by relying on a less ambiguous relationship, game engines relate cultural artifacts and the market in a fundamentally new way. There are implications for this arrangement, both for creation and for criticism. Intellectual property relations can be modified and interpreted by law, and effective criticism of games as cultural works may need to take the licensing operation into account in understanding how a work functions discursively. If there was ever any doubt about the political economy of works of art, game engines end that doubt.

Similarly, the common material and functional basis of games made from the same engines collapses literary critical notions of metaphor and analogy into encapsulated unit operations. *Quake* and *Half-Life* are different in some ways, but they share the same material basis: the same core code. The low-level routines that render objects, manage collision, fire projectiles, and model physical interactions between characters and objects are fundamentally, explicitly identical. While intellectual property implicates a state and an economy in the game, materiality implicates a set of softer cultural, social, and microeconomic forces.

In the recent past, questionable labor practices have haunted the largest developers in the videogame industry.[13] Accusations of oppressively long work hours with no overtime pay and little consideration for out-of-work obligations have led to calls for class-action suits against the worst violators.[14] If we imagine that the programmers working on a hypothetical game engine were forced to work hundred-hour weeks under afflictive working conditions to ship a product, that working condition becomes embedded into the resulting product, just as sweatshop textile labor "taints" the clothing that it produces. In 2003, California supermarkets were disrupted for 141 days by a worker's strike based on unfair benefits practices.[15] Many Californians chose to avoid the offending markets, rather than contribute their financial support to the employers who allegedly perpetrated these practices. However, these people could not track down those who did patronize the markets during the strike and avoid *their* businesses, at least not in broad measure. In the case of the game engine produced under this condition, the common material basis of one game is formally embedded in the other, and thus derivative works inherit the material conditions of their production. A more mundane example might entail a security or functional defect in the engine that, because of its common, encapsulated codebase, would cascade through any games created on that engine.

A more interesting question surrounds the discursive relationship between games built on common engines. *Half-Life* can and does alter or adjust parameters on the unit operations the *Quake Engine* provides. *Counter-Strike* allows players to combat one another in a hypothetical world of moonlike gravity and friction. Unit operations like physics, ballistics, and refractive luminance may not seem like important or even interesting properties to heed when analyzing games. The "S" in FPS does stand for "shooter," so we shouldn't be surprised that the speech such games enact is usually replete with violent depictions of fantastic battles of good versus evil. There is a cultural place for such works, just as there is a place for popcorn action films. The FPS game engine was born from the market opportunity to perpetuate the power fantasy among a videogame market almost entirely dominated by young men. But unlike linear media such as film, discursive prescription has proven less punitive for videogames built on engines. Whereas film studios have experimented with formula fusion—made famous by stereotypical producer pitch room incantations like "it's *The Godfather* meets *When Harry Met Sally*"—some game developers have used FPS engines as a reflexive window on the very notion of the "shooter." Following the lead of Hideo Kojima's 1987 classic *Metal Gear,* third-person games like the *Metal Gear Solid* series and the *Rainbow Six* and *Splinter Cell*[16] series focus on stealth over violence as the preferred—often the only—way to accomplish the game's objective. But it was Looking Glass Studios's *Thief* series that turned the traditional discursive mode of the FPS on its head.[17] The plot of most first-person shooter games is to wage as much slaughter as possible; in *Thief,* the main goal is to *avoid* conflict, sneaking through shadows and darknesd to avoid detection.

Deus Ex, also principally designed by *Thief*'s Warren Spector and built on the *Unreal* game engine, extends *Thief*'s design to include forms of goal-reaching beyond both combat and stealth. *Deus Ex* adds character interaction and skill use as alternative, nonviolent ways to traverse the same narrative space; in fact, the player has access to numerous solutions for any one challenge the game provides. The particular innovation of *Deus Ex* is its addition of a moral tenor: each violent *and* nonviolent player decision affects the outcome of the game.

The discursive carriage of the FPS will change further as game engines, tools, and libraries move beyond killing, racing, and visual effects to emotional conflict, jealousy, and disappointment. As part of their interactive drama *Façade,* Michael Mateas and Andrew Stern have begun to develop an engine for these more subtle human acts.[18] *Façade* uses a set of software subsystems to manage interactions between Grace and Trip, in-game characters involved in a complex marital crisis, and the player, who takes the role of a longtime friend of the couple visiting them after having fallen out of touch. As part of its architecture *Façade* integrates A Behavior Language (ABL), a compilable "reactive planning language" based on Hap, a previous computational system for goal-directed activity developed at Carnegie Mellon University.[19] *Façade* underscores the importance of recognizing the material and functional details of unit operations exposed by game engines. There is already much to debate about how a body reacts to a bullet's impact in a game: is it realistic? Does it desensitize players to the reality of violence? Surely there will be even more to say about how the softer side of human experience is represented through generic unit operations.

In this regard, the discursivity of games is changed by the capabilities of game engines. The kinds of works, and the nature of these works, have material and functional limitations and capabilities—the unit operations the game engine exposes. These limitations and capabilities influence the kind of discourse the works can create, the ways they create them, and the ways users interact with them. For better or worse, the capabilities of game engines have been limited to visual and physical experience, rather than emotional and interpersonal experience.

In August 2003, the consumer PC magazine *Maximum PC* reported on the new features of the widely anticipated *Half-Life 2,* including improved bump mapping, particle effects, fresnel effects, and volumetric effects.[20] All of these features are visual; none has to do with people, save the player's phenomenal encounter with them. The article continues to describe developer Valve's goal for the engine: "to make everything in the game look positively life-like (if not otherworldly)." The focus here is on appearance, not function, not interaction. Game designer Chris Crawford thinks social representation is weak in games because "most game designers are socially incompetent geeks whose social reasoning skills are microscopic."[21]

In *Remediation,* Bolter and Grusin suggest that even though humans write code, because computers execute it, computer programs "can operate without human intervention." "Programming," suggest the two, "employs erasure or effacement . . . .programmers seek to remove the traces of their presence in order to give the program the greatest possible autonomy."[22] Bolter and Grusin often return to disappearance as a goal of new media, from the disappearing worlds of virtual reality (VR) to the verisimilitude of computer-animated films like *Toy Story.* The two argue that digital media "multiply mediation" to create "the reproduction of the feeling of resemblance or identification between two beings."[23]

I agree with this characterization insofar as representations of any kind are informed by their creators' interactions with previous forms of representation. But I would argue that something unique takes place in computational works that distinguishes them from other sorts of production, digital or nondigital: computational systems are not the only kinds of works that exhibit the logic of unit operations, but such systems rely on unit operations as their *primary* mode of representation, and thus unit operations have a special role in how works like videogames function. This function is rooted in a mode of discursive authorship quite different from the one Bolter and Grusin characterize. In the case of a game engine, a code framework, or an SDK (software development kit), the programmer does not seek to remove the traces of his or her presence, but rather seeks to embed that presence into object-oriented systems that both enable and limit any works that instantiate them.

In Michael Mateas's goal-directive language ABL, no work is created. *Façade* uses a compiled behavioral application written in ABL, but ABL itself is a computer language that compiles to an ABL agent API-instantiated in *Façade*'s interactive narrative world. ABL supports synchronized behaviors, which allow the narrative author to make two things happen at once, both of which yield mixed effects when run. ABL supports a number of "features," including preconditions, success tests, priority, atomic behaviors, goals, and subgoals. These primitives are made accessible from the story world via the API, which includes lurid method signatures such as SetGazeTracking() and DoMiscLittleAction(). Mateas and Stern offer this summary of ABL that clarifies its function:

ABL behaviors send simple parameterized action requests to the 3D story world such as "take an angry walk step towards the couch," "look at this object in a coy way," "speak this line of dialog," "do an anxious but smiling facial expression," "do an emphasis hand gesture and nod when I speak," "make my eyes quiver," and so on. ABL behaviors sense the world with queries such as "what is the location of the wedding picture," or "what am I holding in my hand," and receive automatic event notifications such as "you just finished speaking a certain word in your dialog," or "the player just spoke these words," or "the player just picked up a martini glass." The 3D story world is responsible for accomplishing basic performance tasks such as low-level motor control of the body, procedural animation of facial expressions and gaze, lip-sync to dialog, and pathplanning.[24]

Mateas and Stern further break down master narrative into story beats, a term they borrow from screen writing. In film, story beats refer simply to plot points within a larger story; in *Façade,* they refer to short segments of goal-driven, flexible interaction. Beats are the unit operations of the narrative, and the platform queues subsequent beats to progress the experience along a given story arc, a bit like narrative pathfinding.

Unit operations like "look at this object in a coy way" are specific to *Façade,* but the discursive capability offered by ABL goes beyond these specific examples. ABL is a full-fledged computer language, not a game engine, and it requires a separate set of software to manage everything outside the logic for the expressive AI. Nevertheless, it could be incorporated into a complete engine, new or extant.[25] The unit operations of the ABL API encapsulate abstract functions for human discourse, while engines like *Quake II* concentrate on abstract functions for object physics. In both cases, developers who use these engines as the basis for other works are bound to the material, functional, and in many cases intellectual proprietary attributes of the engine. These confines both facilitate and limit discursive production, just as the rules of natural languages bound poetry and the rules of optics bound photography.

Such confines can always be challenged, of course, as evidenced by poets like e. e. cummings and photographers like Jan Saudek. In such disciplines, material analysis often accompanies content analysis. Given their even greater conflation of materiality, functionality, propriety, and discursivity, the same must be true of videogames.

Games and Narratives

Games like *Façade* that recreate human experiences normally reserved for stage, print, or cinema raise questions about the relationship between videogames and traditional media. Aarseth recognizes adventure games like *Adventure* and *Zork* as objectified systems that generate units of textual meaning. Between the lines of Aarseth's reading of adventure games are poignant insights into the proto-object design those systems exhibit, and how such architecture affects the kind of textual output the works create. Writing on the evolution of *Adventure,* he observes,

once the parser and database tools have been developed, these can be reused for several games, and game development then becomes much like planning and writing a piece of short fiction. . . . Since the source code for *Adventure* was available, many game developers simply ported it to any new computer that came along. Creating a new version is mainly a matter of editing and then recompiling a program file; the end result can be as similar or different from the original as the programmer wants.[26]

But Aarseth avoids discussions of the expressive nature of such artifacts in their specific configurations. Markku Eskelinen praises this aspect of cybertextual theory because, in his words, "Aarseth's theory focuses on functional differences within media instead of making essentialist claims."[27]

Aarseth's and Eskelinen's preference for formal analysis underscores a long-standing debate within game studies that continues to fester: what is the relationship between the study of games (ludology) and the study of narrative (narratology)? This "ludology vs. narratology debate" has played itself out in many public and private forums. Writing in the first edition of the first peer-reviewed game studies journal, Jesper Juul sees the issue as an all-or-nothing wager: "Do games tell stories? Answering this should tell us both how to study games and who should study them. The affirmative answer suggests that games are easily studied from within existing paradigms. The negative implies that we must start afresh."[28] Juul concedes that games and narratives share common properties: we use narratives to make sense of experiences, and games have embedded stories and backstories that are undeniably narrative. Juul shows how even a "simple" game like *Space Invaders* relies on a narrative backstory to motivate gameplay, in this case the prehistory of an alien invasion. As structures independent of medium, Juul argues that if games are narratives, they must be translatable from other mediums, such as film. Juul then shows how the narrative coherence of a film like *Star Wars* becomes occluded its video game incarnation. The game version of *Star Wars,* argues Juul, does not provide enough narrative equivalence to recreate the story of the film. Instead, the game offers only an abstract experience of three space battles—the game re-creates neither characterization nor motivation for narrative action.

Juul's fundamental point is that games disturb the relation between reader and story that narratives require. In a game, "the player inhabits a twilight zone where he/she is both an empirical subject outside the game *and* undertakes a role inside the game."[29] Whereas narratives create "cognitive identification" with generally human or anthropomorphic characters, games implicate the player personally in the work. A game like *Tetris,* observes Juul, has no ostensible narrative in the usual sense.

Like Aarseth and Eskelinen, Juul seems to believe that the principal benefit of eschewing narratological analysis is to achieve a kind of "clean break" from the baggage of the linguistic turn in literary studies. "Relying too heavily on existing theories," says Juul, "will make us forget what makes games games: Such as rules, goals, player activity, the projection of the player's actions into the game world, the way the game defines the possible actions of the player."[30]

One could mount several objections to Juul's argument against narrative. The filmic rendition of a work like *The Crying of Lot 49,* for example, could be said to utterly lose the narratives of the textual medium through the same modes of selection and editing Juul points out in the 1983 game *Star Wars.* Likewise, many critics hailed the recent filmic rendition of *The Lord of the Rings* specifically for its ability to preserve the narratives of the textual medium through some of the same kind of obligatory selective reproduction that the *Star Wars* arcade developers must have endured. There is no reason to assume that adaptation of narrative works would neceearily seek to reproduce narrative coherence.

"Ludology vs. Narratology" may be a nice shorthand for the tension between rule-based systems and story-based systems, but as Gonzalo Frasca has pointed out, *narratology* is a somewhat vague contender in this prize match—the debate does not seem to orient ludology against followers of traditional narratologists like Todorov or Genette.[31] Ludology has been characterized by its coverage of the unique features of games, and narratology in the traditional sense of the word is the study of narratives across media, including oral and written language, gestures, and music. Interestingly, this variety of narratology is much more similar to ludology than its detractors may acknowledge. Narratology owes a deep debt to structuralism in general, and Lévi-Strauss, Roland Barthes, and Vladimir Propp all took highly structural approaches to their studies, focusing primarily on the formal properties of narrative.[32] Even the Russian formalists' approach to narrative through *fabula* and *sjuzet* implies rule-based analyses of narrative discourse. If both terms are taken in their strongest sense, narratology is just as formalist and reductionist a practice as ludology. Frasca observes such a common formalism in his original conception of ludology: "Just like narratology, *ludology* should also be independent from the medium that supports the activity."[33] Frasca relates elements of ludus to elements of narrative (game goal to narrative plot, for example), hoping to leverage some of the long-standing formalist utility of narratology to the field of game studies.

The study of the formal properties of narrative or games, then, is quite different from studying the expressive output of either form. Janet Murray reminds us that oral modes of ancient epic storytelling relied extensively on "patterning language into units" for easier recall.[34] Poetic meter (dactylic hexameter in the case of epic poetry) also helped the orator reconstruct segments of discourse without recourse to written record. Likewise, Murray observes that Vladimir Propp's morphology of folktales offers a formulaic, structural grammar from which "satisfying stories can be generated by substituting and rearranging formulaic units."[35]

However, the procedural generation of new genres of digital stories—the principal future vision of Murray's book—represents only a subset of the representational possibility space for unit operations. Examples like epic poetry and folktale suggest that stories are *instances* of unit-operational expression, not a superset of it. However, discussions of formal properties of games and narratives have often become conflated with the expressive quality of instances of games and narratives. Murray's later rumination on possible interactive narratives of the future returns to a reproduction of the film's narrative progression. In her hypothetical "new narrative experience" of the film *Casablanca,* she breaks down the film into units of plot progression: "arrival in Casablanca . . , offer of letters of transit, offer of sexual encounter, meeting with the SS, offer or resistance activities" and so forth.[36] Frasca suggests the term "narrativism" instead of "narratology" to characterize this particular kind of criticism, one that privileges narrative over simulation as the configurative output of a digital work.[37]

Henry Jenkins has observed that many other media maintain a tension between performance and exposition: musicals, action films, and commedia dell'arte among them.[38] Jenkins suggests that narrative might enter games in "localized incidents," a phenomenon he names "micronarratives."[39] Jenkins's principal example is Sergei Eisenstein's famous "Odessa Steps" scene in *Battleship Potemkin:*

Eisenstein intensifies our emotional engagement . . . through a series of short narrative units. Each of these units builds upon stock characters or situations drawn from the repertoire of melodrama. . . . Eisenstein used the word "attractions" broadly to describe any element within a work that produces a profound emotional impact, and theorized that the themes of the work could be communicated across and through these discrete elements.[40]

At first blush, Jenkins seems to be suggesting that something akin to narrative unit operations are at work in Eisenstein's film. A central belief operates here: Jenkins argues that the form these units take is necessarily narrative in nature. Later, Jenkins relies on fabula as the logical catalyst for understanding such structures: "narrative comprehension is an active process by which viewers assemble and make hypotheses about likely narrative developments on the basis of information drawn from textual cues and clues."[41] The narrative reassembly of unit operations is thus taken for granted. Jenkins's arguments call to mind recent research that attempts to align narrative with cognition. AI researcher Roger Schank explicitly argues that "we think in stories."[42] In Schank's conception, humans simply process units of meaning in story form: "seeing a particular story as an instance of a more general and universally known story causes the teller of the story to forget the differences between the particular and the general."[43] Similarly, Mark Turner has argued that humans possess a "literary mind," a cognitive propensity for stories.[44]

The admittedly questionable role of cognitive science in criticism notwithstanding, other neuroscientists offer a different perspective on the relationship between cognition and generic understanding. Most notably, Giacomo Rizzolatti's discovery of "mirror neurons" suggests a relationship between cognitive understanding and discrete, nonnarrative actions.[45] Rizolatti recorded the brain activity in monkeys and observed that certain cells would fire when one monkey watched another monkey (or a human!) perform a specific action, such as picking up and eating a nut. Rizolatti then demonstrated that these same cells fire when the observing monkey performs the action himself. Further research has suggested that mirror neurons also structure human cognition, and their function has been conjectured to explain empathy and some causes of autism.[46] Some neuroscientists have argued that mirror neurons might explain, and therefore precede, the evolution of language,[47] although few are willing to argue that mirror neurons alone can explain such a development.[48]

Mirror neurons suggest ways of understanding units of representational meaning that do not necessarily have recourse to narrative. On the one hand, ludology in the strongest form, if it even exists, would seek to divest games of any engagement whatsoever with human experience; they would become mere abstract rule systems. Even the most extreme structuralists don't take a position this strong. On the other hand, narrativism in the strongest form, again if it even exists, would see games only as producers of narratives, no matter what kind of configurative, unit-operational structures might underlie such production. Each of these extremes is haunted by a functionalist ideology, albeit a very different one in each case.

A reformulated version of the question of ludology versus narratology might ask if games *need* to produce stories, while acknowledging that they might be able to do so. Mateas and Stern's interactive drama *Façade* musters a great many core technologies toward the production of a legitimate generative narrative, among them natural language processing, goal-directed behavior management, procedural facial animation, and drama management. Of these, only drama management is fundamentally related to narrative.

We should attempt to evaluate all texts as configurative systems built out of expressive units. This entails training ourselves not only to "understand simulations as interpretations of the world," as Janet Murray suggests, but also to understand narrative texts as simulation.[49] Videogames can be played as individual linear experiences that might in turn be describable in narrative form, but such analysis is useful only as an exemplar for the broader abstract meaning the text's unit operations elucidate. For example, the story threads in *The Terminal* do take the form of coherent micronarratives, to use Jenkins's term, but their significance comes not from the individual stories they tell, but from the general unit operations they expose. *Casablanca* does indeed have a narrative progression—Ilsa and Victor's struggle to escape Casablanca—but the film has more to do with Rick Blaine's struggle to escape cynical bitterness. Murray's tacit assumption that a digital edition of the film would have to reproduce its plot progression is not so much an artistic strategy, as an ideology. Instead, we need to read unit operations as discursive in their own right, outside and before the grammars of specific creative strategies.

Encounters across Platforms

As part of the evolution of game studies, and to further the resistance to the overly simple opposition of functionalist versus expressive analyses, we ought to spend time looking at how other kinds of cultural artifacts implement their expression through unit operations. This exploration need not equate literature, poetry, or film with videogames. Rather, it should strive for the kind of understanding Janet Murray hopes for: "something as true to the human condition, and as beautifully expressed, as the life that Shakespeare captured on the Elizabethan stage."[1]

The concept of the *chance encounter* is a founding archetype of modernity. I want to explore this concept through four cultural artifacts spanning 150 years: a well-known poem by French modernist Charles Baudelaire; another poem written about 100 years later by American poet Charles Bukowski; Jean-Pierre Jeunet's film *Amélie;* and Will Wright's bestselling game *The Sims* and its expansion pack *Hot Date.*

By chance encounter, I mean that random, anonymous meeting one has in modern environments, usually but not always with a subject of desire. My contention is that as this very modern experience moves from an experience of crisis in the mid-nineteenth century to an experience of banality in the twenty-first century, it becomes compressed into more and more compact modes of representation. Baudelaire does not merely author a poem; he also creates a unit of cultural memory, a tool that others can make fungible as a performance of the modern life. During its 150-year lifespan, this unit operation marks two important transitions. First, by the time Charles Bukowski is writing poetry in the mid-twentieth century, the figure retains its original function as a way to resist the alienation of modern experience but achieves a level of familiarity that leads to significant poetic condensation. Second, by the turn of the next century, Baudelaire's strategy begins to wane, and Jeunet's and Wright's works expose the potentially objectionable qualities of this unit of modern experience, calling those very rules into question.

Baudelaire required the richly expressive format of the lyric poem, with its complex psychological structures, to combat what Walter Benjamin called a "breakdown" of experience. Benjamin's notion of the decline of the aura in natural objects and in works of visual art amounts to a decoupling of the natural vista or the creative work from its place in ritual, or in the continuity of representation. But Benjamin also articulates a decline in the aura of human experience. Like natural objects and objects of tradition, human experience decouples from the continuity of ritual and social abundance. In practice, this force contributed significantly—indeed perhaps most significantly—to the feeling of alienation that Baudelaire so famously recounts. As modern cities brought more people together in closer quarters, the social and interpersonal relationships between individuals became more incidental, more aleatory. Baudelaire's Paris had been torn down and reconstructed with unidentifiable monuments that undermined and erased his sense of place. Urbanization only created alienation, indeed even alienation from the city's very failure.

Benjamin locates these sociohistorical gaps of the mid-nineteenth century at the tip of Baudelaire's quill: "He envisioned blank spaces which he filled in with his poems."[2] These gaps represented impositions, struggles the poet attempted to combat for his narrator. Baudelaire tried to resist alienation through his poetry, both creating a record of his contemporary strategies and tools for combating estrangement and formalizing those very tools into a framework, a kind of scaffolding for modern experience that remains with us today. These tools include *flânerie,* self-isolation, and resistance—especially to memory. Together, Baudelaire's lyric encapsulates these figures and tropes into a framework, or rule set, for living the modern life. Benjamin calls these rules *motifs.* I would call them unit operations.

Since Benjamin, the output of this collection and dissemination has been considered to be beneficial for the city, imbued with positive intent, probably because our own urban experiences today still seek to mimic the *flâneur* as hero. The *flâneur* is that wandering modern dandy whose path through the city arbitrarily couples and decouples with otherwise unknown, anonymous individuals. And yet Benjamin characterizes the *flâneur*'s role as representative of the simultaneous shock and intoxication of the city: The *flâneur*, he writes, "becomes accomplice [to the crowd] even as he dissociates himself from them. He becomes deeply involved with them, only to relegate them to oblivion with a single glance of contempt."[3] This ambiguous movement between the celebration and rejection of the modern experience is arguably the strongest motif we inherit from Baudelaire.

I am most interested in how Baudelaire creates tools for living modern life—strategies that function procedurally even more than they do lyrically. As a figure in transition across an anonymous urban expanse, the *flâneur*'s role is fundamentally a configurative one. His passage through the city constantly opens up new paths, new glances at passersby, new storefronts and sidewalks, just as it closes down others. Because *flânerie* is fundamentally a passage through a space, it bears much similarity to the configurative structure of procedural texts. Writing about the distinction between a cybertext and its specific instantiations, Aarseth observes that "when you read from a cybertext, you are constantly reminded of inaccessible strategies and paths not taken, voices not heard."[4] Aarseth further describes such configurative structures in terms of the multicursal medieval labyrinth, one in which "the maze wanderer faces a series of critical choices."[5] The modern city also resembles the multicursal maze, and the flâneur acts as its wanderer. However, the decision points faced by the *flâneur* far exceed mere cartographic decision; he chooses not only which streets, alleys, and arcades to traverse, but also which tobacconist to visit, which passersby to watch or ignore, which carriage to take, which puddle to step in or avoid.

The work of the *flâneur* is constructed of these individual unit operations, some of which he configures as he traverses the city, some which configure themselves for him based on the emergent effect of actions taken by all the other individuals in the vicinity. This fundamental urban configuration remains unchanged. Residents of large contemporary cities experience these unit operations every day; they explain why you might see the same people commuting in to work as you wait for the subway, or why you might stop at the same food cart after your morning jog.

Let's take a look at one of Baudelaire's most famous sonnets, "A une passante," which embodies many of the figures I've already described.

La rue assourdissante autour de moi hurlait.
Longue, mince, en grand deuil, douleur majestueuse,

Une femme passa, d'une main fastueuse
Soulevant, balançant le feston et l'ourlet;

Agile et noble, avec sa jambe de statue.
Moi, je buvais, crispé comme un extravagant,
Dans son œil, ciel livide où germe l'ouragon,
La douceur qui fascine et le plaisir qui tue.

Un éclair . . . puis la nuit!—Fugitive beauté
Dont le regard m'a fait soudainement renaître,
Ne te verrai-je plus que dans l'éternité?

Ailleurs, bien loin d'ici! trop tard! *Jamais* peut-être!
Car j'ignore où tu fuis, tu ne sais où je vais,
O toi que j'eusse aimée, ô toi qui le savais!

The deafening street was shrieking around me.
Tall, slender, grieving majestically in her widow's veil,
A woman passed, with a delicate carriage
Lifting up and swinging her skirttails;

Sprightly and noble, her arms were like a statue's.
As for me, I was drinking, restless like an eccentric,
In her eyes, I saw the livid sky where hurricanes begin,
The sweetness that charms and the pleasure that kills.

A flash . . . then night!—Fleeting beauty
Whose glance suddenly gave birth to me again,
Will I see you again only in eternity?

Somewhere else, far from here! Too long! Maybe never!
I don't know where you're running, nor do you me,
Oh you who I would have loved! And you who knew it too! [6]

We have all had something like this experience. It is so familiar that it is hard to imagine what it would be like to experience it for the first time, to have to think about this encounter deliberately in order to make sense of it. The first line sets the stage for the poem, an example of the raucous streets of nineteenth-century Paris. The rest of the poem acts as a subterfuge to help the narrator accommodate the "change in the nature of experience" that Benjamin argues embodies Baudelaire's lyric.[7] Critic Jérome Thélot asks of Baudelaire's narrator why he does not stop the woman; after all, what conflict prevents him?[8] Benjamin's answer is worth repeating in context:

What this sonnet communicates is simply this: Far from experiencing the crowd as an opposed, antagonistic element, this very crowd brings to the city dweller the figure that fascinates. The delight of the urban poet is love—not at first sight, but at last sight. It is a farewell forever which coincides in the poem with the moment of enchantment.[9]

The poem expresses a unit operation for contending with the chance encounter. On the one hand, it is the crowd that thrusts the narrator into the new confusion his situation exposes. On the other hand, that very exposure reveals a useful tool, what Benjamin calls a *figure that fascinates.* As Benjamin expresses, the poem's narrator delights in the "farewell forever"—not the woman herself.[10] Through "A une passante," Baudelaire marks a strategy of lonely love, not erotic love, to come to grips with the shock of modern life, the inability to find meaningful social engagement in this constantly reconfiguring world. This experience, again in Benjamin's words, "one might not infrequently say . . . was spared, rather than denied, fulfillment."[11]

Benjamin showed how mechanical reproduction reduced the *aura,* or the cultural authenticity, of art during this age of mechanical reproduction. The kind of experience Baudelaire describes in "A une passante" is an example of a decline of *natural aura.* Benjamin calls natural aura the "phenomenon of a distance," which when reproduced replaces the old ethos of deferential awe with a new one of relaxed expertise.[12] Elsewhere, Benjamin clarifies the function of the aura in human relationships: "The person we look at, or who feels he is being looked at, looks at us in turn. To perceive the aura of an object we look at means to invest it with the ability to look at us in turn."[13] But the salve for the modern chance encounter comes only if the subject resists this return. According to Baudelaire's strategy, out of that resistance comes a kind of pleasure, different from other pleasures, a figure that fascinates. In the alienating confusion of the procedural city, Baudelaire's lyric posits the figure that fascinates as a replacement for the woman's companionship.

Baudelaire and his characters pay dearly for their access to this figure. By maintaining his separation from the crowd and its inhabitants, by opening a rift in traditional experience to make way for this new kind of experience, the poet is waging a war he can never win, for he has no recourse to consummate the encounter. Baudelaire thus infuses his verses with defeat. That the woman of "A une passante" is in mourning, bearing her widow's veil, amplifies the subject's resistance by drawing attention to the woman's solitude in terms of the narrator's own solitude. Both poet and *passante* are alone, without counterpart. The narrator has responded to this encounter not to court her, but to resist her, to fashion her into a figure that fascinates. Even though the woman is in "majestic sadness," the narrator can be sure that she, like he himself, will find emptiness at the end of her journey, this time the emptiness left both by death and by the empty home that death implies.

Benjamin relies on Henri Bergson's *Matter and Memory* as a model for the way Baudelaire represents experience. Under Benjamin's reading of Bergson, experience becomes "a convergence in memory of accumulated and frequently unconscious data." Benjamin sees Baudelaire's response to the failures of ritual practice as the principal function of his poetry. But he cannot predict how Baudelaire's poetry will function later in its historical trajectory. By the mid-twentieth century, American poet Charles Bukowski still finds himself entrenched in the same urban breakdown that afflicted Baudelaire.[14] Yet, his poetic representation of the experience of the chance encounter shifts from a struggle to understand alienation to an acceptance of its inevitability. Still Bukowski's poem "A woman on the street" bears a striking resemblance to "A une passante."

her shoes themselves
would light my room
like many candles.

she walks like all things
shining on glass,
like all things
that make a difference.

she walks away.[15]

Baudelaire's "figure that fascinates" is carried over in Bukowski's chance encounter; the poet draws an explicit connection between his narrator and his female counterpart, taking his pleasure from the abstinence of her company. What is most striking about this poem is the compactness of its representation. Baudelaire appeals to the classical modes of elegy, including the form of the sonnet; Bukowski adopts only two figures to mark the woman's significance, the trifles that separate her from the urban crowd.[16]

Both poems also pay special attention to the women's feet. Bukowski's narrator explicitly makes note of her shoes as objects which might bring light to his otherwise dark surroundings, and Baudelaire's implicitly watches his passerby's ankles appear from under her skirt hem, perhaps as she steps into a carriage. In both cases, the gaze is not lascivious, nor even mildly erotic; instead, it holds the woman in suspense, keeping her at the distance required for the figure that fascinates to function. Bukowski's explicit insertion of his own potential relationship with the woman seems to take on the same function as the *passante*'s veil of mourning; it draws attention to the mutual emptiness of their actual relationship: "her shoes alone/would light my room/like many candles." But this time, it is not the woman's death-torn home, but her shoes alone that are enough to saturate the narrator's world; this fact holds the woman's desire in reserve. This time, even if the two were to realize their admiration, the narrator himself would be no less dead than the *passante*'s bereaved. Moreover, whereas Baudelaire draws attention to the emptiness of the woman's room, an emptiness wrought by death, Bukowski underscores the emptiness of his own home. The darkness of the widow's veil is transferred to the darkness of the room, a darkness that would be extinguished merely by the woman's shoes.

I would argue that the similarities between these two poems are not accidental. Bukowski is not simply mimicking Baudelaire's treatment of the modern experience; rather, that strategy, the figure that fascinates, has itself compacted and become embodied as a unit of cultural currency. As a device for modern living, the figure that fascinates becomes instantiated and reexpressed in Bukowski's poem. As Benjamin predicted, Baudelaire's lyric has resisted tradition, only to create a new kind of ritual practice, the ineffectual closure of chance encounters. A century later, Bukowski is still acting out the same Baudelairean strategy, knowing that love at first sight implies a whole set of new conflicts, a mass of problems and uncertainties that never guarantee any emotional benefit.

The infancy of the modern city requires much more commentary on the part of Baudelaire, who reminds us that both woman and poet may never see the other again, but the love's possibility remains within them. Despite its brevity, Bukowski's poem conveys the same message: everything Baudelaire expresses in the final tercet is contained within the received, ritual experience Baudelaire creates in the figure that fascinates. The woman of "A woman on the street" seems to walk *only* to "walk away."

In the time between the two poems' writing, the figure that fascinates has become an effective unit operation, a tool for engaging modern life. It would be overzealous to equate this figure that fascinates with a software subsystem, a piece of compiled code that Bukowski instantiates into his poem. Such a reading would only validate Kittler's objections that we are slaves to technological representation. What is important about Bukowski's representation of the figure that fascinates is not that it could be construed as a software system, but rather that Bukowski's poem relies on a consolidated version of Baudelaire's figure, that it enacts this figure by playing by its rules. Moreover, the figure does not exist in one stable place—not merely as a literary device, nor as a historical condition, nor as a faculty of the mind, nor as a social convention. What "A woman on the street" shows us is that a material frame can be drawn around the complex experience of the chance encounter and yet still succeed at representing something meaningful. This potential for a formal material framework is essential to understanding the poems, and more fundamentally, our own experience of the world.

Baudelaire and Bukowski want to invoke the rules of chance encounter in order to maintain the distance required to muster the figure that fascinates. But the unit-operational logic of the chance encounter becomes more visible when it starts to break down. Jean-Pierre Jeunet's film *Amélie* both reinforces and responds to this common material framework. The film quickly introduces its main characters in a formal but unusual way, through a series of rapid-fire vignettes. The narrator describes each character as a highly encapsulated figure, taking advantage of the unusual yet familiar archetypes upon which each is based: Amélie's neurotic-obsessive mother; her cold but caring neurotic-obsessive father; her hypochondriac coworker. Amélie herself dreams "of escaping a dead world." In her pursuit, she takes pleasure in a series of inconsequential acts that configure her experience in much the same way as the modern city configures the habits of its residents. Amélie likes cracking crème brulée with her spoon, plunging her hand in a bucket of grain at the market, and skipping stones. She enjoys looking at the faces of the other people in the darkness of the cinema, and she wonders "how many couples are having an orgasm right now?"

The film takes place in contemporary Paris, but it looks and feels much closer to Baudelaire's Paris. As one critic put it, "It's a bit surprising for example that there is no telephone ringing to pollute the streets of a city whose inhabitants now appear to be born with a cell phone grafted to their hands."[17] Symbols and archetypes of Paris reign throughout the film, from Yann Tiersen's accordion-heavy score to the whir of Nino Quincampoix's moped to the street bistro to the steps of Montmartre.[18] These are clichéd, almost parodic figures for anyone who has spent any time in modern Paris; arguably these figures serve only to create connections between the modern city and its nineteenth-century complement. This historical anamorphosis also helps Amélie seat her desire to maintain the nineteenth-century distance of her encounters with others. Baudelaire and Bukowski rely primarily on the potential relationships with women to constitute the figure that fascinates, but Amélie has achieved a level of abstraction that extends to a wealth of possible, but not actual encounters.

Driven by a chance discovery, Amélie decides to construct fully realized experiences around her. Her purpose is ostensibly benevolent, or at least this is the message the film telegraphs. In fact, Amélie creates ornate plans to introduce satisfaction in the lives of those around her only to maintain her own distance from that satisfaction, and to capture for herself the figure that fascinates in new forms.

The first of these encounters comes after Amélie discovers an old box of childhood mementos behind a floorboard in her flat. She makes inquiries of neighbors and old residents, trying to locate the man who once hid away these treasures as a boy. When she finally locates him, she coordinates a chance encounter—an antithetical notion indeed—through which the now aging man might be reunited with this box of treasures. After she successfully delivers her payload, the film depicts Amélie seated next to the man at a bar; he now considers rekindling a lost relationship with his son due to this provocation. Amélie says nothing, but downs her drink and leaves.

Even though Amélie appears to act out of generosity, the purpose of her project is not to rekindle the man's affection for his childhood and family, but to construct an experience that satisfies her fantasy through chance encounter. Amélie is no longer the subject of the encounters she creates; instead she is their designer, so versed in the logic of modern experience that she crafts representations in blood and flesh that Baudelaire and Bukowski had to encounter for themselves, then document. Amélie shows us that the chance encounter is such a replete structure that it can be acted out as a unit operation. She has become the programmer of her own procedural urban encounters.

As Amélie instantiates more figures that fascinate, the film also allows the viewer to enjoy them in the same manner; they are charming and endearing, and the viewer does not hesitate to receive them as such. At the same time, Jeunet sends signs of the problems with Amélie's strategy. Most of the encounters she constructs are manipulative, even illegal. She breaks into and vandalizes the grocer's flat because he treats his simpleton clerk poorly. She sets up a false longing between one coworker and another's estranged former lover. She sends her father's esteemed garden gnome on an adventure around the world, instructing recipients to mail home photos of the gnome's journey. Jeunet maintains deliberate ambiguity between the benevolence and malice of these acts, although most of the films viewers and critics see only the former, just like Amélie.

As the film wears on, Amélie finds herself trapped in one of her chance encounters with a young man, Nino Quincampoix, who shares her obsessive interests (he collects the disposed shards of photos left near the metro photo booths). For a time, Amélie tries to maintain the distance of the figure that fascinates between herself and Nino. The film changes focus; now it is about Amélie's struggle to maintain this distance, her struggle to remain faithful to the unit operation's rules. This struggle unravels through a series of exchanges with her neighbor, an old man with a bone disease that prevents him from leaving the house, and thus earning the name "L'homme de verre" (Glass Man). The Glass Man spends every day indoors, and each year he paints a new copy of Renoir's *Dejeuner des canotiers*.[19] Through this painting—by a contemporary of Baudelaire, often considered the voyeur of the impressionists—he coerces Amélie to question the logic of the figure that fascinates. The Glass Man points out the girl in the center of the painting, drinking from a glass, and says, "After all these years, the only character I cannot understand is the girl holding the glass of water. She is in the center, but somehow outside."

Amélie   Vous savez la fille au verre d'eau? Si elle a l'air un peu à côté, c'est p'têtre parce qu'elle est en train de penser à quelqu'un.

Homme de verre   Quelqu'un du tableau?

Amélie   Non, plutôt un garçon qu'elle a croisé ailleurs. Elle a l'impression qu'ils sont un peu pareils elle et lui.

Homme de verre   Autrement dit, elle préfère s'imaginer une relation avec quelqu'un d'absent, plutôt que de créer des liens avec ceux qui sont présents.

Amélie   Non, p'têtre même qu'au contraire elle se met en quatre pour arranger les cafouillages de la vie des autres.

Homme de verre   Mais elle, et les cafouillages de la sienne, de vie, qui va s'en occuper?

. . .

Homme de verre   Elle est amoureuse de lui.

Amélie   Oui.

Homme de verre   Et bien je crois que le moment est venu pour elle de prendre un vrai risque.

Amélie   Justement, elle y pense. Elle est en train de réfléchir à un stratagème

. . .

Homme de verre   Ah elle aime bien ça les stratagèmes! En fait, elle est un peu lâche. Je crois que c'est pour ça que j'ai du mal à saisir son regard.

Amélie   *You know the girl with the glass of water? If she seems a bit out of place, maybe it's because she's thinking about someone else.*

Glass Man   *Someone in the painting?*

Amélie   *No, probably a boy she crossed paths with somewhere else. She had the sense that he and she were a bit alike.*

Glass Man   *In other words, she prefers to imagine a relationship with someone who isn't there, instead of creating real bonds with people around her.*

Amélie   *No, maybe she even goes out of her way to arrange other peoples' messed up lives.*

Glass Man   *But what about her own messed up life? Who's going to worry about that?*

. . .

Glass Man   *She's in love with him.*

Amélie   *Yes.*

Glass Man   *Well, I think it's time for her to take a real risk.*

Amélie   *Actually, she's thinking about it. She's just now in process of devising a stratagem.*

Glass Man   *Oh, she likes stratagems! In fact, she's a bit of a coward. I think that's why I have a hard time pinning down her glance.*[20]

The "stratagem" is precisely the Baudelairean unit operation, the figure that fascinates. Importantly, this scene forces Amélie to reveal her plans as mere ploys or subterfuges—not strategies, but stratagems—intended for deception instead of reward. It is an instance of this figure, and a representation of Amélie's understanding of that figure in its abstract form, and Amélie realizes that she is duped by her own ploy.

Suddenly, the entire film exposes itself as a struggle between totalizing systems and individual actions. The child Amélie's goldfish is sacrificed so its suicidal crises don't unnerve her mother; Amélie's excited response to her father's rare touch during her monthly physical is misinterpreted as a heart condition that keeps her forever at home; the obsessive ex-boyfriend Joseph, who seeks to document everything his former love does; the hypochondriac Georgette, who seeks to map every oscillation in her body to a systemic disease. All stand as instances of the same unit operation, the attempt to sacrifice the present for the perverse indulgence of its forfeit.

Despite its popular reception, *Amélie* is hardly a film about an innocent girl making good in the world; it is about the struggle to reject a hundred-year-old obsession with Baudelaire's bequeathed way of using modern life. At the end of the film, Amélie welcomes Nino Quincampoix on his own terms, in an admittedly touching scene where she wonders if she's lost him, only to find him return to her door moment later. This moment of panic marks Amélie's abandonment of the figure that fascinates.

Around the same time *Amélie* found her way to the theater to watch the faces in the audience, Will Wright's studio Maxis released what would become the bestselling PC game ever—*The Sims*.[21] The game allows players to create and model a modern individual's life, giving him or her a house, a job, and specific characteristics. *The Sims* spawned numerous add-on packages that provide additional behavior, scenarios, or objects in the game. One such expansion pack is the 2001 release *The Sims: Hot Date*. *Hot Date* is essentially a courtship add-on for *The Sims*. It adds a "downtown" area that Sims can visit to meet or woo potential love interests. But to understand how *Hot Date* works, it is important to understand *The Sims*.[22]

The Sims is a daily life simulator, a game that allows the player to manage a household of simulated people, or "Sims." The game itself allows for complex customization of the environment, including building houses and customizing interior spaces with objects like televisions, chairs, and paintings. The main purpose of the game is to manage or administer the individual and communal lives of the players' characters. After defining the sims' personality types (a subject I'm not going to discuss here), players direct their sims by dictating interactions between the characters and other people or objects in the environment. A series of gauges represent various critical factors in each sim's life, such as hunger and energy. For example, a player can direct his sim to eat by clicking on a refrigerator placed in the game and selecting the menu option, "have a snack."

Will Wright has explained that some of the interaction design of *The Sims* is based on Scott McCloud's principles of comic design. McCloud argues that in comics, the reader fills in the spaces between the panels, projecting themselves into their reading and interpretation of the story.[23] Some of the abstraction in *The Sims* is built into the simulation—sims speak gibberish, and their spoken and nonspoken thoughts are represented ichnographically. Talking about this use of abstraction, Wright said the following:

Especially right now with current technology, there are a lot of limitations in terms of what we can do with character simulation. So, to me that seemed like a really good use of the abstraction because there are certain things we just cannot simulate on a computer, but on the other hand that people are very good at simulating in their heads. So we just take that part of the simulation and offload it from the computer into the player's head.[24]

As a simulated model of daily life, *The Sims* makes certain decisions about what kinds of representations to include, and what to leave out. This "weakness" is also a strength, because it increases the game's possibility space. Whether or not the game supports or critiques a specific approach to daily life management is largely up to the player; the game provides a tool set in which it is possible to explore some of these ideologies—for example, whether to dedicate a sim's life to work or to zoning out on distractions. Nevertheless, the game does privilege certain values over others. Gonzalo Frasca offers this commentary about *The Sims*'s celebration of consumer capitalism:

Literally, the amount of virtual friends that you have depends on the amount of goods that you own (obviously, the bigger your house, the better). Nevertheless, I met some people that firmly believe that *The Sims* is a parody and, therefore, it is actually a critique of consumerism. Personally, I disagree. While the game is definitively cartoonish, I am not able to find satire within it. Certainly, the game may be making fun of suburban Americans, but since it rewards the player every time she buys new stuff, I do not think this could be considered parody.[25]

The issue is certainly an open one, but it underscores the game's fertility as a representative medium.

The *Hot Date* expansion pack is important because it moves the sims outside of their homes, out of the virtual dollhouse and into a simulated urban environment. In this "downtown," sims can meet "townies," characters generated entirely by the simulation rather than created by the player. Because *The Sims* is a game, players have an opportunity to explore the conditions, assumptions, and outcomes of the simulation through interaction, something impossible in the poems of Baudelaire and Bukowski. But like their poetry, *The Sims* relies on a set of rules that define how the simulation unfolds. *Hot Date* adds the ability to model and interact with sims' romantic encounters. And because it offers an urban social space filled with game-generated characters, the expansion pack makes it possible to simulate chance encounters.

Unlike "A une passante" and "A Woman on the Street," which offer poetic significance by their formal characteristics, meaning in *The Sims* comes solely from the generative effect of numerous codified rule sets. Events can be interpreted out of the interaction or sequence of these rules, but the player's control requires him to embody and act in units of compressed meaning rather than in streams of narrative meaning. At the same time, *Hot Date* codifies a set of privileged rules that presumably represent what players would most enjoy accomplishing in the game. Built into the main game are eight basic character needs, including hunger, hygiene, energy, and fun. Each sim's status is determined through contribution curves, or need regulators, that normalize the character's relative level for each of their basic needs.

While it is possible to adjust a sim's characteristics, every sim has to fulfill each of these basic needs. If the player ignores any of them, the simulation will take over, directing the sim to take the required action automatically. For example, if the player fails to take care of his sim's need to empty his bladder, then the game will direct the character to find the nearest bathroom to return the simulation to stability. That said, it is possible to create scenarios in which the AI cannot compensate for player negligence. If I place my toilet-needy sim in a room with no doors, eventually he will die of starvation—or possibly explode.

Hot Date allows players to experiment with the sims' need for social interaction. The game itself is built on the assumption that players will want to take their sims out on dates, or to pick up potential love interests. In its design, and perhaps unwittingly, the game's designers have encapsulated the modern experience of chance encounters, taking the representation of the figure that fascinates and instantiating it in a combination of procedural actions and need contribution curves.

When a sim goes downtown to interact with other sims, he is thrust into a highly formalized representation of the modern social space, a representation directly inherited from models like Baudelaire's. Downtown, the sim can enter an arcade, sit on a street corner, visit the beach, or stop by a club. In any of these venues, both the sim and the player are presented with countless "woman on the street"-type experiences, chance encounters for both the player and the sim.

In this context, the player chooses whether or not to approach another sim and strike up a conversation by executing specific software-enabled actions through menu interfaces.

When Bukowski instantiates the inherited figure that fascinates into his real encounters, he affirms the ritualization of Baudelaire's strategy. When Amélie meticulously plans her contrived encounters, she explicitly recognizes this ritual. *The Sims: Hot Date* finally takes the ultimate step in representing the chance encounter as a unit operation: it encapsulates it into the code of a simulation. What the game allows that the literary medium cannot is interactivity, the direct manipulation of the "narrator" in the simulated world. Because the sim waits for the player's input by default, the game affords a unique perspective on chance encounters in the simulated and real world. On the one hand, the player is forced to register the event not only from the perspective of the character (*does that sim look like someone I'd like to meet?*), but also from the perspective of the simulation (*what are the social rules to which my sim conforms?*). Otherwise said, the simulation exposes the various strategies the player can choose in approaching his sim's situation. One option is to exercise the opportunity; to approach and talk to anyone the player chooses. Another option is to sit around and watch potential love interests pass by forever, never to return—like Baudelaire's and Bukowski's narrators.

In the simulation, the player has at his fingertips a limited set of procedural rules that reveal the set of strategies available for manipulating a sim's reaction to the chance encounter. On the one hand, these strategies are encapsulated into specific actions that the player can and cannot take. For example, the player can talk to another sim or even kiss one, but he cannot pass by, brushing gently against her. To be fair, the player also cannot explicitly enact the figure that fascinates—there is no command for "watching the sim walk away." However, the gaps in the simulation that the player fills in "in his head" function equally well no matter how the player directs his sim.

That said, *The Sims'* very structure of character encounters in code exposes the chance encounter as a unit operation ready for conceptual retirement. *The Sims* uses a scripting engine called Edith to define the ways sims and objects in the world interact. Objects imply both tangibles—chairs, refrigerators, pinball machines—and intangibles—weather, character spawn logic, and, most important, social interactions.[26] Sims objects "advertise" their capabilities to the simulation around them, which matches the fluctuating needs of individual sims with the capabilities of the object. In the game's architecture, the code to interact with an object is contained in the object itself, not in the sim, which is inherently ignorant of the world around him. In the case of person-to-person interactions, a social interactions "object" brokers messages between two sims characters, whether user- or computer-controlled. In each case, the game posits a mediator between the player and his interactor, a black box for social logic that has been compressed into a social rule that exists independently of the interactors.

Ultimately, *Hot Date* allows the player to experiment with the breakdown of the new ritual strategy for chance encounters we inherit from Baudelaire. Even if there is no room for parody in *The Sims'* representation of consumer capitalism, there is a clear ambiguity of ideology in *Hot Date*. On the one hand, the game seeks to capitalize on contemporary culture's fascination with matchmaking. On the other hand, the game challenges its players to bear witness to the strange ritual practice of chance encounters in social spaces. As a virtual downtown, *Hot Date* allows its players to experiment with the ways they choose to negotiate the chance encounter, and the ways they do not. Talking about the inspiration for *The Sims,* Will Wright offers:

One of the biggest things that I wanted to show was how, basically, the real resource everybody has in life is time. You can convert time to a lot of other things—you can convert it into money, objects, and friends—but how you choose to spend your time is how you're playing the game of life. That's the one thing that you don't get more of, really. So, time management was a big thing I wanted to at least make people more aware of. It's not so much preaching, "Here's how you should spend your time." It's just interesting when you sit back and think about how you choose to spend every minute of your day.[27]

In this sense, the game expresses a set of options available to the sim and to the player in negotiating human experience. By encapsulating the framework of the modern social challenge into unit operations, the player's decisions not only establish or reinforce a character behavior but also confer a value judgment on that behavior. By asking players to understand these decisions, *The Sims* has the potential to act as a challenge to social norms. It is a struggle against the receipt of the stratagems of Baudelaire, rather than the barrenness of modernity. The game provides a low-consequence environment where players are finally asked to look objectively about their experience of the crowd and of the chance encounter, and to experiment with the consequences of their perspectives.

Of course, *Hot Date* does not try to model the subtlety of real-world outcomes, but not since Baudelaire has there been a new tool specifically designed to offer practical advice on the modern experience. By laying bare the figure of the chance encounter in the form of software, *The Sims* invites players to examine their own satisfaction with this 150-year-old social rubric, and to choose for themselves how to act—or how not to act—in the material world. This model suggests that videogames, like art of all kinds, has the power to influence and change human experience.

III

Procedural Subjectivity

Cellular Automata and Simulation

Chaos theory describes dynamic systems that are sensitive to an initial state, such as plate tectonics or a double pendulum. Because their behavior depends on initial conditions, chaotic systems are deterministic, even if unpredictable. Recently, many fields of scientific and social inquiry have become interested in complex systems theory, a related discipline that attempts to explain adaptive systems with simple components but complex overall behavior. Most recently, physicist and entrepreneur Stephen Wolfram published his magnum opus *A New Kind of Science,* the product of some twenty years of reclusive and secretive research. Wolfram, who also invented *Mathematica,* the world's leading computer software for complex mathematical modeling and diagramming, based his 1,200-page work on a relatively simple concept directly related to complex networks and unit operations.

Since the early 1980s, Wolfram has been a proponent of *cellular automata.* A cellular automaton is a simple program (an automaton) isolated into small units (cells). These units interact with one another, exposing what scientists—computer scientists especially—have hoped to exploit as a viable model for artificial life. Wolfram takes the approach several steps further. Using simple computer models developed in his own program Mathematica, Wolfram attempts to reinvent every discipline of the sciences, from biology to motion dynamics, according to simple logics. The complexity of these systems, argues Wolfram, "is generated by the cooperative effect of many simple identical components."[1] Cellular automata offer another example of the logic of unit operations at work.

A broad category of games and related computational systems known as simulations are based on unit operations of the cellular-automatic kind. But more than merely seeking to model the function of the material world, simulations also mark a meeting place between unit-based rules and subjective experiences.

Cellular Automata

Despite the credentials behind scientists like Stephen Wolfram, cellular automata are relatively simple to understand. An automaton is any kind of machine or device—electric, electronic, biological, chemical, or otherwise—that performs rote tasks. Despite its tight correlation with the life sciences, the word *cellular* indicates isolation or compartmentalization rather than biology.[2] Cellular automata are mechanized systems that perform a single, simple, isolatable task, and then transmit their output to a neighboring cell. These neighboring cells perform their own automation, transmit their output, and so forth. The sum total effect of these individual unit operations yields tremendous complexity. For example, the patterns of many seashells are composed by a cellular automaton; cells of the shell secrete or inhibit pigment based on the similar behavior of neighboring cells.

Cellular automata offer a way to understand complex systems by breaking down large-scale behavior into simple generative rules. They key difference between this approach and traditional scientific or mathematical modeling is that the complexity of cellular automatic systems as a whole exceeds the complexity of each automaton. This is why Wolfram calls cellular automata "simple mathematical idealizations of natural systems."[3] Wolfram and others have shown how complex natural systems, such as the construction of snowflakes and leaves, generate from elementary or one-dimensional cellular automata.[4] Because cellular automata are simple input–output machines, they are intimately related to computation; in Wolfram's words, "Their discrete nature also allows an important analogy with digital computers: cellular automata may be viewed as parallel-processing computers of simple construction."[5]

Consequently, cellular automata offer a helpful way to get at the heart of complex representations of the world in terms of relatively simply described rules. Wolfram sees cellular automata as information-processing systems, like parallel computers.[6] In such machines, individual cells perform calculations on an initial configuration, typically based on a seed value, and then continually process the resulting output values over time, as long as the system is allowed to run. The ability for cellular automata to be directly applied via information-processing systems like computers leads Wolfram to conclude that "cellular automata may . . . provide efficient media for practical simulations of many natural systems."[7]

While Wolfram attempts to determine how the natural world functions according to simple algorithmic programs, others have used cellular automata to create incomplete models of the natural world, or a subset of it. These simulations differ from Wolfram's work on "pure" cellular automata in an important way: they draw on human intervention, rather than natural law, to generate discursive meaning. Software and videogames can likewise give voice to this kind of expression.

The oldest and best-known cellular automatic simulation is Cambridge mathematician John Conway's *Game of Life*.[8] The game simulates the growth (and death) of a living organism over time. Although *Life* has been translated into computer program form many times during the last thirty-five years, the game does not require computational assistance. Using a checkers or Go board, the player lays out any kind of pattern she chooses for the initial state of the organisms and then adjusts that pattern each turn according to three simple rules:

1. *Survivals* Every counter with two or three neighboring counters survives for the next generation.

2. *Deaths* Each counter with four or more neighbors dies (is removed) from overpopulation. Every counter with one neighbor or none dies from isolation.

3. *Births* Each empty cell adjacent to exactly three neighbors—no more, no fewer—is a birth cell. A counter is placed on it at the next move.[9]

With the aid of a computer to speed up the simulation, Conway and others quickly began to observe common patterns in the game, such as "flip-flops" of oscillating figures and "gliders" that move diagonally across the board. The *Game of Life* is an example of a emergent system, in which simple rules combine to lead to consequences unpredictable from those rules. *Life* is compelling as a "game" because it allows the player to understand a complex model in terms of a much simpler system. I'll return to the importance of this characteristic of simulations in a moment.

First, I want to look at a more complex videogame based on cellular automata. Will Wright's game *Sim City* allows the player to create and manage a simulated urban environment. Acting as a simplified but all-powerful Mayor, the player chooses land zoning, tax rates, and location and funding of city services. For those who haven't played the game before, it is a surprisingly active experience. Ted Friedman offers this helpful summary of the play experience:

Playing *SimCity* is a very different experience from playing an adventure game like *King's Quest*. The interaction between player and computer is constant and intense. Gameplaying is a continuous flow—it can be very hard to stop, because you're always in the middle of dozens of different projects: nurturing a new residential zone in one corner of the map, building an airport in another, saving up money to buy a new power plant, monitoring the crime rate in a particularly troubled neighborhood, and so on. Meanwhile, the city is continually changing, as the simulation inexorably chugs forward from one month to the next (unless you put the game on pause to handle a crisis). By the time you've made a complete pass through the city, a whole new batch of problems and opportunities have developed. If the pace of the city's development is moving too fast to keep up with, the simulation can be slowed down (i.e., it'll wait longer in real-time to move from one month to the next); if you're waiting around for things to happen, the simulation can be speeded up.[10]

Author and Clinton administration adviser Paul Starr traces the origins of *Sim City* to trends in "social simulation" crafted during the 1960s by sociologist James S. Coleman and others.[11] Urban planner Jay W. Forrester's 1969 book *Urban Dynamics* directly influenced Will Wright's design of *Sim City,* but the game is engineered on the same kind of cellular automata as *Life,* although the number and complexity of these interactions are far greater in the former.[12]

The algorithms and design strategies Wright has implemented in *Sim City* are based on "concentric rings," with industry, commerce, and residence at the center, and traffic, energy, water, and other systems surrounding the core. The simulation runs continuously, but updates itself in discrete "turns" that correspond with the passage of time in the game world. *Life* offers only one meaningful state change between turns: organisms can either live or die based on the simple rules about the squares surrounding them. *Sim City* increases the subtlety of these rules and their consequences. For example, the number of jobs in a particular region affects the demand for residential space. Higher unemployment will reduce the demand for housing, eventually accelerating unemployment and causing residents to leave the city.[13]

Games like *Life* and *Sim City* are called "simulations" because they leverage simplified principles to render complex scenarios in reference to real-world systems. *Sim City* is more complex than *Life* by virtue of the number and subtlety of these interactions. Both games begin not by identifying the narrative output of an individual game session, but by defining the rule-units that underpin such individual experiences.

Critics have said much about modes of interpretation for unit meanings in simulations. When playing *Sim City,* says critic Starr, "the models deliberately exaggerate effects to provide feedback to the player; in real life, the effects of many decisions would be imperceptible. The purpose of *Sim City* is not accuracy of prediction but communication."[14] Ted Friedman makes a similar observation:

Learning and winning (or, in the case of a non-competitive "software toy," "reaching one's goals at") a computer game is a process of demystification: one succeeds by discovering how the software is put together. The player molds her or his strategy through trial-and-error experimentation to see "what works"—which actions are rewarded and which are punished.[15]

On initial inspection, these sentiments are consistent with one of Stephen Wolfram's suggested uses of cellular automata–based simulations, "efficient media for practical simulations of many kinds of natural systems." However, there are two critical differences between Wolfram's work on cellular automata, and cellular automata based games like *Life* and *Sim City*. First, Wolfram's work strives to become a viable model for explaining the way the natural world functions; *Life* and *Sim City* are only interested in a very small subset of the natural world. Second, as a scientist, Wolfram necessarily strives to perform this modeling in a comprehensive and nonbiased fashion.[16] Videogames strive to fulfill neither of these goals; instead, they explicitly choose to represent some small subset of the natural world, in a necessarily biased manner. *Bias* is an especially important characteristic to ascribe to simulations, and I will return to it shortly.

In his discussion of *Life,* mathematician Paul Callahan helps to elucidate the differences between the scientific and the discursive modeling of the world as units:

In Life, as in nature, we observe many fascinating phenomena. Nature, however, is complicated and we aren't sure of all the rules. The game of Life lets us observe a system where we know all the rules. Just like we can study simple animals (like worms) to discover things about more complex animals (like humans), people can study the game of Life to learn about patterns and behaviors in more complex systems.[17]

Callahan's understanding of *Life* shares much in common with Gonzalo Frasca's definition of simulation. Frasca argues that computational simulation amends narrative expression with the ability to "model behavior."[18] Frasca defines simulations this way: "to simulate is to model a (source) system through a different system which maintains to somebody some of the behaviors of the original system."[19] Frasca further clarifies that simulations are indeed narrative, in that "for an external observer, the outcome of a simulation is narration."[20] Frasca privileges simulation over narrative, the former providing an interactive experience for representations, the latter providing, at best, a more distant and less "first-hand" experience of the representation in question. Janet Murray calls this phenomenon of first-handedness *immersion,* or the ability to construct new beliefs through interaction with computational media.[21]

However, according to Callahan's casual account of *Life,* that game's simulation serves at least three purposes. First, it offers a window into the unknowable complexity of nature. Second, it provides a simplified representation of that complexity, such that it can be meaningfully experienced. Third, it provides (potentially) fungible insight into the nature of real life, through the successful use and interpretation of the game. Each of these purposes is a special sort of the one, general purpose Frasca exposes in his simple definition: the simulation represents the real world *in part,* but not in whole.

Generalizing this characterization of simulation, one might revise and add to Frasca's definition as follows:

A simulation is a representation of a source system via a less complex system that informs the user's understanding of the source system in a subjective way.

As Frasca notes, this kind of simulation is subtly different from the field of computer simulation, which typically seeks to model accurately some referent in the material world, the simulation serving the sole purpose of informing the observer's opinion or knowledge about the real system.

An example of the traditional type of computer simulation is *BioChemFX,* created by military simulation developer 3D Pipeline.[22] In its stock demonstration form, *BioChemFX* models the dispersion of sarin gas released around the UC Berkeley campus. In such a simulation, certain elements of the material world need to be preserved, for example, weather conditions, geographical topology, the size and height of buildings in the area, the density and dispersion characteristics of sarin gas, and so forth. This kind of simulation is more familiar to most people than the kind of simulation a game like *Sim City* performs, even though both simulations rely on equally contentious assumptions. The reason for this is simple to state, but complex to explain: the relationship or feedback loop between the simulation game and its player are bound up with a set of values; no simulation can escape some ideological context.

Videogames and Ideology

Interaction with simulation in games demands a critical approach slightly different than reading a traditional text. Earlier, I discussed the conflict between ludology and narratology in game studies. Ludologists respond in part to the relationship the player has with the game in a simulation, whose unit-operational rules form the entire basis of the resulting gameplay. Any narration of the game must acknowledge the unit-operational rules that generate a given experience. Any narration that such systems generate is indebted to the user's effort in constituting that narrative via the instantiation of unit-operational rules. While Aarseth argues that computational works are better understood as cybernetic systems than as new, electronic versions of other kinds of texts, he scarcely acknowledges that an ergodic work might synthesize in a manner similar to a literary text.

Even cellular automatic systems like Wolfram's can be appreciated only in synthesized form, as the mathematical rules when applied render patterns that structure a leaf or a snowflake, which then take on biological and social roles. It is thus the two notions of *synthesis* and *subjectivity* that my understanding adds to these previous conceptions. What simulation games create are *biased, nonobjective* modes of expression that cannot escape the grasp of subjectivity and ideology.

Frasca hints at this idea in his definition that simulations represent something *to somebody,* but I think this point needs to be much stronger. Videogames require critical interpretation to mediate our experience of the simulation, to ground it in a set of coherent and expressive values, responses, or understandings that constitute effects of the work. In this process, the unit operations of a simulation embody themselves in a player's understanding. This is the place where rules can be grasped, where instantiated code enters the material world via human players' faculty of reason. In my mind, it is the most important moment in the study of a videogame.

Here is an example of the challenge at hand. A classic conflict between narration and simulation comes from two different readings of the popular puzzle game *Tetris*. Frasca sees the game as entirely nonrepresentative, with no foot whatsoever in the real world: "it is not simulating reality but just creating an abstract environment where the player can test her skills."[23] Janet Murray, on the other hand, sees a specific narrative in *Tetris,* which she explains in *Hamlet on the Holodeck:*

Tetris is a perfect enactment of the overtasked lives of Americans in the 1990s—of the constant bombardment of tasks that demand our attention and that we must somehow fit into our overcrowded schedules and clear off our desks in order to make room for the next onslaught.[24]

Frasca uses this example as convincing evidence that simulations can have different interpretations, different *readings* in poststructuralist literary-critical rubric. Everyone might not share Murray's unique and endearing experience of the game, but the interpretation is certainly a viable one. It suggests the variety of interpretations available to players of the game. Markku Eskelinen offers a less magnanimous response.

It would be equally far beside the point if someone interpreted chess as a perfect American game because there's a constant struggle between hierarchically organized white and black communities, genders are not equal, and there's no health care for the stricken pieces.[25] Of course, there's one crucial difference: after this kind of analysis you'd have no intellectual future in the chess-playing community.

Instead of studying the actual game Murray tries to interpret its supposed content, or better yet, project her favourite content on it; consequently we don't learn anything of the features that make Tetris a game. The explanation for this interpretative violence seems to be equally horrid: the determination to find or forge a story at any cost, as games can't be games because if they were, they apparently couldn't be studied at all.[26]

Eskelinen goes on to contrast Murray's undesirable narrative reading with his own analysis, one that evaluates the temporal relations of games (order, speed, frequency, duration, simultaneity, and time of the action). Eskelinen lays these relations out in a table that hashmarks and characterizes *Tetris*'s participation in these six properties.

If Murray's interpretation is "horrid" because it is determined to find a story at any cost, perhaps Eskelinen's is horrid because it is determined to conceal worldly reference at any cost. In both interpretations, something is lacking. Eskelinen is interested in formal categories that will advance the formal analysis of games. Murray is interested in interpretation and content analysis, to be sure, but she is also interested in rules, since her interpretation is grounded in rules, even if that grounding is unspoken.

Only a few basic functional unit operations drive *Tetris:* the player can turn a piece, move it, or drop it. The game mechanics add perhaps two more unit operations: a completed line of pieces disappears, and each time the player places a block, another one appears immediately after. Janet Murray's interpretation of the game as a representation of the unfettered demands of global capitalism would become much more comprehensible to the uninitiated player if she explicitly correlated the game's unit operations with the real world characteristics she has in mind. For example, the constant bombardment of tasks is correlated to the continuous generation of new blocks, and the need to fit unending work into overcrowded schedules and desks correlates with the completed lines which disappear, but only to give way to another onslaught of work. At the same time, Eskelinen's formal analysis would benefit from player context.

There are several additional unit operations built into *Tetris* that might support Murray's interpretation, or call it into question. For one, the original *Tetris* game I remember came with a "boss key," a special command built into the game's menu. When the player presses the boss key, the game pauses and draws a noninteractive spreadsheet program onto the screen. The purpose of this feature is to protect office workers who might be playing the game at their desks and need a quick rescue in case the boss walks by.

I am not sure if introducing the boss key into Murray's interpretation helps or hinders it. On the one hand, the fact that the game is structured as a break from the hectic workday Murray characterizes might suggest that its rules explicitly do *not* participate in the enactment of an overtaxed life. On the other hand, the "bridge" between play and work that the boss key creates might further support Murray's alignment of the game with the burdens of life. Murray's interpretation of the game accounts for a biased, subjective response in the player, one of the key components of simulation response I described above. Perhaps this response is the active recognition of the Sisyphean life Murray underscores, one that might even engender revolutionary opposition; or perhaps it is a subconscious reinforcement of that life, a sort of Freudian repetition compulsion enacted through simulation. No matter; Murray's interpretation takes into account a larger system that the game represents in smaller part, the function of the unit-operational rules of the simulation, and a subjective response to the simulation that embeds an ideology.

Frasca suggests a revised type of Peircean semiotics to help bring clarity to this friction point between rules and referents in games. Frasca conjoins two Peircean concepts, the *representamen,* or the sign, and the *interpretant,* or the concept of the sign, the idea of the sign in the observer's mind. In simulations, the *representamen* undergoes internal changes that depend materially on the observer's concept of the system, or the *interpretant.* Frasca suggests a tool from human–computer interaction (HCI) studies as a possible aid. HCI research suggests that people form mental models of a computer system's apparent capabilities in order to learn how to use the system. Frasca gives the name *interpretamen* to the revised Peircean *interpretant,* or "the idea, or mental model, that an observer has from the representamen."[27]

As I showed earlier in the case of *The Sims,* Will Wright relies on mental modeling as a design technique for games like *Sim City:* "the more accurately you can model that simulation in your head, the better your strategies are going to be going forward. So what we're trying to [do] as designers is build up these mental models in the player."[28] In the last chapter, I mentioned that one of Wright's influences is comic book critic Scott McCloud. McCloud argues that readers understand the intricacies of narrative in a comic by filling in the details that are missing between the frames. Drawing on Scott McCloud's work, Wright purposely leaves out portions of the simulation from the computer model and allows the player to fill in the details in his or her mind. Wright describes the gameplay as a process of "bringing our different mental models into agreement."[29] In the case of a competitive game like Go, agreement means reaching a consensus about victory and defeat. In an open-ended game like *Sim City* (Wright sometimes calls them "software toys"), it means creating an understanding or mental model of the game and its rules.

Ted Friedman musters a similar strategy for understanding *Sim City,* borrowed from spatial theory: *cognitive mapping.* Cognitive mapping has to do with how people construct understandings of the physical space they occupy. Theorists of postmodernity like David Harvey and Fredric Jameson have used cognitive mapping to suggest how space is actually a human *production* rather than a state of affairs humans find themselves in. Says Friedman,

Simulations may be our best opportunity to create what Fredric Jameson calls "an aesthetic of cognitive mapping: a pedagogical political culture which seeks to endow the individual subject with some new heightened sense of its place in the global system." Playing a simulation means becoming engrossed in a systemic logic which connects a myriad array of causes and effects.[30]

Frasca and Friedman suggest ways to use existing theoretical structures, HCI mental models and space-theoretical cognitive maps, to initiate feedback loops between the simulation's unit operations and the player's experience and understanding of the simulation. But these approaches still focus on making sense of the gameplay experience, rather than giving expression to that experience through criticism. Janet Murray's reading of *Tetris* above is perhaps an extreme example of individual expression in games, but *Sim City* has offered more telegraphic insight into the process of giving voice to the subjective relation between the player and the simulation.

I have argued that all simulations are subjective representations that communicate ideology, but *Sim City*'s particular biases have been discussed in theoretical and popular work since the game's release over fifteen years ago. Ted Friedman traces this progression: "*SimCity* has been criticized from both the left and right for its economic model. It assumes that low taxes will encourage growth while high taxes will hasten recessions. It discourages nuclear power, while rewarding investment in mass transit."[31] In one such example, artist Julian Bleeker argued that the game "displaced" issues of race and racism through utterly excluding such conditions from the simulation.[32]

But Paul Starr has a carefully inquisitive perspective on *Sim City* that suggests a way critics can start to make interpretive sense of videogames. Speculating on the game, Starr wonders, "What assumptions were buried in the underlying models? What was their 'hidden curriculum?' Did a conservative or a liberal determine the response to changes in tax rates in SimCity?"[33] Starr sees a danger "when simulations are used to make predictions and evaluate policies" because those decisions are themselves slaved to the rules of the simulation, the specific unit operations the system does (and does not) allow. He gently criticizes the game's "black box" nature and celebrates a possible future version wherein the player could adjust or author the assumptions of the models. For now, the black box simulator requires players to subject themselves to the model's assumptions, to learn how to master them, and possibly—under certain rare circumstances—to question or debate those assumptions. Critical interrogation is the missing link that bothers Starr about *Sim City*. "The critical problem raised by simulation," he argues, "is the black-box nature of the models. In the 'real world' of policy simulation, the models are subject to criticism and debate, at least among professionals."[34] Starr is referring to "real" public policy simulations, mathematical models run on possible policy scenarios that legislators really would need to argue over, since such simulation is meant to serve solely as evidence for a particular policy decision.

Earlier I drew a distinction between computer simulation and videogame simulation. By computer simulation, I mean the kind of simulation that Starr places in contrast to *Sim City,* simulations like the health care reform scores the Congressional Budget Office (CBO) used during Starr's own tenure in the Clinton White House. In his article, Starr explains the intricate and very real power the CBO yields in Congress through the simulation models it authors.

Earlier I also mentioned *BioChemFX,* the simulator designed to model propagation of airborne biological and chemical agents.[35] I have actually experienced this simulation, and I know that it is currently in use by several private agencies and governments worldwide in terror-event response-planning, the intended use for the product. Such a simulation needs numerous noncontroversial unit operations, such as the weight and density of the chemical agent, the effect of wind and weather, and the physical size and shape of buildings in the surrounding area. When put to use, response teams would use the simulation to predict the movement of a chemical agent within a densely populated urban environment, mustering emergency services where they would be needed most.

Watching this simulation run, one condition struck me as noticeably absent: the relative worth of the affected population. Sarin gas wouldn't permanently damage buildings or other infrastructure, but it is fast acting and very fatal. Because the simulation was explicitly located around a university, I wondered if certain faculty of special esteem might be deemed more necessary to save than, say, workers in fast food restaurants just off-campus. Perhaps the simulation should include predictive maps of the movement of the campus's Nobel laureates to account for such an eventuality. Or, perhaps securing the freshman dorms would be a better idea, since Nobel laureates are old and have probably already made their contribution to society, while all those fresh, young minds have their whole lives ahead of them. Plus, the liability associated with parents of freshman is assuredly greater than that of Nobel laureates.[36]

These may seem like foolish examples in light of the seriousness of the simulation itself; this is, after all, a simulation whose potential application feels more real than ever. In my experimentation with the sarin gas simulator and Starr's account with *Sim City,* our experiences construct mental models of the simulation that converge on an interpretation based on what the simulation *includes* and what it *excludes.*

In Frasca's revised-Peircean rubric, both my understanding of *BioChemFX* as a commentary on the value of human life and Starr's understanding of *Sim City* as a fictional representation of real social issues are *interpretamen* of how the simulation functions. Under Wright's looser understanding, my interpretations become mental models that combine game rules with subjective ideas. Under Friedman's post-Harvey/Jameson reading, my interpretations are cognitive maps of the real UC Berkeley or the real contemporary urban space. Friedman's argument for cognitive maps is compelling when real, spatial environments are in question, but it might break down as the simulated environments become more abstract.[37]

Both mental modeling and cognitive mapping show how the interpretation of a game relies as much or more on what the simulation excludes or leaves ambiguous that on what it includes. The idea that a sign derives meaning from how it differs from other signs is certainly nothing new; this is the basis of Saussurean semiotics. Saussure understood language as a "system of differences"—the signifier "dog" has meaning only insofar as it is not the signifier "cat." According to Saussure, these differences are "without positive terms," meaning that there is no way to make manifest the difference *itself*.[38] Derrida revises Saussure's idea of difference, showing how differences are palpable (we can talk about the differences between signs), but at the same differences are not stable identities that persist. Derrida names this new kind of difference *différance,* a neologism that combines the French terms for *differ* and *defer*.[39] In this respect, meaning for Derrida is a relational system, a network of actual and possible things and experiences. *Différance* disrupts the primacy of "originary meaning," or "pure presence," and founds a principal part of Derrida's critique of origins and self-presence in Western culture.[40]

In chapter 2, I explored how semiotics and structuralism function according to a logic of unit operations. There is an important distinction between Saussurean difference, Derridean *différance,* and the unit operations at work in videogames and simulations. For one, unit operations function at a higher level than linguistic signs. Whereas a philologist could easily unpack a linguistic sign like *value* or *office* or *human,* these signs and their differences are embedded into experience at a much lower level than, say, urban zoning or terror-response strategies. Certainly it would be possible to deconstruct *BioChemFX* to show how the software's rescue strategies become unstable once questions of the relative value of human life are brought to the table. However, the nature of the game's embedded system is not as telegraphic as a natural language or even a social custom. Instead, games create complex relations between the player, the work, and the world via unit operations that simultaneously embed material, functional, and discursive modes of representation.

Paul Starr calls this "black-box effect" the "seduction of the sim."[41] He worries that the absence of debate about the unit operations a game like *Sim City* deploys makes the medium as troubling as it is promising. Starr finds some solace in the fact that games like *Sim City* are "children's games," but he urges us not to underestimate their power over "how we communicate ideas and think through problems."[42] These games are, after all, much more similar to the social policy-making simulations that governmental organizations like the CBO use to craft public policy than they are to mere playground toys. In this respect, even though simulation games may function very differently than scientific models, we need to take the same approach to simulations *qua* games that we would to simulations *qua* scientific models: we need to interrogate them through criticism.

The fact that Will Wright explicitly crafts his games such that the player has to fill in important details about the game's complex interrelations of unit operations offers an insight into how we might perform criticism of such games. If the experience of a game takes place in the player's mental model of its unit-operational rules, then game criticism would do well to give voice to these mental models and the ideology they communicate.

Simulation Fever

One of the reasons videogame criticism has been so difficult is that the process of working through the subjectivity of simulated experiences has less history than that of narrative experiences, even though computer-aided simulations have existed as long as computers. The graphical user interface (GUI) of the Macintosh and Windows operating systems are also simulations, representations of information groupings and processes in terms of interactions with a physical working space.

For many people, the use of simulations for specific purposes still breeds mistrust and anxiety. Media theorist Sherry Turkle identifies two kinds of ways simulation users might respond to Paul Starr's simulation seduction:

One can accept simulations on their own terms . . . the stance that Starr was encouraged to take by Washington colleagues who insisted that even if the models are wrong, he needed to use the official models to get anything done. This might be called *simulation resignation.* Or one can reject simulations to whatever degree possible, the position taken by the MIT physicists who saw them as a thoroughly destructive force in science education. This might be called *simulation denial.*[43]

Simulation resignation implies the blind acceptance of the limited results of a simulation, because the system doesn't allow any other model of the source system. This is the kind of response that worries Paul Starr. *Simulation denial* implies the rejection of simulations because they offer only a simplified representation of the source system.

Simulation resignation and simulation denial share certain core properties. The most notable of these relates to the limitations of the simulation. Both of these "conditions" stem from the simulation's partitive nature, or what the system chooses to include and exclude. Both kinds of apprehension likewise derive from subjectivity's encounter with the game's unit operations. Simulation resignation acknowledges that sims are subjective, but refuses to interrogate the implications of that subjectivity. Simulation denial acknowledges that sims are subjective, and concludes that they are therefore useless, untrustworthy, or even dangerous tools.

Earlier, I offered this definition of simulation:

A simulation is a representation of a source system via a less complex system that informs the user's understanding of the source system in a subjective way.

Simulation resignation and simulation rejection are two sides of the same coin, a coin forged in the subjectivity of simulation. There is a space or a gap between which the key to approaching and understanding simulations might be found. This gap constitutes the core representation of simulation, between the work's rules and its reception. I suggest a further revision of my provisional definition of simulation that would highlight the importance of this gap:

A simulation is the gap between the rule-based representation of a source system and a user's subjectivity.

There are many precedents for gaps as the basis of meaning making. Plato's *khorismos* is the original gap that separates the material world from its ideal forms. Saussurian semiotics claims that the spaces or differences between linguistic signs constitute their meaning, and Derrida temporalizes this difference in his notion of *différance*. Lacan's *objet a* founds desire in the uncrossable distance between the subject and the unattainable object of fantasy. Badiou's void allows for situations to restructure.

Writing about authority and origin in writing in general, Derrida has argued that archivization, in written and other forms, always implies inclusion and exclusion, the preservation of something to remember, and the omission of something to forget. Derrida gives a name to this obsession to return to stable remembrance: he calls it *mal d'archive,* or "archive fever," a "a compulsive, repetitive, and nostalgic desire for the archive, an irrepressible desire to return to the origin, a homesickness, a nostalgia for the return to the most archaic place of absolute commencement."[44] Archive fever is the simultaneous drive toward and fear of archivization.

The cure to archive fever is a process of working through this discomfort. Together, we might call Turkle's two kinds of responses to simulations *simulation anxiety,* or following Derrida, *simulation fever.* Turkle envisions a pedagogical revisionist strategy to help combat this frenzy:

> one can imagine a third response. This would take the cultural pervasiveness of simulation as a challenge to develop a new social criticism. This new criticism would discriminate among simulations. It would take as its goal the development of simulations that help their users understand and challenge their model's built-in assumptions.[45]

Turkle recounts the story of Marcia, a tenth grader she interviewed about *Sim City.* Marcia had developed a set of guidelines for playing the game, including this one: "Raising taxes always leads to riots."[46] Turkle worries gravely about Marcia's inability to conceive of a simulation in which the rules would differ, in which, for example, "increased taxes led to increased productivity and social harmony."[47] Turkle calls for a new kind of literacy that would teach Marcia and her peers how to develop a reading competency of simulation.

Of course, simulations are not exactly like textual or electronic archives. Markku Eskelinen offers a summary of Aarseth's understanding of the difference between games and literature: "the dominant user function in literature, theatre and film is interpretative, but in games it is a configurative one."[48] And yet, configuration in videogames does not automatically entail interpretation; we must also make room for interpretive strategies that remain faithful to the configurative properties of games. One method would encourage player critics to work through the simulation anxiety a simulation generates. Part of this process takes place within the gameplay, as the player goes through cycles of configuring the game by engaging its unit operations. Another part of this process of configuration has to do with working through the player's subjective response to the game, the internalizations of its cybernetic feedback loops. For a game, this kind of subjectivity becomes manifest in the space between the unit operations the game allows, and the conceptual understanding of the gameplay process.

Derrida points out that the only way to preserve work in an archive is to expose that work to its possible destruction ("The archive always works, and a priori, against itself").[49] Choosing what to include and what to exclude is not an impartial process. Working through simulation fever means learning how to express what simulations choose to embed and to exclude. Starr and Turkle suggest that part of the cure entails creating new simulations that revise or rethink the ambiguities, omissions, errors, or controversies of previous simulations. This is indeed a worthwhile project.[50] But, a more accessible and readily fungible strategy is to create a body of criticism for simulations that relate their rules to their subjective experiences and configurations.

Simulation fever can also be related to Badiou's event, the rupture of stability in a situation and the reconfiguration of its multiplicities. The confrontation with the event is one of "commitment" and renewal. Badiou even reserves the title of "subject" for individuals who respond to the void of a situation and choose to consider and respond to its implications. This process is interminable, and thus Badiou reserves the name "truth" for an endless "fidelity" to the restructuring of an event.[51] To illustrate how this can be done, I'd like to take a look at several recent simulations that proved to be especially virulent strains of simulation fever, through the lens of a genre of games that tries explicitly to foreground the subjective experience of simulation, and in so doing to function as art.

An Alternative to Fun

Film and literature touch both popular culture and the arts, even if their relationships with each domain are often troubled. Some may not particularly enjoy reading James Fenimore Cooper's *Leatherstocking Tales* or watching Fritz Lang's *Metropolis,* but the historical importance of these artifacts in their respective media histories is indisputable.[1] Some critics may decry the novels of Danielle Steel or the films of Michael Bay as pop culture drivel, pure entertainment with scarce contemplative value—at best a Rabelaisian release of unexpressed carnal pleasures, at worst a prurient surrender of introspection.

Historically, a culture's art has often been read as a cipher for its values. Walter Benjamin articulated a particular property of the work of art that resists reproduction, its presence in time and space, its "unique existence at the place where it happens to be."[2] Benjamin uses the example of a statue of Venus, which the Greeks revered as an homage to the divine and the medievals saw as an portentous figure of idolatry. The ritualistic uses of art can be traced back to the earliest man-made artworks, in the cave paintings of Lascaux and Chauvet, created between 15,000 and 30,000 years ago. These works of art expose what Benjamin calls cult value; they serve as ceremonial works, instruments of magic meant to speak to the spirits, not to man. These artifacts become artworks only retrospectively, viewed through a historical lens that distances their cult value from their exposition value. Earlier I discussed aura as it relates to human experience in Baudelaire's modern Paris. Benjamin also names this exalted uniqueness of the artwork *aura;* aura is that which integrates the artwork in a tradition, "the unique phenomenon of a distance, however close it may be."

As artworks become reproducible, exposition value becomes paramount and cult value recedes. Benjamin calls this recession of cult value in artwork the *decline* or *withering* of the aura, although he intends for this withering to serve a liberating function. Mechanical reproducibility, says Benjamin, "emancipates the work of art from its parasitical dependence on ritual."[3] As art breaks from cult practice, it gains a new function, that of politics. In particular, mechanically reproducible art "changes the reaction of the masses toward art." Especially in the case of film, art becomes accessible as a new kind of collective social criticism. Says Benjamin:

The reactionary attitude toward a Picasso painting changes into the progressive reaction toward a Chaplin movie. The progressive reaction is characterized by the direct, intimate fusion of visual and emotional enjoyment with the orientation of the expert. Such fusion is of great social significance. The greater the decrease in the social significance of an art form, the sharper the distinction between criticism and enjoyment by the public. The conventional is uncritically enjoyed, and the truly new is criticized with aversion. With regard to the screen the critical and the receptive attitudes of the public coincide. The decisive reason for this is that individual reactions are predetermined by the mass audience response they are about to produce, and this is nowhere more pronounced than in the film.[4]

In particular, Benjamin observes that film has enlarged the representational possibility space. Benjamin underscores film's ability to illustrate Freudian theory in particular, but more generally he means to draw attention to film's capacity to create more subtly analyzable behavior than arts like theater and painting, primarily thanks to the camera's ability to isolate individual statements, movements, and situations. Earlier I drew a correlation between unit operations, psychoanalytic practice, and the structures of object technology; Benjamin suggests a further ligature between psychoanalysis as a unit-operational practice and film as a unit-operational practice. For Benjamin, film's importance rests less in its service of narrative expression, and more in its ability to penetrate into individual units of human activity:

By close-ups of the things around us, by focusing on hidden details of familiar objects, by exploring commonplace milieus under the ingenious guidance of the camera, the film, on the one hand, extends our comprehension of the necessities which rule our lives; on the other hand, it manages to assure us of an immense and unexpected field of action.[5]

In particular, Benjamin highlights film's ability to uncover the mechanics behind specific everyday actions:

Even if one has a general knowledge of the way people walk, one knows nothing of a person's posture during the fractional second of a stride. The act of reaching for a lighter or a spoon is familiar routine, yet we hardly know what really goes on between hand and metal, not to mention how this fluctuates with our moods. Here the camera intervenes with the resources of its lowerings and liftings, its interruptions and isolations, its extensions and accelerations, its enlargements and reductions. The camera introduces us to unconscious optics as does psychoanalysis to unconscious impulses.[6]

In essence, Benjamin is articulating the film camera's properties of procedural recombination, which make possible unit-operational visual observations of the lifting of a spoon, the lighting of a cigarette, the stride of a step.

It comes as no surprise that Benjamin would see film as a tool of unit-operational expression, given his great uncompleted work, *The Arcades Project* (*Das Passegenwerk*), a massive montage of quotes, observations, and aphorisms about nineteenth-century Paris arcades—a kind of covered street, the predecessor of the shopping mall—that helped constitute the modern experience, underwriting the movement of the *flâneur* as Baudelaire recorded it.[7] Benjamin committed suicide trying to escape Nazi Germany in 1940, and the work was never finished; exists only as a massive collection of meticulously compiled notes. Some presume that the manuscript was merely a collection of notes and citations, a kind of notebook for a book to be written. But given his affinity for units of structural meaning, it is reasonable to conclude that Benjamin had this very structure in mind, an experiment in a text of reconfigurable, unit-operational aphorisms. It is clear that the figure of the montage served some kind of purposeful, structural frame for *Passagenwerk*. Like the filmmaker, Benjamin endeavored to connect numerous individual commentaries on important social and cultural referents of the nineteenth century. Critic Susan Buck-Morss takes this latter view, arguing that *Passagenwerk* is inherently a work of disjoined units:

Because of the deliberate unconnectedness of these constructions, Benjamin's insights are not—and never would have been—lodged in a rigid narrational or discursive structure. Instead, they are easily moved about in changing arrangements and trial combinations, in response to the altered demands of the changing "present."[8]

Fragmentary representation allowed Benjamin to unpack his social and cultural referents as abstract ideas, as aphorisms that broke from their particular contexts and took on the role of cultural unit operations, rather than cultural histories. Buck-Morss calls these images "politically charged monads," a merger of Leibnizian unary being and discursive cultural production.[9] Benjamin's project was to uncover and concretize general cultural moments through repetitive, individually constructed examples—the prostitute, the *flâneur,* the arcade, their shocking disconnections mirroring the very cultural form he sought to critique.[10] Benjamin's ultimate form of cultural criticism was to take the same form as the art forms he valorized, and indeed he intended this work to serve the same ends as mechanically reproducible art—political critique. In Buck-Morss's words, *Passagenwerk* is "intended to provide a political education for Benjamin's own generation."[11]

The profusion of videogames in contemporary popular culture shares parallels with film under Benjamin's analytical eye. Like film, videogames also underwrite what Benjamin called "progressive reaction," the increased confluence of criticism and enjoyment. As procedural systems, videogames extend Benjamin's unit-operational logic of film—games create abstract representations of precise units of human experience. Where videogames and the film of Benjamin's writing diverge is in their material practice. Already in the 1930s, Benjamin observed film evolving into a capitalist business practice more than a form of revolutionary art: "So long as the movie-makers' capital sets the fashion as a rule no other revolutionary merit can be accredited to today's film than the promotion of a revolutionary criticism of traditional concepts of art."[12]

Despite Benjamin's hopes for art's ability to spur widespread Marxist revolution, today the forces of capital are orders of magnitude more pronounced than they were seventy years ago. In 2004, videogame software contributed $7.3 billion of the $28 billion "entertainment software" industry.[13] The industry's major U.S. lobbying association, the Entertainment Software Association (ESA) explicitly aligns itself with the production of leisure, not revolution. If the ESA's name implies a direct correlation between videogames and entertainment, the organization's mission statement seals their affinity: "The Entertainment Software Association (ESA) is the U.S. association exclusively dedicated to serving the business and public affairs needs of companies that publish video and computer games for video game consoles, personal computers, and the Internet."[14] In the spirit of the Hollywood film industry, the ESA's unspoken ligature between "entertainment software" and "video and computer games" reveals contemporary culture's inherited ideology for games: they are amusements, distractions that have no place provoking thought.

The chasm between videogames and revolutionary art is most helpfully unpacked through the notion of *play.* Dutch historian Johan Huizinga serves an important role in the prehistory of our received notion of games *qua* entertainment. In *Homo ludens,* his study of play and culture, Huizinga offers a definition of play that separates the playful and the serious. For Huizinga, play is

a free activity standing quite consciously outside "ordinary" life as being "not serious," but at the same time absorbing the player intensely and utterly. It is an activity connected with no material interest, and no profit can be gained by it. It proceeds within its own proper boundaries of time and space according to fixed rules and in an orderly manner. It promotes the formation of social groupings, which tend to surround themselves with secrecy and to stress their difference from the common world by disguise or other means.[15]

At first glance, Huizinga's understanding of play seems clearly aligned against cultural production of the material and political type. Play, he argues, is "not serious" and moreover is disconnected from matters of material gain; such categories would seem utterly at odds with Benjamin's understanding of reproducible art as a progenitor of political revolution. At the same time, Huizinga seeks to expose play as a metacultural phenomenon where entirely serious practices like law, war, and politics find root. Despite Huizinga's attempt to undermine the dichotomy of seriousness and play, his readers sometimes fail to take into account the scare quotes around "not serious" in Huizinga's definition. Although Huizinga has become required reading among scholars interested in the ontology of games, the complex relationship between play and seriousness is frequently trivialized. In Eric Zimmerman and Katie Salen's comprehensive study of game design, Huizinga's definition is unpacked into a bullet list of properties of play, of which "not serious" is left unanalyzed.[16]

But rather than contrasting play and seriousness, Huizinga's characterization of play bears more similarity to the kind of ritualistic activity Benjamin calls cult practice. Huizinga asserts that play "promotes the formation of social groupings," groups whose cultural meanings persist after, or outside, the place of play itself. The construction of social groups in games suggests a potential correlation between the uses of play and the uses of art.

Unfortunately, later play theorists further increased the conceptual divide between games and cultural production. French sociologist Roger Callois expanded on Huizinga's work, offering his own concept of play in *Man, Play, and Games*. Most notably, Callois extends Huizinga's argument that play resides "outside everyday life." For Callois, play is *make-believe*, "accompanied by a special awareness of a second reality or of a free unreality, as *against real life*."[17] There is clearly an affinity between the idea of play as separate from and contrary to everyday life. Functionalist perspectives on religion such as Emile Durkheim's notion of the sacred and the profane[18] or Rudolf Otto's concept of the numinous are obvious examples.[19] Despite both Callois's and Huizinga's insistence that play structures and organizes human culture, both segregate play into a "pure space" freed from daily production. Huizinga calls this isolated space the "magic circle," a concept that has become central to many contemporary theories of games and to which I will return later.

In Huizinga's and Callois's struggle to locate play at the very foundation of human culture, they threaten to separate these two domains at their very junction. Unlike Huizinga and Callois, Hans Gadamer focuses on the role of play in the work of art. Gadamer limits his interest in play to aesthetics, borrowing Huizinga's idea of play as a system of "fixed rules" and applying such structure to the work of art. Play, argues Gadamer, serves as the artwork's "transformation into structure," or in Heideggerean terms its "unconcealment."[20] Unlike Derrida's understanding of play as the catalyst for deconstruction, Gadamer retains Huizinga's important gesture of the unit-operational nature of play—"fixed rules"—but disputes the isolationist view that play and cultural production remain separate.

In our contemporary situation, the relationship between play and cultural production inherits this basic segregationism. The ESA has made important strides to extend the reach of videogames, but it still implicitly aligns videogames of any kind with "entertainment," a testament to our deeply ideological relationship with play.[21] Neil Postman first traced this trend of a "media-metaphor shift" in relation to television. Postman argued that the shift from books to television has created a public discourse of increasingly "dangerous nonsense."[22] Although Postman does not share Benjamin's vision for the political applications of mechanically reproducible art, he does acknowledge that such imagery has begun to overtake written language as our primary means for "construing, understanding, and testing reality."[23] Interestingly, Postman relates this social change to a form of play, and more specifically a child's game; he calls the post-typographic era the "Peek-a-Boo World," a world in which mechanically reproduced images appear and disappear rapidly as in a game of peek-a-boo. This progression reaches a pinnacle of "dangerous perfection" in television.[24] The quality that isolates television from the actionable world is strikingly similar to that which isolates play: it is a safe space, without consequence, that is entirely self-contained. With the space of television, according to Postman, we sacrifice interrogation and dissent for entertainment, for fun. Benjamin had already begun to critique the capitalist renovation of film into show business, and Postman takes up this critique at a time that segues seamlessly into the contemporary culture of videogames. Bizarrely, Huizinga's own words help dissolve the relationship between play and social structures. "The fun of playing," wrote Huizinga, "resists all analysis, all logical interpretation. As a concept, it cannot be reduced to any other mental category."[25] Although the purpose of this sentiment serves to underscore Huizinga's radical claim that play precedes all cultural structures, it could just as easily be mustered in support of Postman's apocalyptic vision of the death of self-reflection and cultural interrogation at the hands of television.

Videogames are thus subject to two equally strong forces opposing their use as tools for social commentary, social change, or other more "revolutionary" matters. On the one hand, the anthropological history of games has set the precedent for their separation from the material world. On the other hand, videogames inherit a mass-market entertainment culture whose primary purpose is the production of low-reflection, high-gloss entertainment.

Even earnest attempts by game critics and developers to overturn this received conception of videogames can be shown to reinforce rather than challenge the status quo. Raph Koster, Sony Online Entertainment Chief Creative Officer and lead designer of popular massively multiplayer online games *Ultima Online* and *Star Wars Galaxies,* offered a recent such effort, a unique book of cartoon sketches and semi-aphoristic insights called *A Theory of Fun for Game Design.* The book's title already implies Koster's adoption of "fun" as a yardstick for games, but, in an attempt fraught with hazard, he tries to recuperate the term for broader purposes than the production of anonymous desire.

In his attempt to preserve "fun" at the center of the experience of games, Koster musters loose principles from cognitive science; fun, he argues, is the sensation of "our brains feeling good."[26] Koster opposes critiques of fun like Postman's, arguing that we "migrate" fun into contexts.[27] In particular, the primary kind of fun that games produce comes from mastery of a task. In their representational form, what I call unit operations Koster calls "abstract models of reality."[28] For Koster, fun is very nearly a pedagogical category, "the feedback the brain gives us when we are absorbing patterns for learning purposes."[29]

This general approach allows Koster to mount a welcome argument in favor of expanded purposes for games. Like Huizinga, Koster argues that games structure cultural behavior, but Koster explicitly maps such behavior to practice-oriented mental mastery of problems of a general kind. Admirably, Koster uses this position to issue a call for videogames that attempt to build unit-operational models for situations beyond the current genres of war, alien invasions, driving, and sports. He issues a call for the use of games as an "expressive medium," offering *Beowulf* and *Guernica* as legitimate models for game-based expression. "No other artistic medium," argues Koster, "defines itself around an intended *effect* on the user, such as 'fun.' They all embrace a wider array of emotional impact."[30] One of Koster's cartoon illustrations depicts a well-dressed bearded man at the counter of a videogame store. "Hey, is *Custody Battle 3* out yet?" he asks. A poster of top sellers behind the cashier suggests other potential games: *Hamlet, Sim Gandhi, Against Racism.*[31]

Unfortunately, Koster's reliance on fun as a first principle for games forces him into a corner. On the one hand, he makes a convincing call for games that fulfill goals beyond mere entertainment. This call is especially constructive given Koster's relative celebrity in the game design community. On the other hand, he argues that the effect games produce in their players—all games, and all players—is "fun." This reliance on a single output for games contradicts his earlier, apparently reproachful observation that a singular expressive goal limits the medium. The reliance on fun poses a conceptual problem for Koster, who must retrofit the revolutionary potential of games to mate properly with the concept of fun that serves as his engine. Anticipating possible objections to games that go beyond fun in the usual and popular sense, Koster finds himself attributing a wide array of possible responses to the realm of the fun. "One of the commonest points I hear about why videogames are not an art form," says Koster, "is that they are just for fun. They are just entertainment. Hopefully I've made it clear why that is a dangerous underestimation of fun."[32] This moment marks Koster's inversion of games and their expressive output; here fun becomes the primary term, with videogame-based expression enslaved to it. Koster admits that "we may be running into definitional questions for the word 'fun' here," but he prefers a "formalist perspective to actually arrive at the basic building blocks of the medium."[33] Like Benjamin, Koster hopes to open a space between uncritical enjoyment and antagonistic critique. Despite these intentions, Koster is hard pressed to avoid the rhetoric of fun as the superficial conveyance of capital so often associated with the entertainment industry, the goal that Benjamin foresees and Postman critiques.

Koster's understanding of fun decouples the outcome of gameplay from pleasure in the ordinary sense, enabling other kinds of responses. But in the same gesture Koster insists that these outcomes still entail fun, albeit fun of a different kind. We might call Koster's alternate fun *fun'* (fun prime), a kind of alternate-reality fun that entails the social, political, and even revolutionary critique that Benjamin first envisioned for mechanically reproducible art.[34] Despite this conceptual similarity, Koster's insistence on grouping meaningful responses of any kind under the rubric of "fun" is simply perverse. One need go no further than everyday experience to recognize how absurd the notion of fun' is: "I couldn't believe it when I walked in on her and Jim. I know our relationship has been mostly fun' lately, but I didn't realize it was over." Or: "I heard Mary's husband had another heart attack. And so soon after her mother died . . . they've really been going through a lot of fun' this year." Chris Crawford recognizes this limitation and observes its inappropriateness as a measure for the impact of a videogame. "Fun," observes Crawford, "doesn't quite fit the adult's experience."[35]

Biased Videogames

In late 2003, Gonzalo Frasca released a small Web-based game called *September 12,* the first in a series he calls Newsgaming. The Newsgaming series is an attempt to make social and political statements with games, much like political cartoons. *September 12* is a very simple game; it depicts a Middle Eastern town, rendered in colorful cartoonlike detail. People wander around the town by foot; a few of these people are terrorists. The player controls a reticle on the screen, which can be moved around to target terrorists. Clicking the mouse sends a missile to the selected target, after a short time delay. Missiles wreak significant damage, and each missile destroys not only the targeted terrorist (if the player's timing is right), but also any nearby buildings and innocent people. When innocents die, surrounding people mourn over the body and then turn into terrorists themselves. The game's message is simple: bombing towns is not a viable response to the terrorist threat; it begets more violence. Specimens like *September 12* suggest that games can be noteworthy rhetorical devices; within the gap between game rules and subjectivity, players complete and refine their understanding of the game's representation, implicating themselves inside that experience. This power of the medium has gone untapped because the market has focused primarily on entertaining players, rather than engaging them in important topics.

Games like *Sim City* do have the secondary effect of teaching players something about urban planning and local governance. Military simulations like *Full Spectrum Warrior* and *America's Army* and training simulation games such as *Virtual U* impart a more explicit pedagogy. *America's Army* is a military recruitment tool funded by the U.S. Army that puts the player in the shoes of a soldier in various "realistic" army missions. *Virtual U* is a university administration simulation funded by the Alfred P. Sloan foundation that teaches players about the management practices in various kinds of American universities. These games seek to create a correlation between the player's mental model of the game rules and his understanding of the real world. The same gap between subjectivity and unit-operational rules that motivates criticism also underlies the rhetorical and educational possibilities of games.

Other game-based social commentaries have come in the form of videogame "mods," alterations of existing commercial games. In 1999, Anne-Marie Schleiner and her collaborators designed a mod called *Velvet-Strike* for the popular multiplayer first-person shooter *Counter-Strike*.[36] *Velvet-Strike* allowed players to spray virtual posters with political messages such as "Hostage of an Online Fantasy" and "You are your most dangerous enemy." In 2001, artist Josh On created *Antiwargame*, a simulation that allows the player to explore how policy decisions affect presidential popularity. The player allocates government funds to military, social, and foreign targets. On injects his own view that U.S. policy exists only for "securing the interests of the U.S. ruling class in the world" into the game's logic.[37] As a result, deployed troops lean toward desertion, and the homefront populations destabilize as social spending decreases. On uses *Antiwargame* to communicate his personal perspective on U.S. foreign policy.

One commercial game that takes on a social challenge through gameplay proper was Chris Crawford's *Balance of the Planet*. Released on Earth Day 1990, *Balance of the Planet* is a simulation game that models environmental issues and their consequences. In Crawford's words, the game deals with "the complexity of environmental issues and their entwinement with each other and with economic issues. . . .everything is connected, [and] simplistic approaches always fail."[38] In the game, the player makes choices about a multitude of settings, from lake acidity to radiation to oil spills. The game even requires the player to place a value on human lives—and separate values for third-world lives and urban industrial lives. *Sim Health,* a 1994 game from the designers of *Sim City,* allows the player to model the kind of health care system the United States should have. Games like *Balance of the Planet* and *Sim Health* allow the player to simulate an adjustable value system, to witness the effects of that value system, and to carry that perception beyond the gameplay experience.

Gonzalo Frasca generalizes the social function conveyed by such games to simulations in general. "Simulation authors," says Frasca, "do not represent a particular event, but a set of potential events. Because of this, they have to think about their objects as systems and consider which are the laws that rule their behaviors. In a similar way, people who interpret simulations create a mental model of it by inferring the rules that govern it." In such simulations, says Frasca, "the goal of the player would be to analyze, contest and revise the model's rules according to his personal ideas and beliefs."[39] Under this rubric, games become rhetorical opinion texts whose positions players explore rather than merely take to be true.

Some might object that videogames about political and social practices risk becoming merely didactic rather than reflective.[40] Such an objection assumes that a videogame that performs a rhetorical function is a closed system, devoid of simulation fever. This objection also raises an aesthetic challenge: it proposes emergence as a design strategy for games. Earlier I discussed cellular automata as emergent systems; examples of emergence outside of games include traffic patterns, brain chemistry, and the spread of disease. Jesper Juul contrasts emergent games with what he calls "progressive games," or games in which the player performs sequential actions to reach the game's end, such as action/adventure games.[41] Juul rightly argues that emergent games necessitate strategic tactics and therefore yield high replayability, whereas progressive games require that only the player finish all the game's sequential challenges, and therefore yield low replayability.

There are reasons to privilege emergence over progression as a design strategy; the former inherently requires more configurative gameplay and therefore would appear to maximize the expressive affordances of the medium. But Juul risks falling into a trap: like Koster's call for art games that maximize "fun," Juul's call for emergent games that maximize replayability privileges the formal quality of the game over its expressive potential. As the value proposition of entertainment gaming, fun and emergence both imply a kind of accounting, a return on investment for the player. In such an economy, a high degree of nonrepeating interactivity might indeed suggest more total "potential fun."

However, as I have been arguing, videogames need not participate in such an economy. Rather, they may strive to make highly isolated statements that pursue specific goals through the gameplay experience.

In the context of advocacy and especially politics, replayability need not even entail a repetition of the gameplay experience, as it would in leisure games. Rather, replayability might manifest in the same way as does powerfully rhetorical work of traditional art, film, or print: by causing the player to revisit the game's rhetorical claims and thereby to influence the player's judgments. Replayability in this sense implies self-reflection, debate, dispute, and a host of other contentious activities. It is a special kind of simulation fever, an openness to the unresolved crises such representations create.

Writing about responses to *September 12* in a research/practice crossover column, Frasca observes:

I think that a big part of this critique is due to the fact that political videogaming is not yet a well-established genre. Nobody would ever criticize a printed political cartoon on the basis of being too simplistic: caricatures are simplifications by definition. In spite of this, cartoons make a point and this is why they remain a useful journalistic tool.[42]

This comment suggests that collectively, we are not yet acclimated to the conditions of simulation fever. In an online discussion about *September 12, Virtual U* co-designer Ben Sawyer writes, "I think that in positioning it as a 'simulation' they invite the sort of valid attacks people have already begun to make [on this blog]. If it was focused more on being pitched as an editorial cartoon in the form of game media I don't think those attacks would be as open."[43] Sawyer's comment, however, might be plagued by its own kind of simulation fever. He seems to suggest that games *as such* might not be able to function as highly encapsulated commentary, since simulations are by definition scientific rather than emotional systems. More likely Sawyer is pointing out the problematic nature of the word "simulation" as it applies to videogames and artifacts like Paul Starr's CBO models. Nevertheless, this problematic itself points to a highly engrained preconception about what games and simulations should and should not do. This raises a question about our understanding of games in general. Typically, the claim is, simulations like *BioChemFX* and Paul Starr's CBO tools strive for objective representation, whereas games hope only for subjective representation.[44]

But as vehicles for simulation fever, I don't believe any game can make such a distinction between objective and subjective representation; there is no such thing as an objective simulation, or an objective game. Like literature, editorial, public oration, and countless other forms of rhetorical speech, videogames participate in the struggle between authorial intent and interpretive freedom. Videogames require players to create a subjective understanding of the synthesis of one or more unit operations. Games demand that players be capable of making this synthesis palpable in their own experience.

This process of engagement with artworks can constitute an event in Badiou's sense of the word, and in so doing it constitutes a subject and commences the process of fidelity at the heart of his theory of truth. Badiou gives special attention to poetry, whose breaks from the ordinary use of language he finds particularly disruptive.[45] Like mathematics, poetry offers formal categorizations, and in its frenzied structure poetry also enables—even invites—reconfiguration. These features of formality, abstractness, and disjointedness also characterize procedural media like videogames, allowing the kind of disruptive recombination that characterizes Badiou's understanding of the purpose of art. Videogames thus challenge any stable view of themselves as artifacts of purely commercial entertainment value. Fun' characterizes games that produce especially salient simulation fever.

Against Fun

A useful example of fun' at work can be found in Raph Koster's games. Upon the publication of *A Theory of Fun for Games,* many players of his most recent game, *Star Wars Galaxies* (SWG), reviled the book in public forums and online bookseller reviews. Most of these critics responded not to the book but to Koster's design of SWG. Along with many other massively multiplayer online games (MMOGs), SWG was criticized for the tremendous amount of work required to successfully develop and advance ("level" or "level up," in MMOG jargon) a character. This attitude is perhaps best summarized in the first comment posted alongside popular Web site Slashdot.org's review of *A Theory of Fun:* "If Raph Koster is an expert on anything, as many *Star Wars Galaxies* players can attest to, it's making a game NOT fun."[46]

In their analysis of sociability in SWG, Nicolas Ducheneaut, Robert J. Moore, and Eric Nickell analyze the game's attempt to engineer social interactions.[47] In particular, SWG attempts to recreate the "corner bar" in the form of a cantina, an abstraction of the recognizable Tatooine bar first introduced in George Lucas's first *Star Wars* film. Ducheneaut et al. describe the principal function of the cantina in the game:

In the many cities of SWG . . . there is always a cantina to be found. These locations serve an important instrumental game function. Indeed, they are one of the few places where the "entertainer" character class can perform their services. Entertainers dance or play music mostly in cantinas. And as watching a dancer, or listening to a musician, are both the only ways of recuperating from "battle fatigue," most players have to visit cantinas on a regular basis.[48]

Koster and his team designed the cantinas to encourage downtime, requiring injured combatants to stay in the cantinas while they solicit the healing services of entertainers.[49] But inevitably, many players use the game's built-in macros to automate healing rather than engaging in conversation. Ducheneaut et al. call these "instrumental" players and contrast them with the "social" players who come to heal and to converse. The researchers perform an intricate quantitative analysis of unique utterances in these cantinas, finding that the majority of players use the cantinas like "battle fatigue drive-thrus," utilities for recovering from combat.

In addition to entertainers, SWG offers another character class devoted to a noncombat profession, the artisan. Artisans are craftspeople, able to advance to professions like armorsmith, architect, tailor, or droid engineer. To create basic items, artisans must first find and extract resources and then use tools to craft artifacts. Finished products can be sold at a bazaar to other players who need armor, weapons, and the like to perform combat tasks. The bazaar serves the whole galaxy of SWG, but players do not have access to it whenever they want. To buy or sell items, players must access special terminals inside SWG cities. Brawlers and marksmen might often find themselves in SWG cities, but artisans spend much of their time searching for resources or assembling artifacts on remote planets. Artisans then must commute to cities to get their wares into the bazaar. Likewise, when a customer wants to purchase an item, he must travel to the terminal on which the item is being sold to retrieve it. In either case, artisan crafts create incentives for players to traverse the galaxy. Like the cantinas, then, the bazaar is intended as a social engineering tool, facilitating otherwise unnecessary player interactions. In practice, however, buying and selling at the bazaar requires a great deal of empty transit time, especially for artisans.

Since MMOGs often function as social spaces as much as games, it is tempting to call the cantina and bazaar design defects, failed efforts to create meaningful social spaces. The tedious, empty play that healing and commerce require seem to emulate work, not play, thus eliciting comments like that of the Slashdot pundit. Such reactions arise mainly from the assumption that fun is a first principle of games and that SWG, as a game, must produce empty gratification.

But instead, we might think of SWG as a game that challenges certain contemporary social practices. The cantinas, filled with mindless, preprogrammed jabber, could represent a number of anonymous public social encounters; but especially it represents the unit operation of waiting tables. Etymologically, "waiter" comes from the notion of courtly attendance, as a lady-in-waiting might attend to a royal. But in more colloquial terms, waiting tables often connotes a kind of provisional occupation, a stopgap between jobs, a second job, or a supplement to other long-term work, as an actor or a student might wait tables while pursuing another more "serious" career. When considered in this context, paying a monthly subscription to perform the virtual equivalent of waiting tables in a fantasy galaxy seems rather bizarre, even perverse. But waiting tables also offers a built-in motivation—a moment-by-moment reminder and reinforcement of some external goal that justifies the job itself.

The production of such external motivation seems to be tied directly to the ambivalence of interactions between waiter and customer; although waiting tables might for some be a satisfying profession of deep interpersonal relationships, such an attitude is rare, at least in its contemporary mythology outside of high-end restaurants and clubs. Indeed, the fundamental unit operation of waiting tables needed to fulfill the waitperson's goals outside the pub, café, or restaurant might come precisely in the form of absent, anonymous, even meaningless short-term interpersonal interactions. SWG is able to offer the apotheosis of such an experience: cantina customers controlled exclusively by simplistic preprogrammed macros meant only to service the instrumental need of healing. As a unit operation of simplistic automatism, there are few better designs than a robotic customer programmed to utter the same statement until sated. Worse yet, like a waiter, the SWG entertainer relies mostly on tips for income.

One might wonder if the SWG entertainer is actually a cynical, downtrodden player type, one meant to reveal the discouraging nature of playing the game itself and thus encourage the player to seek satisfaction elsewhere. Even within the game, an entertainer character's player has no recourse to broader goals than the specific role in which he is cast; the game offers no recourse to a broader dream than entertaining. By drawing attention to the unit operation of the dysfunctional waiter–customer relationship, the cantina can be understood as a meditation on the budding artist's idealistic dream in a reality of few successes.

If the cantina underscores SWG's critique of the idealistic goals of the artist, the bazaar emphasizes the futility of a much broader array of contemporary urbanity. In their study of cantina visitation practices on two SWG planets, Ducheneaut et al. observe that SWG's design sets up widely distributed centers of activity with large distances in between. Player cities, they observe, "are isolated in the 'suburbs.' If players were allowed to live in high-density apartments close (or even above) each cantina in the main cities, patterns of visits would probably change."[50] The difficulty in reaching cantinas could be extended to bazaar terminals, which demand similar treks across large swaths of anonymous galaxy.

Ducheneaut et al.'s observation that SWG players are "stuck in the suburbs" is a productive one. Whether or not spatial expanse was intended to enable more sociability in the game, the task of transgressing entire star systems to visit a cantina or retrieve a purchased artifact becomes a unit operation for the long-distance errand. SWG simply requires a great deal of commuting to complete simple tasks. Those of us who live or have lived in large cities are all too familiar with the dread that accompanies even the simplest of daily errands. For residents of automobile-reliant cities like Los Angeles and Atlanta, simple five-mile in-town trips might entail forty-five minutes of bumper-to-bumper traffic in either direction. By recreating empty commuting in a virtual space that could just as easily collapse distance infinitely, SWG enforces commuting as a prerequisite for successful commercialism.

Taken together, SWG's cantina and bazaar culture could be taken as unit operations for one real-world referent in particular: Southern California. The region's massive urban sprawl[51] and lack of affordable housing—only 17 percent of Angelenos could afford a home in March 2005, compared with 53 percent for the rest of the nation—have forced more and more middle-class families to live increasingly farther away from their workplaces.[52] Together, Los Angeles, San Bernardino, Orange County, and San Diego also have the worst traffic congestion in the nation, increasing the burden of long-distance commutes.[53] Moreover, the Hollywood film industry helps create and maintain a massive culture of waiting tables in Southern California; waiters and waitresses rank in the top ten occupations for job growth in Los Angeles County projected through 2008.[54] When Raph Koster was named Chief Creative Officer of Sony Online

Entertainment in 2003, he moved to the company's headquarters to work on *Star Wars Galaxies*—in San Diego, California.[55]

It would be inappropriate to call SWG a complete and coherent critique of contemporary Southern Californian life. But two key design innovations in the game, cantinas and bazaar terminals, serve as convincing representations of particularly salient dissatisfactions in that region. *Star Wars Galaxies* may not service Benjamin's longing for artworks that serve revolutionary ends, but the game does break from its supposedly primary role as entertainment software and become social commentary. This type of experience would still count as "fun" for Koster—the player gains new knowledge about social structures through their representation as key unit operations in the game—but it is that perverse kind of fun I call fun'. It should be clear now that neither fun nor fun' is an appropriate moniker for the sort of critical interrogation videogames like *Star Wars Galaxies* encourage in their players. Forcing videogames to share their potential as social critique with their potential as absent-minded distraction will inevitably constrain the power of players' simulation fever to the game itself, rather than allowing that anxiety to play out in their daily lives.

The Simulation Gap

Like some poststructuralist strategies, unit analysis is especially concerned with response; the crux of this experience takes place where unit operations meet subjectivity, in the crisis of simulation fever. But further, videogames radically increase the importance of player response. Espen Aarseth makes this point in *Cybertext:*

The concept of cybertext focuses on the mechanical organization of the text, by positing the intricacies of the medium as an integral part of the literary exchange. However, it also centers attention on the consumer, or user, of the text, as a more integrated figure than even reader-response theorists would claim.[1]

However, where reader-response theorists, deconstructionists, and other poststructuralists privilege the position of the *reader,* Aarseth's cybertexts privilege the position of the *work.* A cybertext, Aarseth says, is a "machine for the production of a variety of expressions."[2] Reader-response criticism shares some of the same properties of unpacking a text as cybertextual criticism; both focus on the ongoing responses and cognitive functions of the reader or player. In reader-response rubric, the meaning of the text is a production of the reader, not the text, even if the text can "constrain" that reading. For example, in critic Wolfgang Iser's conception of reader-response, the text provides controls for the reader's experience, like signposts, but leaves "gaps" that the reader must fill in. Roland Barthes's notion of the "death of the author" frees the reader to approach a text unburdened by the limits of authority.[3] Deconstruction dismantles textual signification into purely relational elements, mediating the irresolvable interrelations between these elements, a process of continuous subjective effort. In all of these approaches, interpretation becomes a process of invoking a text from a particular point of view, making the reader the central figure of post-structuralist criticism.

The reader (or user, or player) is still critical in Aarseth's account of cyber-texts. In the process of interacting with a cybertext, "the user will have effectu-ated a semiotic sequence, and this selective movement is a work of physical construction that the various concepts of 'reading' do not account for."[4] But this "work" is what qualifies texts as "ergodic." Even though Aarseth insists that cy-bertexts go *beyond* reader-response criticism's focus on the user of the text, he fol-lows Barthes in collapsing this property of use back onto the works themselves; these are ergodic pieces of *literature,* not ergodic experiences or ergodic encoun-ters.[5] The user never disappears from the cybertextual experience, but Aarseth shifts the focus of the ergodic experience from the user to the text.

Shortly after the passages cited above, Aarseth characterizes cybertext as "various kinds of literary communication systems where the functional differ-ences among the mechanical parts play a defining role in determining the aes-thetic process."[6] *Cybertext* implies a cybernetic feedback loop between user and machine,[7] but Aarseth mainly considers the embodiment of this cybernetic re-lationship to be a property of what he calls a "perspective" on textual forms.[8] This cyborg relationship is, according to Aarseth, a "kind of machine, a sym-biosis of sign, operator, and medium."[9] Cybertext theory does open up a mode for approaching texts that takes into account the indispensability of these three components. However, in so doing, cybertext theory also risks undermining the importance of the user's individual subjectivity. Responding to an approach to cybertext theory by Markku Eskelinen, N. Katherine Hayles notes this elision of individual media into one master medium:

Like all functionalist theories, cybertext theory elides materiality in order to create a template based on function, generally casting a blind eye to how these functions are in-stantiated in particular media. Cybernetics made much the same move when it reduced complex physiological and biological processes to "functions" and then claimed there were no essential differences between biological organisms and machines, because both carried out the same functions. Despite the frequency with which Aarseth and Eskeli-nen use the word "material," in an important sense cybertext theory is very immaterial, for it largely ignores the material differences between, say, computer-generated text, the *I Ching,* and print novels. Of course the generality it attains by doing so accounts for its power as a theory. But material differences between media do matter, and matter significantly, if one wishes to account for the specificity of reading practices, the responses of users or readers to particular texts, and the nuanced effects that different kinds of texts can achieve.[10]

Just as Hayles sees cybertext theory as diminishing material specificity, I see it as diminishing subjective specificity. As a computational strategy, unit operations embody representations of the world inside abstract, formal containers. These units are not anonymous forms bereft of ideology. Thinking of cybertexts as a mode of understanding, a "perspective," threatens to close down the feedback loops of individual user experience. At the extreme, cybertext theory becomes a system operation, forgoing all the gradations of a work's subjective uses in favor of their common roles as configurations. For this reason, exploring the manifestation of game rules in player experience is perhaps the most important type of work game criticism can do.

Since most games are commercial works focused on "fun" and measured by commercial success more than critical acclaim, criticism in the popular media tends to focus on subjectivity's lowest common denominator: player enjoyment.[11] Games like *September 12* heighten simulation fever, and by doing so they become easier to critique than some other kinds of games. After *September 12's* release, game designer Greg Costikyan posted a scathing response on his personal weblog:

There are no victory conditions. Essentially, you continue until everyone is dead and the city is a smouldering pile of rubble—or you don't, and everyone just toddles about the city until you become bored and go play Nethack or something.

Now . . . I see. Terrorists are perfectly peaceable people who toddle around until nasty, evil Western imperialists destroy them and half of their neighbors through indiscriminate missile attacks.[12]

The terrorists don't perform any actual terrorism in the game. They are identified by their appearance, but their terrorist deeds are omitted from the simulation. Costikyan's response signals a possible case of Sherry Turkle's simulation denial. Costikyan's concerns stem from his discomfort with this representation; terrorists, after all, don't just "toddle about" innocently. But the simulation's model excludes actual terrorist activity, to focus instead on the response to terrorism.

Earlier I talked about the importance of what simulations exclude as much as what they include. In this case, Costikyan is responding based on his presupposition that terrorism cannot be discussed in this one-sided fashion. In the present case, this response is personal, and perhaps psychological. Costikyan lives a block from the former site of the World Trade Center and has even published a detailed, personal account of his experience on September 11.[13] This may be why Costikyan's response to *September 12* is so provocative; he wears his simulation fever on his sleeve. Costikyan makes the assumption that the simulation's failure to render acts of terrorism in the game is a kind of revisionism: terrorism never really happened. He continues:

But to call this a "simulation," as the creators do, is fucking obscene. Simulation of what? Where's the research? What systems are simulated? What intellectual depth is brought to the consideration? What is the point—and have they even though[t] through their point, smug, superior schmucks that they are?[14]

If simulation fever is the struggle between the omissions and inclusions of a source system and the player's subjective response to those decisions, then Costikyan's position shows how very ill he is with the condition. This is not a criticism—simulation fever is a condition more at home in psychoanalysis than in physiology. Costikyan objects to the game's simplicity: it does not model, for example, the worldwide financial networks behind terrorist activity; nor does it model the complex religious and historical backdrop in which such terrorism occurs.

What it models instead—and in an admittedly simplistic way—is the way the West's response to the terrorism of September 11 seems content also to ignore all these other conditions, reverting to the simplicity of military destruction. The game's argument could be interpreted to include this failure to consider the political and historical context for terrorism and states' responses to terrorism, replacing those systems with a single unit operation: squeezing the trigger button.

Some players of *September 12* did a better job working through their conditions of simulation fever. Another player offered this rather subtle explanation of an encounter with his own simulation fever:

Interesting . . . I found myself first thinking "wow, this is a lot of work to go to in order to say one 'little' thing." Which led me to believe that that's not what the authors were trying to do. Which led me to think about the fact that I don't necessarily care what the authors were trying to do, it's how I incorporate it into my own context that is what matters more to me. Which led me to realize that even a simple simulation gives me room to actively participate in creating meaning in a different way than static textual or visual presentations like editorials and cartoons. Which led me to think more deeply about these issues.[15]

In this player's perspective, the various ways to play the game, and the various subjective embodiments of the simulation's effect, suggest a richer experience. The key to the experience he describes is not the realism of the simulation, or its correspondence with a set of validated and internationally accepted models for international politics; instead the value of his experience comes directly from his willingness to allow the multiple subjective experiences of the simulation's rules play against one another. The result of this indeterminacy is not the failure of signification, but the reflection of debate. The subject matter and simplicity of *September 12* teaches several lessons about simulation fever.

First, unit operations are biased. Starting with Aristotle, universals have been taken to be representations within human experience, accessible through reason. Because of their ubiquity and incredible computational power, computers often make us forget that they use forms of human representation, rather than transcendent formalisms. After von Neumann's conditional control transfer, the representational power of computation increased the number of forms of representation computers could perform, just as structuralism increased the number of forms of representation linguistic analysis could perform. The transfer of representations from less to more encapsulation increases the controversy surrounding those representations. Sometimes this increase is immediately manifest, as in the case of *September 12*. In *September 12,* there is only one player rule; players can shoot or not. But the game embeds several additional simulation rules. For example: missiles are inexact weapons that can't help but destroy more than they intend to. Additionally, they impose a delay between the time they are fired and the time they hit their target; during this delay, the terrorists may have moved and been replaced by innocent citizens. Together, these rules contribute to a highly encapsulated unit operation for current U.S. foreign policy. In other cases, the increase is suppressed. Ideology is less discernible, and interpretation needs to work harder to make its case. *Tetris* falls into this category, as do many commercial videogames, including *Star Wars Galaxies.*

Second, the dialectic between unit operations and subjectivity that constitutes simulation fever is extrinsic, not intrinsic, to the game. This means that all games entail some kind of subjective embodiment that transgresses the game itself. In some games, this transgression is very easy to trace. In others, like *Tetris* again, it is not so easy to trace—thus Janet Murray's interpretation of the game is less immediately credible than just about any response to *September 12*.

A Gap in the Magic Circle

Play theorist Johan Huizinga has articulated a structure he calls the *magic circle,* a safe place of play: "The arena, the card table, the magic circle . . . all are in form and function playgrounds, i.e. forbidden spots, isolated, hedged round, hallowed, within which special rules obtain. All are temporary worlds within the ordinary world, dedicated to the performance of an act apart."[16] During this "act apart," the magic circle delineates a place of predictability and order in an otherwise chaotic world. The figure of the magic circle has been popular in contemporary discussions of games, where it often prefigures a claim about the safety of games. Game designer Chris Crawford cites a form of the magic circle in his four characteristics of computer games: *representation, interaction, conflict,* and *safety.*[17] Crawford clarifies the last of these characteristics carefully: "a game is an artifice for providing the psychological experiences of conflict and danger while excluding their physical realizations. In short, a game is a safe way to experience reality."[18]

But if all games are both ideological and extrinsically subjective, then the magic circle cannot maintain its status as a hallowed, isolated safe place, at least not entirely. I think both Huizinga and Crawford paint compelling pictures of how games work. However, an adjustment to our understanding of the magic circle is in order.

Huizinga treats the subject of play rather broadly. For Huizinga, play is an act of cultural production and transformation, in which communal secrecy creates rifts in the status quo. In fact, Huizinga is mainly interested in how such play activities persist after the game is abandoned: "the feeling of being 'apart together' in an exceptional situation, of sharing something important, of mutually withdrawing from the rest of the world and rejecting the usual norms, retains its magic beyond the duration of the individual game."[19] This suggests that the magic circle of the game world ruptures into the material world, but yet it does not disappear entirely. Such an understanding of the magic circle disrupts the notion that play space possesses a stable interiority and exteriority. The idea that "you're either playing a game or you're not" or that games offer an "artificial space" that contrasts sharply with the material world needs to be revised in light of this new understanding of the magic circle.[20]

Huizinga defines play as "a voluntary activity or occupation executed within certain fixed limits of time and place, according to rules freely accepted, but absolutely binding, having its aim in itself and accompanied by a feeling of tension, joy and the consciousness that it is 'different' from 'ordinary life.'"[21] Elsewhere, he calls play a "*stepping out* of 'real' life into a temporary sphere of activity with a disposition all of its own."[22] As a spatially and temporally finite object, the magic circle of play thus implies an entry and an exit, a disruption in its very skin through which the game's players can move between the game world and the real world, a bridge across which the actual cultural production takes place. Far from an unbiased activity, then, games take a position much more akin to Michel de Certeau's idea of the practice of everyday life, in which individual and group actions can reclaim the autonomy lost to statist and commercial structures.[23]

Earlier I argued that there is no distinction between subjective and objective representation, in contrast to Chris Crawford's characterization of the difference between games and simulations. The objective simulation is a myth because games cannot help but carry the baggage of ideology. The same is true of the magic circle. Instead of standing outside the world in utter isolation, games provide a two-way street through which players and their ideas can enter and exit the game, taking and leaving their residue in both directions. There is a gap in the magic circle through which players carry subjectivity in and out of the game space. If the magic circle were really some kind of isolated antithesis to the world, it would never be possible to access it at all.

When Chris Crawford claims that *safety* is a core characteristic of games, he is referring to a different kind of safety than that of Huizinga's magic circle. Crawford suggests that the consequences of in-game actions do not spill over into the real world *analogously.* Crawford clarifies:

A player can blast the monsters all day long and risk only her quarter. She can amass huge financial empires and lose them in an hour without risking her piggy bank. She can lead great armies into desperate battles on which hang the fate of nations, all without shedding a drop of blood. In a world of relentless cause and effect, of tragic linkages and inevitable consequences, the disassociation of actions from consequences is a compelling feature of games.[24]

Crawford argues that the player is safe from the consequences of the actions produced within the game, which are not mirrored in the real world. Crawford does allow for certain other real-world consequences of games, such as the loss of dignity or reward upon a player's defeat. But by the letter of Crawford's definition, it is not clear to me if he would consider a player's changed mental state—at the time of play or long after—a possibly unsafe characteristic. The loss of dignity, for example, which Crawford mentions in particular, might send a player into a rage. Is this result a safe feature of games?

All games convey ideas, and those ideas may instill a process of subjective interrogation and altered mental state. The history of serious consequences to cultural works from Socrates to Mao has not gone unnoticed by world civilization. The legitimacy of the media effects debate notwithstanding, videogames have sparked considerable controversy regarding the effects of representational violence and hatred. Recently, accusations of defamatory comments against Haitians in the bestselling game *Grand Theft Auto: Vice City* led to protests[25] and hate crime investigations in Florida. For participants in that historical trajectory, it is naive to think that games are safe havens of representation—or that we would want them to be. Huizinga himself writes about the magic circle from within Nazi captivity, in whose hands he would eventually die.

Crawford's definition can also be read more subtly. Games provide safe ways to experience reality, but that safety is not necessarily preserved once the game ends and the player slips through the gap in the magic circle, into the sincerity of his or her own mind. Games do provide a protected space, in which players are spared all the physical consequences of their actions. But for the magic circle to couple with the world, it must not be hermetic; it must have a breach through which the game world and the real world spill over into one another. The residue of this interaction infects both spheres, causing what I earlier called simulation fever, the nervous discomfort caused by the interaction of the game's unit-operational representations of a segment of the real world and the player's subjective understanding of that representation. Huizinga lamented the fact that play in modern society has become relegated almost entirely to sport, a field of mere distraction. The idea of simulation fever insinuates seriousness back into play and suggests that games help us expose and explore complicated human conditions, rather than offering mere interruption and diversion.

IV

From Design to Configuration

Complex Networks

Complex adaptive systems theory is an amalgam of the hard and social sciences, including mathematicians Leonhard Euler's[1] and Paul Erdős's[2] research on graph theory and sociologists Stanley Milgram's[3] and Mark Granovetter's studies on social networks.[4] Complexity touches chaos theory, artificial life, computation, genetics, human systems, and many other fields, and it is characterized by its focus on patterns of emergence. As with Stephen Wolfram's cellular automata, complex systems self-organize through adaptation and emergence, in which disaggregated unit operations coalesce to create structured systems.

Complexity theory offers a framework from which to approach the work of Gilles Deleuze and Félix Guattari, especially the second volume of their capitalism and schizophrenia twosome, *A Thousand Plateaus,* and specifically their notion of the *rhizome* and the practice of *nomadism.*[5] The rhizome gained a sudden boost in popularity in the 1990s, first as a potentially useful device for understanding new electronic hypertexts and later as a compelling theoretical model for the Internet.[6] Since then, theorists, critics, and artists have engaged *A Thousand Plateaus* as a theoretical framework for creating or analyzing electronic art, both the digital and virtual-reality/installation varieties.[7] Despite this close history with digital media criticism and practice, there are important differences between Deleuze and Guattari's approach and that of unit operations.

Throughout their work, together and individually, Deleuze and Guattari demonstrate a lingering fascination with madmen, wanderers, and mechanical connections. Like Stephen Wolfram, Deleuze and Guattari critique the ordering principles of major fields of human thought. But where Wolfram seeks to revise the sciences in general, Deleuze and Guattari seek specifically to revise the human sciences. In *A Thousand Plateaus,* the two try to upset the basic notions of meaning, particularly those surrounding the subject, the body, and language. To do this, they seek to topple three Goliaths of meaning-making: psychoanalysis, physiology, and semiotics. *A Thousand Plateaus* suggests "liberation strategies" by which individuals can oppose such regimes. To do this, Deleuze and Guattari concentrate on disrupting unities of meaning and replacing them with assemblages of singular states of meaning.

Two concepts from *A Thousand Plateaus* have proven especially salient to interpretation and application, namely, *rhizome* and *nomadism.* The rhizome is a plant-growth model, according to which growth spreads by nonhierarchical tubers instead of hierarchical roots. Deleuze and Guattari use the rhizome both as an object lesson and as a theoretical model for their later analysis. Deleuze and Guattari create an expansive and somewhat baroque system to drive the machinery of their analysis, concentrated around a large number of charged terminologies. Throughout, Deleuze and Guattari expand the rhizome, adding jargon to describe the free-form movement of an entity within a rhizomatic structure. One name they give to this logic is *nomadism.*[8]

Named for the nomadic lifestyle of tribes of the Asiatic steppes who move from locale to locale rather than settling and expanding in a few localized regions, Deleuze and Guattari's notion of nomadism encapsulates the operation of the rhizome: a logic of free-form attraction between bodies. Deleuze and Guattari oppose nomad space with state space; the former is "smooth" or open ended, whereas the latter is "striated" or fixed to a grid. State space focuses on organization, be it cultural, religious, sexual, psychological, psychoanalytic, familiar, or commercial. Occupying nomad space is a way to evade or protest statist machines.

Deleuze and Guattari suggest that their theory might become a kind of practice, presumably a revolutionary one. This is a hard sell, since the theory itself is rarely grounded in immediately comprehensible human experience. It is nevertheless possible to underscore an implementation strategy for nomadism. The authors borrow the term *plateau* from Gregory Bateson, who uses it in reference to systems that seek not to interrupt or terminate their intensity through either external intervention or internal climax. Deleuze and Guattari call these plateaus "components of passage," each plateau lined up in succession or divergence with another plateau, allowing free movement.[9] The rhizome is the structure along which activity moves between plateaus. These heightened energies inject themselves into other actions through a moment of *deterritorialization,* along what Deleuze and Guattari call *lines of flight.* Deterritorialization is the uprooting of a thing along the vector of a rhizome that decodes it, or changes the circumstances and actions affecting it. Deterritorialization leads to a reterritorialization, in which the thing is reimplanted and reincoded in a new circumstance. This recoding is called an "overcoding"; it creates a new insertion of the object into a different level or assemblage, from which it can again uproot and reconstitute itself through a rupture in its center.

Like the movement of nomadic tribespeople, nomadism itself goes through fluxes of motion and rest. These "waves" move, in Deleuze and Guattari's words, "from the central layer to the periphery, then from the new center to the new periphery, falling back to the old center and launching forth to the new."[10] As with Derrida, structures and actions gain meaning based not on their nature but on their limits and what escapes them.[11] But, in contrast with Derrida, Deleuze and Guattari focus on the intersecting forces on and between bodies in dictating the nature of and response to this relation of difference. Rather than thinking of difference as an externally constituting and insurmountable force, Deleuze and Guattari insist that the subject is an empty category through which forces interact, moving from one plane of existence, one plateau, to another. Nomads do stay at rest, and thus nomadism does not imply a hasty frenzy from one state to another. Nomad thought allows for free movement between states of being, along any of a multitude of arbitrary axes, but it endorses such movement only when it is logically consistent with the relationship between a body and its external conditions.

The practice of nomadism is thus one of receptivity to possible escape paths from one state into another. Deleuze and Guattari insist that it is possible to use this practice to unseat their three targets, the subject, the body, and language. Language becomes a supple structure that changes in variation to social and cultural context. The body becomes an arbitrary structure organized entirely by flows of desire. These "desiring machines" connect or disconnect with other bodies irrespective of social and political tenets of union. The subject becomes a smooth structure that modifies, amends, and obliterates portions of itself as it interacts with and wraps around other subjects, objects, and structures. Critic and *A Thousand Plateaus* translator Brian Massumi offers this summary:

Nomad thought replaces the closed equation of representation, $x = x = $ not y (I = I = not you) with an open equation: $\ldots + y + z + a + \ldots$. Rather than analyzing the world into discrete components, reducing their manyness to the One (= Two) of self-reflection, and ordering them by rank, it sums up a set of disparate circumstances in a shattering blow. It synthesizes a multiplicity of elements without effacing their heterogeneity or hindering their potential for future rearranging.[12]

In Massumi's analysis the fundamental difference between nomadism and unit analysis comes to the fore: nomad thought resists thinking of the world in discrete components, devouring individual decision into an amorphous whole. This obstacle stands in the way of nomadism's embrace of unit operations, despite the apparent similarity of their attempt to disrupt unities of meaning. Deleuze and Guattari endorse assemblages that make individuated changes in constant progression. These assemblages create and destroy broader contexts and structures, but they always return their allegiance to the flow.

Alain Badiou has argued that Deleuze's insistence on continuity implies an eternal return to the same.[13] In Badiou's reading, Deleuze maintains a connection between the singular units of a flow, returning all deterritorializations and reterritorializations to a single, overall whole: "contrary to the commonly accepted image (Deleuze as liberating the anarchic multiple of desires and errant drifts), contrary even to the apparent indications of his work that play on the opposition multiple/multiplicities . . . it is the occurrence of the One . . . that forms the supreme destination of thought and to which thought is accordingly consecrated."[14] Under Badiou's critique, the assemblages of subjectivity that appear to characterize nomadism always remain bound to an overall process, a system operation. Massumi's matheme "$\ldots + y + z + a + \ldots$" explicates Deleuze and Guattari's insistence on sameness: here it is the continuous mathematical series, not the disjunctive mathematical set, that best characterizes being. Nomadism implies stasis as much as it implies movement. One might observe that the unitarity in nomadism comes in the actual movement from y to z, from z to a. But Deleuze and Guattari do not locate the significance of nomadic movement in the gaps between states, as Badiou locates the significance of subjectivity in the restructuring of an event. Nomadism thus risks becoming a system operation.

This tendency toward holism is at work in the figure of the nomad and the rhizome, upon which Deleuze and Guattari do not ascribe even the tangible movement of a tuber's sprout or the passage of the nomad tribe. The nomad and the rhizome appear to be only metaphoric figures for Deleuze and Guattari. A nomad is a real person, or a historical one at least, who appears to act according to normal conceptions of subjectivity. But when Deleuze and Guattari speak of the nomad, they do not appear to mean a real individual, but rather something else, a kind of nomadic spirit. Subjectivity is replaced by *assemblages* and *machines*. Here is how Deleuze characterizes the assemblage:

What is an assemblage? It is a multiplicity which is made up of many heterogeneous terms and which establishes liaisons, relations between them, across ages, sexes and reigns—different natures. Thus, the assemblage's only unity is that of co-functioning: it is symbiosis, a "sympathy." It is never filiations which are important, but alliances, alloys; these are not successions, lines of descent, but contagions, epidemics, the wind.[15]

The subject's replacement binds desiring forces with their objects. The heavy plow, say Deleuze and Guattari, exists only "in a constellation" between field, oxen, soil, and mouth.[16] Assemblages are intermingled with desire, such that decision and determinacy become swallowed up in the assemblage of bodies and other bodies. "Desire," say Deleuze and Guattari, "has nothing to do with a natural or spontaneous determination; there is no desire but assembling, assembled desire."[17] Machines are the places where flows enter or leave structures. Deleuze and Guattari offer the first example of a machine in *Anti-Oedipus,* a baby's mouth, which they characterize as a mouth machine meeting a breast machine. Desiring machines connect to a body without organs, organized systems that control flows. And yet, the act of plowing, grazing, or breastfeeding ceases to exist as such for Deleuze and Guattari.

The nomadic subject, then, is a singularity where desiring machines distribute their flows. Deleuze and Guattari call this point of movement between states the *local.* The movement from point to point is a flow, part and parcel of the constitution of the nomad. Subjectivity is replaced by "an infinite succession of local operations."[18]

Deleuze and Guattari's local operations seem to be increasingly less similar to unit operations. Even though the deliberateness of individuality is excluded from Deleuze and Guattari's understanding of the nomadic subject, ruptures within assemblages still take an individuated, autonomous form at these points between flows. Unlike decision, local operation is not a process of preordination or deliberation. Rather, Deleuze relates this kind of expression to vectors, along which assemblages "enunciate."[19]

To be closer to unit operations, nomadism would require some kind of ratification at points along the vector of an assemblage where the nomadic subject is constituted. This structure would find affinity with Badiou's event but on a less consequential scale; at this ratification point, a unit operation experiences an acknowledgment of the gesture that just took place, and its foundational structure relies on that acknowledgment. In Badiou's philosophy, this acknowledgment is called fidelity, and continuous fidelity entails truth. Like Deleuze, Badiou also articulates a continuous process, but unlike Deleuze, he takes that process to be made up of discrete moments—unit operations whose aggregate effect creates fidelity to an initial event. Where Deleuze and Guattari privilege aggregate flows over discrete unit operations, Badiou privileges the latter over the former. In Badiou's philosophy, the units have precedence. Even though Badiou's truth develops through continued fidelity to an event, that continuance is far less developed than Deleuze and Guattari's nomadism. A fungible theory of unit operations requires a commitment both to the individualism of discrete units and to the meaningful and durable connections between those units.

Deleuze and Guattari remain ambivalent to the relationship between flows and the unit operations comprised by them. While Badiou's rejoinder seems quite valid, Deleuze and Guattari do offer occasional allowances for gaps or pauses in the nomad's progress. The nomad, they argue, "has a territory; he follows customary paths; he goes from one point to another; he is not ignorant of points."[20] Deleuze and Guattari give a number of names to the oscillation between movement and rest: nomad versus state space; smooth versus striated space; deterritorialization versus reterritorialization. In the end, however, it is not the movement from one toward or against the other that fascinate these thinkers. Near the end of *A Thousand Plateaus,* Deleuze and Guattari make a statement that I would offer as its most fungible practical guideline: "What interests us in operations of striation and smoothing are precisely the passages or combinations: how the forces at work within space continually striate it, and how in the course of its striation it develops other forces and emits new smooth spaces."[21] The punctuations between deterritorializations and reterritorializations appear to come closest to demarcating the individual "units" of a flow.

Complex Networks

One could compare unit operations' structured relation to the whole they make up to Wolfram's cellular automata, which execute simple, discrete, individual rules to construct larger, holistic systems. In computer science and digital circuits, one application of automata is in finite state machines (FSMs), models of behavior that proceed in discrete steps from one state to another. An FSM's state relies on its past history of inputs as well as its current inputs. For example, an artificial intelligence (AI) specification for a character in a game might have three states: Wander, Attack, and Retreat. In its Wander state, it might meander around an environment and check for an enemy. If it finds one, the FSM would change its state to Attack. In this state, the character might attack, then check its and its opponent's health state. If the opponent were dead, the character would return to the Wander state. If the character's health approached zero, it might shift to a Retreat state. FSMs operate in discrete unit operations whose aggregate effects represent a coherent behavior.

Progressions of individuated movements within complex systems are likewise the subjects of complex adaptive systems, or complex network theory. Complex networks operate by similar principles as the cellular automata I discussed in chapter 7. Exploiting a four-century-old field of mathematics called graph theory, complexity theory attempts to model patterns out of chaos through the complex, individuated interrelation of many simple parts. Complex systems explain how relatively few components, say 35,000 genes or 100 urban youths, can create tremendously complex effects, such as human beings or the latest nationwide fad. Each cell (or "node" in graph theory jargon) makes autonomous, individual gestures that spill over its borders, extending its influence. Complexity arises not from the number of connections or "links" these nodes draft, but from the configurations those many interconnected nodes form. In the case of the human genome, it is not our 35,000 genes that makes humans more complex than wheat (which contains a relatively commensurate 20,000 genes), but the complex, fault-tolerant systems those 35,000 units create. As I showed earlier, the Human Genome Project makes the rash assumption that knowing what all the genes look like—rather than what they do and how they interact—is the key to understanding their biological function.

In the middle of the last century, two Hungarian mathematicians named Paul Erdős and Alfred Renyi took a mathematical perspective on a social question. Suppose you are at a party with a hundred other partygoers. None of you knows each other initially, but one of you knows that the host has an especially desirable bottle of wine, snuck in among all the cheap stuff being served out in the open. As the evening progresses, everyone begins chatting in pairs, then small groups. Everyone likes to mingle at a party, and the guests work the room, gradually moving between groups and meeting new people. Word will certainly get out about the wine, but can it spread enough to run the bottle to the dregs?

Common sense would suggest that even if you could meet one person every five minutes, meeting all ninety-nine of the partygoers would be nearly impossible within the time limits of an ordinary party. So, the wine would remain safe from all harm. Erdős and Renyi disagreed. By the end of the evening, they argued, each partygoer indeed would not have met everyone else individually. But it would be possible to trace a connection between all of them, through the links they had forged. This web or network of partygoers constitutes a much more complex and powerful structure than each casual relationship between individuals.

Today, the most common entry point into complex network theory is through the notion of *six degrees of separation*. Before the play, film,[22] software application,[23] and Kevin Bacon parody,[24] there was Stanley Milgram's 1967 study of the distance between people in the United States.[25] Participants in the study were given a set of postcards and the name of a target person somewhere in the United States. If they knew the target person, they were to send the entire dossier directly to him. Otherwise, they were asked to send the dossier to someone they knew personally, who was more likely to have a direct relationship with the target person. Milgram found that the average number of hops from start to finish was 5.5, or roughly "six degrees of separation."[26] In this case, the structure that described what seemed like an infinitely complex social network turned out to be very simple and compact.

Around the same time Milgram was conducting his famous experiment, Harvard sociologist Mark Granovetter was developing a related study on the importance of "weak ties" in social relationships. In his seminal paper "The Strength of Weak Ties," Granovetter argued that when people leverage their social network for the purposes of finding a job or launching a product, acquaintances are far more valuable than strong friendships.[27] Granovetter showed that strong relationships like our close friends often represent smaller, closed systems. Our friends are often friends with one another, and when it comes to getting a job or spreading the word about a new restaurant, friends may not provide much greater reach than we could achieve on our own. Weak ties allow us access to other closely clustered relationships outside our immediate reach. The strength of weak ties not only explains why most people find jobs through acquaintances, not close friends, but also sheds light on the six degrees of separation problem. Weak ties connect us with massive numbers of people in the world, leading to the six degrees or "small world" phenomenon. Strong ties usually connect us to only a few handfuls of people, most of whom probably know one another already.

In the ecosystem of weak ties, many networks exhibit strong nodes, or hubs, that connect a much larger number of individuals than other nodes in the network. When finding a job, the certain high-powered "networkers" often provide the most introductions to the most people. In networks that grow (that add more nodes), new nodes attach themselves to hubs more often than any other kind of node. Complexity theorists call this preferential attachment.[28] In common parlance, we often call it the "80/20 rule," or the "rich get richer" phenomenon. Networks that are structured in this way do not exhibit the same connectivity or *scale* from node to node (that is to say, each node does not have a proportional, or scaled, number of connections to any other node). Consequently, complexity theorists call such networks *scale-free networks*. Scale-free networks distribute their connections on a power-law curve rather than a bell curve. The route map in any airline magazine provides a good lesson in scale-free networks. A few cities like Dallas, Chicago, Atlanta, San Francisco, Houston, New York, and several others account for a large percentage of the flight routes, while a large number of cities like Seattle, Omaha, Indianapolis, and Albuquerque account for a small percentage. The high traffic airports are called hubs, just like the powerful social networkers.

Researchers in a variety of fields, from physics to sociology, have since showed how interconnected complex networks, and especially scale-free networks, underlie many kinds of phenomena, from the worldwide outbreak of AIDS in the 1980s to the spread of the latest teenage fad. Scale-free networks also happen to be very strong, resilient structures, because breaks in individual ties do not lead to chain reactions like cascading failures that destroy the entire system. This is why the Internet is a much stronger system than the electrical power grid, and why terrorist networks are much stronger than statist or guerilla regimes. While many scientists remain convinced that the nature of life lies in the structure of individual genes, others believe that the real key will be found in the interrelated function of genes.[29] The unpredictable network relations produce elegant or stable patterns through emergence. Through emergence, complex networks achieve meaningful order through the correlated (but not controlled) unit operations between individual interacting parts.

Recently, a multitude of social network services Web sites have been launched, software applications that let people make manifest the scale-free complex networks that govern their interactions in order to better exploit them. Among the most popular is *Friendster,* a service that lets people find new friends among their friends' friends.[30] *Friendster* bills itself as a social service best used for dating and socializing. When users sign up for the service, they create a profile that describes their interests, location, and other basic information. The service then encourages subscribers to invite their friends to join. Each member can search or browse through the network of friends and friends' friends. If they find someone whom they'd like to meet, the service facilitates a permission-based introduction through the links that connect the two parties. Other services like *Ryze* allow people to make connections with any other member, without permission.[31] Following Mark Granovetter's original model, *LinkedIn*[32] and *Ecademy*[33] facilitate business relationships instead of arbitrary personal ones, with a special focus placed on deal making, job hunting, and recruiting.

While the end result of each of these services is the same—a manifestation of social complex networks—the importance and subtlety of each comes from the ways in which users are able to follow individual links in their network. Complex network theory often focuses on end results and emergent outcomes instead of the individual unit operations that collectively make up such outcomes. Social software creator Ross Mayfield has evaluated these services and categorized them into four models for social network operations: declarative *(Ryze),* in-person *(Meetup),* conversational (weblogs), and referral *(Friendster, LinkedIn).*[34] Mayfield recognizes that the important characteristics of these tools include not only their underlying structure, but also the nature of the individual gestures by which people traverse that structure.

Social Software design fosters specific social norms by regulating possible behavior. Regulation is a good thing. A stem cell can grow into any cell in the human body not by hard coded instructions of what to become, but regulators telling it what not to become. Simple rules in complex adaptive systems, like social networks, yield complex results . . . . Social Software encodes political bargains that are required because of natural social tension.[35]

In complex networks, discrete unit operations form the foundation for emergent structures. In the case of social software, the individual relationships between friends or colleagues form the groundwork for a social network, not the other way around. The observable nature or final product of the system may indeed rely on its generative nature, but the individual actions do all the real work.

At their core, complex network theory and nomadism share common fundamental principles. Deleuze and Guattari seek to remove the idea of boundaries as primary creators of meaning. For Deleuze and Guattari, liberation is not total chaos, but free individuated movements from one stratum to another. Although their "local operation" fails to account for the discreteness and reflection that I require of unit operations, the two have similarities. Complex networks show us how many stable structures are actually built from a myriad of individual, free-form connections between nodes, which are also unit operations.

But unlike proponents of network theory, Deleuze and Guattari strive for a new kind of everyday practice. Nomadism is not about following one's whims arbitrarily; rather, it is a statement that subjectivity should overcome isolation and constitute itself in assemblages of relation, along the lines of something like what mathematicians and information theorists call a network. Within that network of possible decisions, unit operations regulate movement between nodes, or impulses between intensities. This is why madmen like Judge Schreber and Antonin Artaud are such operative models for Deleuze and Guattari's analysis: they are unaffected by the systemic, overarching burden of institutionalized sanity.

But despite Deleuze and Guattari's wide readership, applications of nomadism or schizoanalysis as a viable praxis have been limited.[36] Understanding nomadism as a kind of complex network theory helps lay a viable groundwork for using *Capitalism and Schizophrenia*. Complexity and nomadism underscore the importance of free-form, localized maneuvers that constitute larger systems through creative configuration. Emergence in complex networks relies on individual gestures, not on coordinating system operations.

Go, the 3,000-year-old Chinese game played with black and white stones on a wooden board, has only two rules: players each place a single stone on alternating turns, and if one player's stones completely surround the opponent's, the surrounded stones are captured. Players are forbidden from making a move that would sacrifice their stone. From these simple rules, hundreds of thousands of possible Go games emerge, each different from one another. Videogames often exhibit emergence too, accelerated by the computational power of the computer. Games like *The Sims* and *Sim City,* discussed earlier, use a fixed set of rules to generate a wide range of game options and outcomes. In a game of Go or *Sim City,* the game as a whole is never lost on the rational player; he will always find context by conceptualizing the board's current configurations with its possible future states. In Go, this context points toward the final winner of the game. In *Sim City,* this context converges asymptotically on a particular player goal, which may shift over time. But the only control the player actually has in these games relates to individual unit operations, that is, moves and actions: placing a stone, demolishing a building, lowering taxes, zoning a property.

In the last chapter, I discussed Jesper Juul's distinction between emergent games and progressive games. Juul calls emergence "the primordial game structure," in contrast to progressive games wherein the player "has to perform a predefined set of actions in order to complete the game."[37] Juul goes on to characterize several "levels" of emergence, from the simplest, rule interaction, to the most complex, "true" emergence, as in Go. Juul makes the implicit value judgment that more emergence yields more variation and thereby more universal value ("emergence is the more interesting structure").[38] Go, Chess, and Mancala are good examples of "true" emergent games.

Juul focuses more on the generative effect of emergence than on the individual interactions between player and game that make up that emergence. Emergent structures are elegant and aesthetically appealing, perhaps even seductive or sublime, and it is understandable that one should admire the simplistic elegance of Go. Stephen Wolfram's opus on emergent automata includes full-color plates of the graceful structures his cellular automata generate inside *Mathematica*. As aesthetic structures, emergent systems are undeniably captivating, although perhaps only as instances of the sublime, not the expressive.

For this reason, one must take great care when assigning value to such systems. Juul's formalist commitment to emergence provokes visions of other aestheticized and fetishized systems of computational representation. Cybernetics and virtual reality are appealing examples of liberation technology because they promise some future ability to rewire the ordered system of life-decisions; in so doing, they hope to control such systems. This dream of control is often the tragic flaw of modern science fiction, the hubris that causes the system's operator to eventually lose control and become subverted by his creation, like Richard in *Galatea 2.2,* or Case in *Neuromancer. Virtual reality* refers to the dream of wiring ourselves—literally and figuratively—to operate according to the unit-system relationship of our choosing.

While cyberpunk, virtual reality, and emergence may offer more decadent ways to conceive of humanity's battle with our psychic unit operations, I would argue that more mundane forms of relation are more fungible. Some would claim that videogames are nothing more than a stepping stone to the inevitable "complete" control of virtual reality or artificial intelligence systems that would allow us to fully regulate the unit operations of our own minds, and the videogame industry's continuing obsession with verisimilitude might support such a claim. But videogames also mark an important break in their rejections of "natural" order, like the rejections of Deleuze and Guattari. Subtlety and consequence in games might come more from how we choose to execute game functions within the system's constraints, rather than how we attempt to find repleteness in their formal structures. Put differently: the type, and not the degree, of emergence is the deciding factor in the expressive potential of a complex system.

Complex Worlds

In 1999, Rockstar Games released *Grand Theft Auto III* (GTA) for the popular Playstation 2 console. GTA puts the player in the skin of a criminal who, after a botched bank heist, escapes from prison with his comrade.[1] In the game, the player explores an enormous fictitious world called Liberty City, in which he engages in various forms of behavior, legal and illegal. The main innovation of GTA is its vast virtual urban space and freedom of action in that environment. GTA gives the player the option of following structured missions for the city's criminal underground, or just striking out on his own. The missions require the player to take on criminal assignments from pimps and thugs, earning money to do their dirty work for them. This structure is most similar to a traditional mission-based game, in which a series of bite-size tasks lead the player through an otherwise linear, traditional storyline. However, the player can also choose to meander through the city, performing many ad hoc actions. He can carjack any vehicle on the street. He can bludgeon or rob any passerby he chooses. He can also deliver the sick or injured to the hospital or work as a vigilante. The player can also change modes at whim.

GTA offers a wealth of play modes or styles. One option is to follow the game's missions, which consist of a series of organized crime assignments. As the game's title suggests, the principal crime that enables many others is stealing cars—and the player can steal any vehicle that appears in the game. Organized crime assignments range from picking up your employer's girlfriend, to roughing up a thug who crossed your employer, to taking out hits on various pimps, thugs, and troublemakers. Players can experiment with allegiances for one or many mob bosses, and the game adjusts gang member responses to you based on your previous actions and loyalties.

Another option is to play any of the embedded side missions, structured tasks that also converge and communicate with other modes of play. These include taxi, ambulance, and firefighter missions, all of which appropriate gameplay mechanics from *Crazy Taxi*. Taxi-driving entails picking up and dropping off fares—the player even earns money for delivering the fares successfully. Of course, you have to steal a taxicab before you can reap the benefits. Ambulance missions require the player to deliver injured citizens to the hospital, and fire-fighter missions involve putting out car fires. These missions are basically non-violent, but the player must steal or otherwise acquire a taxicab, ambulance, or fire truck to participate in them.

Yet another option is just to wander the streets of Liberty City, by car or by foot. Nothing compels the player to follow the game's mission-based storyline or to take on any of the side missions. Many players choose to exact random violence on passersby, and the game's controls do encourage violence by providing many combative maneuvers at the touch of a button. Famously, players can even pick up prostitutes.[2]

Much has been written in the popular media about the game's violence. Most critiques—good or bad—are careful to point out that the game is *not* for children, and its ESRB "M" rating is supposed to keep the product out of the hands of minors.[3] Nevertheless, the game has sparked several purported copycat crimes,[4] as well as the previously cited accusations of hate crimes.[5] An activity for the playground or the basement playroom GTA is not.

As a structure of unit operations, GTA does not just provide several different styles of gameplay, it also allows free-form transitions between those play styles. One moment the player is a vicious criminal wielding a rifle against a throng of thugs or bludgeoning a bum senseless with a bat, and the next he is transporting the innocent injured to the hospital, or enjoying a calm sunset over the ocean. While player decisions do have consequences within the game, the core characteristic of GTA is not the varied types of acts the player can carry out, but the rationale for transition between these acts. These transitions take many forms: the introduction of a new crime mission from a gang; an encounter with a parked ambulance; a stroll to a new part of town. In each case, the player makes a conscious and rational decision to follow one path instead of another. Choosing a life of crime has its consequences: the player's character is always on the radar of the police, and committing crimes in their view increases the player's "wanted" status. The police can apprehend and arrest you. If things get really bad, the FBI and the army get involved.

In complex network theory terms, GTA derives its representational power from the links or edges that connect the player's possible unit operations together. Fire a gun, steal a truck, explore a hidden building, bludgeon a cop, explode a car: although important to the games appeal, the specificity of these actions is subordinate to the ease of transition between them, and the conscious player decision associated with that gap. In a short review of the game, Gonzalo Frasca suggests that most players call this ability *freedom,* and they cite it as the most important and compelling feature of the game.[6]

Freedom has a long and complex history. Nomadist thinking sometimes seems to suggest a return to the crude Greek notion of freedom, to "live as you want." Deleuze and Guattari paint a lurid picture of bodies connected to other bodies, bodies connected to machines, and the sudden and disruptive, often violent, often mad disruption from one state to another. A *Thousand Plateaus* refers to babies, madmen, and warriors as paradigms for the practice of nomadism. And the clear rejection of reason in its late enlightenment register finds support elsewhere in Deleuze's work.[7] At the same time, Deleuze and Guattari also warn against excessive zeal in managing one's flows, reminding us "how necessary caution is . . . since overdose is a danger,"[8] and that "a too-sudden destratification may be suicidal, or turn cancerous."[9] This is a terrain reigned by the will, but a will with goals.

One of the alternative structures for desire Deleuze and Guattari suggest is the Body without Organs (BwO).[10] The BwO is a reformation of the physical body that rejects its boundaries in flesh. It is a mass of potential "zones of intensity," but suspended in an indeterminate state, waiting to pass through a state transformation. Deleuze and Guattari give a name to these state transformations, which correspond with the process of deterritorialization and reterritorialization: they call them degrees of intensity, or degrees of freedom. The BwO maintains a higher degree of freedom the more impulses it might consider following. Kant believes that beings are free when they act in accordance with what they should do, and what they should do is universally attainable through reason, via the categorical imperative. Rejecting Kant, Deleuze and Guattari instead follow Spinoza, who conceives of ethics as a process of augmenting existing potentials toward a greater power (*conatus*).[11] The BwO has a tendency to expand its potential continuously, through the desiring machines that crisscross it, rather than imposing boundaries that limit its potential. In Brian Massumi's words, the BwO is "the body outside any determinate state, poised for any action in its repertory."[12] Deleuze and Guattari's project focuses on removing boundaries, in rejecting the idea that boundaries create meaning. Instead, meaning is always provisional, in a state of openness.

Freedom in GTA is thus much more like the freedom of the desiring machine than that of Kantian reason. When players of GTA exercise freedom, it is not just freedom from the real consequence of felony crime. It is also freedom to orient one's conception of right and wrong in relation to a whole host of activities in addition to, or in place of, crude prohibition. One GTA reviewer comments on the unexpected result of this "morality-bending":

before you decide to begin the transformation, consider this: once you start, you can never return. You will discover things about yourself that you may wish you never knew. Maybe you will be a beater, one who shamelessly beats the shit out of innocent passer bys [*sic*]. Or maybe you'll turn out to be a mower and careen around the sidewalks, mercilessly mowing down pedestrians. GTA 3 is an orgy for your amorality, a feast for your darker side. Go ahead, indulge you [*sic*] inner demon. You know you want to. And when you hear the sirens, you will jump guiltily, because you will know, somehow, deep down, you are guilty.[13]

Such is one possible response to the freedom the game allows; a recognition of the inner demons that regulate our behavior as much as our reason. For this player, GTA brings those forces together into an unstable harmony, not for the purpose of rejecting the baseness the game depicts, but for allowing that corruption to intermingle with its rejection.

Machinima artist Jim Munroe offers a more explicit demonstration of how the game allows movement between virtue and corruption.[14] In his short machinima film *My Trip to Liberty City,* Munroe documents his alternative GTA play style in the form of a travelogue. After meeting with mob henchman Luigi, who offers the first gang job of the game, Munroe decides not to take him up on the offer. Instead, he explores the city by foot, finding a hidden staircase to the top of a building, where he enjoys watching the sun set over the Liberty City harbor. Taking advantage of the game's built-in character skin editor, Munroe creates two new appearances for his in-game character, a Canadian Tourist and Priest. In Canadian Tourist garb, Munroe visits various spots in the city, snapping photos with the game's built-in screen-capture utility. Then, donning his priest's habit, he ventures into the more dangerous parts of town, where he prays over the dead and injured victims of the street fights that often break out in such neighborhoods.

My Trip to Liberty City could be held up as an example of how the player can reject the game's violent themes, but this is a mischaracterization. Even though Munroe chooses not to exact any violence by his own hand, his entire experience flows from his choices in relation to both peace and violence. Those who argue that one can "do anything" in Liberty City are mistaken: the game constantly structures freeform experience in relation to criminality. GTA crafts the game experience in terms of a set of relations between possible actions and their consequences; in the gap between these decisions, simulation fever reigns. This is where the player must frame his next action in relation to a web of motivations, fears, and preconceptions, both within and without the game.

In so doing, the game suggests a subtlety of relation that calls to mind Badiou's critique of Deleuze. Both nomadism and complexity rely on unit operations that traverse complex structures in an arbitrary but deliberate way. The elegance of a complex system like human genetics emerges from the interrelated functions of individual genes. The freedom of the nomad materializes from the multitude of opportunities available to consider. These are positive characterizations that focus on generativity. But even if networks offer a multitude of possible paths resulting in a very large number of potential arrangements, any singular arrangement implies a set of definitive decisions that both include and exclude a multitude of other options. Complex systems and nomads are state machines that must persist in *some* form, even if they constantly rearrange themselves. Both complex network theory and nomadism inch toward formalizing their respective structures. The BwO is perhaps the more blatantly formal of the two, a structure of absolute potential and absolute fulfillment, a conceptual space so boundless that it loses all sense of scale.

Complexity theory uses the network more as a shorthand structure than an absolute structure, and in this respect complexity theorists are more aware of the inherent indeterminacy of their subjects than are nomadists. However, complexity's macroscopic vision may threaten to become myopic, forgoing the importance of individual unit operations within a network in favor of exalting the resultant generative structure.

The social network services *Friendster* and *LinkedIn* focus on the emergent system users can create: a massive, realized social structure. However, these services also require the user to explicitly traverse the nodes in the network, a process that makes the effort of linking more deliberate than in casual, "ordinary" social networks. In *LinkedIn,* introducing one business associate to another suddenly becomes a formal unit operation: a set of software interactions that enable bigger professional networks while fixing users' individual experiences. Suddenly, casual introductions become software-mediated affairs with Web forms, emails, and spam filters intermixed. The recent surge in popularity of social network services has spawned numerous critiques that point directly to the medium's ambivalence about the substance and method of individual links. Howard Rheingold, author of the book *Smart Mobs* on mobile technology social networks, argues that fluidity is precisely the missing link in social linking.[15] "Social network literacy," as Rheingold aptly calls it, "is not about how many connections you have, but how well you use them to navigate your life."[16] Fluidity is also Deleuze and Guattari's focus in *A Thousand Plateaus;* nomad space is "smooth space," along which lowered boundaries, not lowered friction, facilitate the vectors of assemblages. Sociologist Barry Wellman agrees, adding that networks in general are bringing us more connectivity, not more ties.[17]

Proponents of networked tools often privilege the structure of networks over the liberated gestures they facilitate. In crude terms, the problem with complexity is that it misses the trees for the forest—an unusual but increasingly common cultural inversion. Nomadism exhibits some of the same problems; Deleuze and Guattari vaunt the power of rhizomatic decision making, but they offer little practical basis for reformulating individual maneuvers. The Grand Theft Auto titles offer more practice in complex relations than *Friendster,* because the games facilitate and require players to reflect on each individual action they take.

Other contemporary games also boast immense worlds and great freedom of movement. One such example is a recent addition to the successful *Legend of Zelda* franchise. The *Zelda* franchise is based on a sword-and-shield epic about a fantasy world in which a young boy, Link (the player), sets out to defeat an evil power called Ganon who seeks to take control over the mythical triforce, a three-part amulet of power, wisdom, and courage. Once in control of the triforce, Ganon intends to use its power to destroy the world. The original *Legend of Zelda* was designed by *Mario Bros.* and *Donkey Kong* creator Shigeru Miyamoto and released in 1986 in Japan, 1987 in the United States. The game boasted numerous technical innovations, including the first on-cartridge read/writable memory, which allowed players to save a game on the cart (previous games required players to enter a long alphanumeric sequence to restore a previous game state).

The Legend of Zelda is revered for its nondirective design. Although the game sports a strong storyline and a definitive set of tasks and quests the player must complete, the gameplay itself is free in much the same way as GTA—the player can meander around a very large map and choose which quests and challenges to pursue. Unlike previous Miyamoto games like *Super Mario Bros.,* the player is not required to complete the game in any particular sequence. The game contains nine dungeons the player must complete, but his chances of success in these areas is mediated by his skill and items he has amassed, allowing a much more fluid, semi-arbitrary game experience. *The Legend of Zelda* became the first game to sell one million units.[18]

In 2003, Nintendo released *The Legend of Zelda: The Wind Waker,* for their fourth-generation Gamecube console, the contemporary of the Sony and Microsoft boxes that run *Grand Theft Auto.* Like its predecessors, *Wind Waker* sports numerous innovations including a new cel-shaded rendering style, but the most noticeable addition is the game's massive physical setting. *Wind Waker* takes place in an enormous expanse of ocean, and the player has to use a small sailboat to move from island to island. The game relies on the same basic story as the original, cast in a different era of the legend.

Like GTA, *Wind Waker* constructs an enormous world that requires considerable real-world time to traverse. Likewise, both games boast considerable freedom of movement. GTA takes place in an urban environment, and the player can walk, run, or drive around it. The possible configurations of movement in *Wind Waker* are arguably much broader than those in GTA; since the former takes place on an ocean, the player can sail in any direction at any time. But the significance of these possible configurations is less rich in *Wind Waker* than in GTA. In GTA, the player can choose from a multitude of functions at any given time, each chosen in reference to specific transitional cues the environment provides. When sailing on the vast ocean of *Wind Waker,* the player has few choices, save which direction to sail, and whether to fight or avoid sea monsters when they crop up. *Wind Waker*'s sea is enormous, and the game offers a wider variety of objects and tools than GTA, including a grappling hook and camera. But the game offers fewer inspirations for the player to reorient his current activities and make meaningful use of those tools. The size of the world and the quantity of possible actions matters less than the significance of those actions. *Wind Waker* is still a terrific adventure game, but it fails to create the complex relations of experience found in GTA, even though the latter boasts no technical achievements whatsoever.[19]

Configurative Literary Spaces

GTA's structured configuration of possible actions within a larger space suggests a broader expressive tactic: space is used not for the repleteness of exploration, but in order to structure smaller, singularly meaningful experiences. One of the characteristic features of the modern is a lack of direction in, or a confused relationship with, time and space. We have already witnessed Baudelaire's response to the configurative properties of the modern city, and his poetry serves as an expression of the difficulty to find meaning in this new spatial reality. In its most extreme form, this process of disassociation and recombination reaches the level of the abstract, as in cubist painting. Poetry too is inherently fragmentary. But the novel had traditionally provided coherent depictions of complete narrative sequences. In the modern novel, coherent sequences of events and the confusion of time and space collide, often through formal changes in the novel itself. In such works, space and time are often decomposed into constituent elements that the novelist recombines into new wholes.

In a particularly crucial moment in Flaubert's novel *Madame Bovary* known as the agricultural fair scene, the adulterous Emma's lover Rodolphe declares his love for her while a provincial country fair takes place around them. In this scene, Flaubert weaves together two distinct incidents, the speeches and awards given on the platform at the fair and the increasingly passionate *tête-à-tête* between Rodolphe and Emma. Flaubert takes on a difficult task in this scene, namely, how to render in prose two contemporaneous spaces which overlap and move between one another. Flaubert devises the following tactic: interrupt the flow of one space with the other, at the key moments of rupture that would most effectively shed light on both. This passage between the two spaces configures Emma's romantic fancy in relation to the crude reality of provincial life.

The scene begins with the long speech of Lieuvain, an overly self-important bureaucrat, during which Rodolphe offers commentary to Emma in response to Lieuvain's claims, all the while affecting his coy seduction. After the speeches conclude, the president begins to announce the fair's prizewinners, and these short exclamations merge with Rodolphe's mounting temptation of Emma and with her fraught replies. Finally, as Emma begins to give in (and as Rodolphe realizes the certainty of his conquest), the two dialogues merge into one indistinguishable speech, at once standing in for two separate events. The entire episode is imbued with Flaubert's familiar causticity, such that the two lovers' absurd romantic banter infects the business of the inane, provincial fair and vice versa.

The reader's attention is split between the speaker on the platform and Rodolphe's or Emma's current effusion. As the scene begins, Lieuvain extols the virtues of the current politic and its effects on the rural populous. Rodolphe's interspersed worries about being spotted with Emma serve to begin his seduction:

"Qu'il me soit permis d'abord . . . sachant d'ailleurs faire respecter la paix comme la guerre, l'industrie, le commerce, l'agriculture et les beaux-arts."
—Je devrais, dit Rodolphe, me reculer un peu.
—Pourquoi? dit Emma.

"May I be permitted first of all . . . knowing, moreover, how to make peace respected as well as war, industry, commerce, agriculture, and the fine arts."
—I ought, said Rodolphe, to get back a little further.
—Why? said Emma.[20]

Flaubert crafts both expressive and material separation between the two threads of discourse. He places white space before and after, creating a spatial separation of the two sets of voices. As an additional typographical clue, the speeches and awards given on the platform are placed between quotation marks, while the dialogues of Rodolphe and Emma are prefaced by em-dashes. A narrator occasionally interrupts the dialogues of the latter, including immediately after the lines just cited ("Mais, à ce moment, la voix du Conseiller d'éleva d'un ton extraordinaire" / "But at this moment, the voice of the councilor rose to an extraordinary pitch").[21] At other times, Rodolphe or Emma simply stop speaking, allowing the speech to come to the foreground once again, for example:

Il se passa la main sur le visage, tel qu'un homme pris d'étourdissement; puis il la laissa retomber sur celle d'Emma. Elle retira la sienne. Mais le Conseiller lisait toujours.

He [Rodolphe] passed his hand over his face, like a man about to faint. Then he let it fall on Emma's. She drew hers back. But the councilor was still reading.[22]

The two take up again not where the speech left off, but where Rodolphe and Emma begin to listen to it again; the absence of the missed portions of the speech indicates the simultaneity of the two events, which cannot both be observed at once.

—Oh! vous vous colomniez, dit Emma.
—Non, non, elle est exécrable, je vous jure.
"Mais, messieurs, poursuivit le Conseiller . . ."

—Oh, you are slandering yourself, said Emma.

—No! It is dreadful, I assure you.

"But, gentlemen," continued the councilor . . . [23]

This spatial framing creates decisive movements between the public speech of Lieuvain and the private speech of Rodolphe. The frame enables the latter's intention by situating it in a banal environment that encourages Emma's susceptibility to seduction, much as Liberty City encourages the player's susceptibility to sociopathic behavior.

In addition to the scene's framing, the subjects of the speeches and of Rodolphe and Emma's dialogues spill over into one another, Rodolphe converting points made in the speech into advances upon Emma. At a particularly dry point in the impressively verbose speech, Lieuvain extols the necessity of duty to the public welfare. Rodolphe capitalizes on this defamation by turning it around in order that he might sway Emma away from her duty as faithful wife:

". . . à l'amélioration commune et au soutien des États, fruit du respect des lois et de la pratique des devoirs . . ."

—Ah! encore, dit Rodolphe. Toujours les devoirs, je suis assommé de ces mots-là. Ils sont un tas de vieilles ganaches en gilet de flanelle, et de bigotes à chaufferette et à chapelet, qui continuellement nous chantent aux oreilles: "Le devoir! le devoir!"

". . . to the common amelioration and to the support of the state, born of respect for law and the practice of duty . . ."

—Ah! again! said Rodolphe. Always "duty." I am sick of the word. They are a lot of old jackasses in woolen vests and old bigots with foot-warmers and rosaries who constantly drone into our ears, "Duty! duty!"[24]

Later, as the awards are handed out, the latent passion between Rodolphe and Emma is about to climax. Flaubert structures the text such that the fair's platform directly intersects the private space around Emma and Rodolphe. A word or action of one of the latter interrupts every other phrase uttered on the platform:

Et il saisit sa main; elle ne la retira pas.

"Ensemble de connes cultures!" cria le président.

—Tantôt, par exemple, quand je suis venu chez vous . . .

"A M. Bizet, de Quincampoix."

—Savais-je que je vous accompagnerais?

"Soixante et dix francs!"

And he seized her hand; she did not withdraw it.

"First prize for general farming!" announced the president.

—Just now, for example, when I went to your home . . .

"To Mr. Bizat of Quincampoix."

—Did I know I would accompany you?

"Seventy francs!"[25]

Flaubert's technique is especially effective here, with awards for manures and livestock intertwining with the equally parodic impassioned gestures of Rodolphe and Emma. As Flaubert's characteristic "coup de vent" impresses itself around Emma, signifying her sexual perkiness, the pace becomes so quick that there is no distinction between the speech and actions on the platform and those between Rodolphe and Emma. Absurdly and impressively, it is during the tedious break in action on the platform during which time the president waits for Catherine Leroux to claim her award for fifty-four years of service that Rodolphe and Emma's flirtation climaxes. Flaubert creates a pure simultaneity by overlapping the speech of the president and others with the final triumph of Rodolphe:

—Vas-y!

—Non.

—A gauche!

—N'aie pas peur!

—Ah! qu'elle est bête!

—Enfin y est-elle? s'écria Tuvache.

—Oui! . . . la voilà!

—Qu'elle approche donc!

—Go ahead!

—No.

—To the left!

—Don't be afraid!

—Oh, how stupid she is!

—Well, is she there? cried Tuvache.

—Yes; here she is.

—Then what's she waiting for?[26]

In his characteristic style, Flaubert's text then gives way to a description of Catherine Leroux, leaving the reader to imagine the lascivious interlude between Rodolphe and Emma.

The agricultural fair scene employs two major techniques to indicate simultaneity: the interruption of one dialogue by another followed by its restitution with middle elements eliminated, and the incorporation of background elements into the progression of the simultaneous foreground action (e.g., Rodolphe's appropriation of the discourse on duty). In the "Wandering Rocks" chapter of James Joyce's *Ulysses,* Joyce extends this technique and complicates it, tracing not two stationary events but dozens of simultaneous, shifting actions.

The chapter is split up into nineteen sections, each concerning either a person or set of people and their current trajectories in Dublin between the hours of 3 and 4 P.M. The first and last sections serve to frame those in the middle: the first details the path of Father Conmee on the way to his walk, during which time he runs into most of the novel's characters in one way or another; the last section describes the procession of the Earl of Dudley's cavalcade as it proceeds from the viceregal lodge to the inauguration of the Mirus Bazaar, also passing most of the novel's characters. Throughout, Joyce employs the Flaubertian technique of interruption (sometimes contemporaneously, other times through flashback or forecast) and of omitting unseen portions of events.

The structure and all of the resonances within the chapter are complex; in addition to the two major links, Father Conmee and the Earl's cavalcade, there are several minor links that travel through Dublin and further bind the scene. These minor links include a one-legged beggar, the Elijah throwaway Bloom disposed of earlier in the day, the Hely's sandwich board men, and a poster of Marie Kendall. Two of these, the Elijah throwaway and the Marie Kendall poster, even come with their own Homeric epithets for easy reference: "A skiff, a crumpled throwaway" and "charming *soubrette,*" respectively. Since there are many events and many connections between them at work in the chapter, I will only explore how several spaces inform and facilitate the actions in one another.

Whereas Flaubert weaves together but one simultaneous moment, Joyce creates a progression of simultaneous events within the space of an hour, some preceding others, some overlapping. The chapter begins with Father Conmee's walk, during which he thinks of Paddy Dignam and his son. He passes Mrs. McGuiness, the pawnbroker, whom Katey and Boody Dedalus have just seen in order to try to sell some of Stephen's books. He passes H. J. O'Neills funeral establishment and sees Corny Kelleher (who appears as the subject of section 2) working. He also passes the pork butchers, where the younger Dignam will later purchase some pork steaks before the cavalcade passes him. Section 2 picks up just after Father Conmee sees Corny Kelleher in O'Neills. Corny closes the daybook Conmee saw him working in, and turns his attention to a coffin in the corner and speaks to a constable who Father Conmee passed just after seeing Corny Kelleher.

In section 1, Father Conmee "passed H. J. O'Neill's funeral establishment where Corny Kelleher totted figures in the daybook while he chewed a blade of hay. A constable on the beat saluted Father Conmee and Father Conmee saluted back."[27] In section 2, after Corny Kelleher turns to the coffin, he sees the same constable: "Constable 57C, on his beat, stood to pass the time of day."[28] The constable, who was traveling in the opposite direction as Father Conmee, arrives at O'Neill's just after passing Conmee, who in turn had just passed O'Neill's going the other way. At the same time, Corny Kelleher sees Father Conmee board the Dollymount tram on Newcomen bridge, which Father Conmee reports doing just after passing the pork butcher in section 1. Thus, a small amount of time has passed, and several simultaneous events have been coalesced into a successive series of singular actions, each point of view configuring what it does not encounter.

In section 3, the singing one-legged sailor (whom Conmee ran into at the outset of section 1) comes around a corner onto a yet unnamed street, passing Katey and Boody Dedalus who are on their way home (4) from the pawnbroker, Mrs. McGuiness. On the way they see the following:

The blind of a window was drawn aside. A card *Unfurnished Apartments* slipped from the sash and fell. A plump bare generous arm shone, was seen, held forth from a white petticoatbodice and taut shiftstraps. A woman's hand flung forth a coin over the area railings. It fell on the path.

One of the urchins ran to it, picked it up, and dropped it into the minstrel's cap, saying:
—There, sir.[29]

It is not immediately clear when and where this event falls with relation to the time and place of other events in the chapter, and therefore what other actions configure and enable it. Joyce leaves a trail somewhat more difficult to follow but much more rewarding than the simple back and forth in Flaubert's agricultural fair scene.

In section 9, we read that "A card *Unfurnished Apartment*s reappeared on the windowsash of number 7 Eccles street."[30] Now we know that Katey and Boody and the beggar have passed Bloom's house, and that Molly Bloom gave the coin to the beggar, and the location is established. The temporal relation is a bit more difficult. In section 3, just as the beggar swings past Katey and Boody, an interrupting phrase reports that "J. J. O'Molloy's white careworn face was told that Mr. Lambert was in the warehouse with a visitor."[31] In section 8, O'Molloy finds Lambert in the ancient council chamber of St. Mary's Abbey with a clergyman. ("Hello Jack, is that yourself? Ned Lambert said.")[32] After a brief dialogue, they leave, and the two see a "young woman with slow care detach from her light skirt a clinging twig."[33]

Meanwhile, in section 4, Katey and Boody return home to find their sister Maggy cleaning her stained shirt. As they arrive, another fragment interrupts the event: "Father Conmee walked through Clongowes fields, his thin-socked ankles ticked by stubble."[34] This is a flashback to the end of section 1, after the Father gets off the tram and begins his walk. Just after he passes through Clongowes field, he reports the following:

A flushed young man came from a gap of a hedge and after him came a young woman with wild nodding daisies in her hand. The young man raised his cap abruptly: the young woman abruptly bent and with slow care detached from her light skirt a clinging twig.[35]

We know that J. J. O'Molloy was looking for Ned Lambert just as Katey and Boody passed number 7 Eccles street. We also know that shortly after that, both Katey and Boody arrive at home and O'Molloy finds Lambert with the clergyman. Just as Katey and Boody get home, Father Conmee walks through Clongowes field, after which he sees the girl detach the twig from her skirt. At about the same, O'Molloy and Lambert see the same girl detach the same twig. So, we can conclude that the episode outside number 7 Eccles street occurred a short while after the O'Neill's episode (which transpired shortly after the outset of the chapter, three o'clock), just enough time afterward that Conmee's tram and feet delivered him to the Clongowes school, just enough time that Katey and Boody returned home from Eccles street, and just enough time that J. J. O'Molloy found Ned Lambert in the council chamber.

Admittedly, this moment is not precise. But it is but one way to discern when the event occurred; there are many more events in the chapter to use as reference points, each interrupting others either through the sort of contamination Flaubert used in making Rodolphe discuss duty at the fair or through explicit proleptic and analeptic descriptions of portions of the text spatially arranged before or after the present section. The longest paths, those of the chapter's two major links, Father Conmee and the Earl's cavalcade, provide themselves as referring maps for the rest of the chapter's events since one or both encounter every event described within the chapter. In section 9, shortly before we see Molly replace the dropped sign *Unfurnished Apartments,* "the gates of the drive opened wide to give egress to the viceregal cavalcade."[36]

"Wandering Rocks" stands as the central chapter of *Ulysses,* itself a small-scale rendition of the entire book. With this in mind, we are offered a strange and appropriately Flaubertian satire of *Ulysses* itself, through Joyce's complex application of the concepts of interruption and restitution of an event with omitted middle and of contamination of events through overlap. In *The Odyssey,* Circe tells Ulysses to avoid the wandering rocks, since they will send him off course (Ulysses heeds her warning). "Wandering Rocks" does not focus on the novel's main characters, Bloom and Stephen, but offers a picture of the urban scenario that grounds their setting. These clergymen, voyeurs, and drunkards structure the Dublin that Bloom and Stephen must navigate elsewhere; they are the structures that configure the two heroes' converging relationship. Each individual action in "Wandering Rocks" structures either a response to a plot movement (Mulligan and Haines's conversation about Stephen) or a character's inner motivations (Stephen's reflection on Dilly's home situation). The spatial configuration of individual relationships is haphazard, but these connections are not insignificant; they influence the mental states of the characters.

Whereas "Wandering Rocks" provides intricate details about interpersonal relationships, GTA fails to maintain credible human responses to shifting player actions. Nonplayer characters (NPCs) in the game are little more than cardboard cutouts, and a relatively small number of character types all respond in nearly identical ways when the player encounters them. Encountering an NPC, for that matter, can lead only to one of two possible actions: beat him up, or bump past him as you run down the street. The game supports the former case, of course, but the latter results in one of a handful of stock phrases. Characters in GTA are thus the most noticeable empty spaces in an otherwise replete urban landscape. Frasca cites the lack of talking NPCs as a design accomplishment that avoids breaking the immersion of the experience; indeed, given the lack of meaningful person-to-person interaction, the game's lack of reliance on credible speech is wise. Perhaps more important, Frasca notes, is that the game's failure to render human characters in any meaningful detail "dehumanizes and objectifies NPC characters."[37] The lack of humanity that the NPCs exhibit could be seen as a testament to the overwhelming technical complexity of believable characters (as discussed in chapter 5 above), or as an implicit declaration of the game's endorsement of sociopathic behavior. Alternately, one could understand the shallow NPCs as the game's primary strategy for alienating the player from productive social interactions, a unit operation for sociopathy.

Both GTA and *Wind Waker* offer fictional worlds that are designed for exploration. But GTA exposes a multitude of relevant player functions at any given time. Moreso than *Wind Waker,* the gameplay experience in GTA comes from the relations of individual decisions rather than a sequence of tasks, even if those tasks are subject to resequencing. In GTA, every decision both includes and excludes another possibility, and thus choosing to drive an ambulance instead of bludgeoning a passerby for some cash to buy a new handgun develops fluid meanings that signify in relation to other possible unit operations. The simulation fever GTA instills arises out of the dissonance between these activities not only within the game itself, but also between the game world and the real world. GTA draws attention to our tenuous relationship with crime and punishment. Kant recognized that human urges are strong and that laws are necessary to recommend the use of reason in matters of public life;[38] our daily encounters typically constantly waver between sociability and antisocialism, mediated as much by the structures of punishment and incarceration as by our own urges toward and away from violent outrage. GTA could be considered the ultimate punctuation of the Foucauldian genealogy of power, an active practice of the relationship between power and discipline.[39] The reviewer who insists that once you play GTA "you can't go back" suggests that the game successfully draws attention to the player's relationship to potential delinquency.

Relational networks of unit-operational meaning might also demand that we rethink the technological goals for rich interactive experiences. For years, scientists and artists have engineered elaborate virtual reality equipment and enclosures, intended to provide richer, more immersive experiences by connecting the user to the work by physical bonds other than sight and sound. Unlike virtual reality installations, which propose to create a liberating immersion by physically enclosing the human subject in a computer system, GTA offers a convincing and meaningful world in a technically bereft environment. GTA suggests how videogames may resist the common opinion that dematerialization of the literal body is a necessary step toward greater interactivity (another theme of *A Thousand Plateaus*). We should be less inclined to condemn works like GTA for their brutality than to try to evolve the core problem they present: how to understand and refine each unit operation of our possible actions so we can interrogate and improve the system of human experience.

Critical Networks

Supporting the study of technology alongside literature and art carries an enormous political tenor. As the original benefactors of technology in the humanities, some English departments feel that they should retain ownership of the field. Having already negotiated the vertex between art theory and practice, design and art departments may cite special privilege to take on electronic texts and videogames. Film departments might feel special entitlement to videogames given their historical experience with an industrial art. And as humanities programs of all kinds continue to struggle against funding cuts, interdisciplinary programs have special appeal as tools for rejuvenating aging fields of study.

Sometimes such conflicts lead quickly to stalemate, with bemused deans denying or diverting funding. Perhaps the most public example of this kind of resistance came from the University of California, Irvine's first effort to create a minor in computer games. *Wired News* published a segment of UCI School of Social Sciences Dean William Schonfeld's response to the faculty proposal:

An academic program of study officially listed as focusing on gaming studies runs, I think, the strong risk of attracting people on the basis of prurient interest. I do not think we should send forth messages of this type if we wish to be a research university of the highest level of distinction.[1]

One can assume that Schonfeld's equation of games and lubricity is more provocation than reasoned argument, but his implication is clear: even if videogames are a viable object of study, any admission of such study in public would offend the institution's traditionalist fancies.

Other institutions have set up programs specifically focused on the study of games, separate from other fields of inquiry. Whether related or not to the American academic puritanism underscored in Shonfeld's response, it happens that many such programs can be found in northern Europe. The IT University of Copenhagen, Denmark, and the University of Tampere, Finland, among others, offer bachelor's, master's, and doctorate degrees exclusively in digital games. Many theorists in this region have been associated with the strong position that the study of games necessarily requires an autonomous terrain completely separate from other fields, among them Espen Aarseth and Frans Mäyrä, whose positions on the matter I discussed in chapter 4.

No matter what objections humanists and social scientists, myself included, might raise to such separatism, there is some evidence that autonomy has been productive. Espen Aarseth founded the medium's first peer-review journal, *Game Studies,* thanks in part to the Norwegian university system, whose structure affords more institutional freedom and faster progression up faculty ranks.[2] Despite the fact that Aarseth has never used the term "ludology" to describe himself or his work, he and other researchers publishing in the early issues of *Game Studies* suggest schism as a first principle of game studies. Says Aarseth in the journal's inaugural issue: "Games are not a kind of cinema, or literature, but colonising attempts from both these fields have already happened, and no doubt will happen again. And again, until computer game studies emerges as a clearly self-sustained academic field."[3]

Aarseth and others' desire to establish a separate, specialized field of research is not unusual. Human complex systems theorist Susanne Lohmann argues that the university's primary purpose is to enable "deep specialization," and specialization has often come by way of fragmentation.[4] Lohmann likens this process to annealing, the slow process of heating and cooling by which metals or glass are made more or less rigid. Through each individual conflict, segments of the university structure were slowly created. Although not emergent in the same way as Stephen Wolfram's fundamental units of science, these plans were not centrally controlled but emerged slowly out of the combinations of individual conflicts.

Although I agree that videogames hold a vital place in the future of both technology and literature, a return to the anxiety of disciplinarity common throughout the 1980s and 1990s hardly seems a viable solution. Instead, I contend that the future of unit analysis relies on a critical strategy that embodies the logic of unit operations itself. Universities are often testaments to system operations: academic departments deal only in specified structures of knowledge, and those departments are highly segregated, resistant to change, and afford few exceptions for innovation. Instead of segregating disciplines into the independent, static divisions that would characterize any new academic department or critical discipline, a meaningful intellectual interrogation of fields like videogames, software technology, and information systems demands flexible organizational units that act more like adaptive networks than stodgy corporations.

In the past twenty years especially, universities have embraced the idea of interdisciplinarity as a way for multiple departments to take advantage of each other's expertise and human and material resources to facilitate convergences between like-minded interests. Comparative literature, which I discussed in chapter 4, almost always leases some or all of their faculty's time from other departments—national languages, film, and so forth. Emerging programs like biotechnology and human complex systems often muster support from a variety of established fields as these new fields evolve. Interdisciplinarity is fraught with difficulties, the most basic of them the complexity of funding and managing groups of people split between often conflicting leadership and goals. Nevertheless, the idea of interdisciplinarity is a positive step toward a unit-operational academy.

Unfortunately, the interdisciplinary relationships only go so far. Interdisciplinarity is, by definition, an exception; it requires stable, formal disciplines between which to construct working relationships. The retention of individual disciplines in the academy still means that the brave people who have tried to forge new connections between fields are inevitably robbing Peter to pay Paul. Attempts at interdisciplinary studies often lead to a deadlock of shared resources for practitioners who don't have enough time for either of their two or three departmental commitments. Even worse, the intellectuals doing the best work are often caught in the undertow of interdepartmental politics, long walks across campus, split social obligations, conflicting curricula, and complex promotion and tenure review politics. These problems unfortunately precede more important questions of pedagogy.

As the seed of a solution to these and other conundrums, I offer the idea of unit-operational academic practice. In the humanities, interdisciplinarity was an easy way to bring neighboring intellectuals into the same neighborhood community: French and Asian studies; English and art history. Extending the circle of interest across widely disparate fields—computer science, psychology, business, music, and so forth—will demand a much more radical shift. A unit-operational university would look like a complex network: a series of constantly changing relations between highly disparate groups, ideas, and resources.

Instead of belonging to static, isolated departments, faculty and students would constantly make and break ties with one another, some indefinite, some lasting only the length of a meeting. Intellectual projects would structure themselves more like software: units of encapsulated production with structured ties to multiple potential applications.

In software technology, traditional object-oriented systems have always been limited by technology platforms. Putting aside the market dynamics and antitrust lawsuits, the struggle between the dominant power of Microsoft and the emerging popularity of Linux has been undermined by the simple problem of compatibility. Windows programs just don't run on other systems, no matter how intricate and complex the networks are between such physically distinct machines. These limitations collapse the complex network of the Internet into a much more localized network driven by individual decision and accident: IT support, purchasing, user preference, and so forth. This is a familiar problem in information technology: getting the computers to "talk to each other" often involves more human engineering than any other aspect of the system architecture.

Recently, a technology standard called Web services has emerged that claims to offer a solution to the problem of interoperability. The idea is simple: the one standard to which every system already adheres is the Internet protocol used to deliver content from computers to human readers on the World Wide Web (hypertext transfer protocol or HTTP). Web services are really just a standard data format for transmitting specialized messages between computers via HTTP. The standardization of the data format and the transfer protocol represents a radical break from the traditional foundational concepts of jargon and intellectual property discussed earlier. Standards have long been the Achilles' heel of information technologies; when a third-party regulating body successfully creates a standard, it often fails to solve the specific problems of individual organizations. More commonly, software architects modify or diverge from standards to offer value-additive services that will distinguish their own version of the standard (an amusing contradiction in terms) from their competitors. Commercial advantage is really just another way to enforce a specific unit of intellectual property as a stand-in for the complex relationship of standards-based engineering. While Web services have not been immune to this sort of modification, the underlying premise of the standard allows it to resist the corruption of jargon and IP in the same way that a complex network keeps the Internet working in the face of local system failure.

Web services transmit data in two common formats, XML and SOAP. XML, or extensible markup language, is a simple, tag-based text format used to render hierarchical, structured data. HTML is structurally similar to XML, but much looser in its formatting requirements. SOAP, or simple object access protocol, is a particular kind of XML-formatted message structured specifically for executing object technology–style requests from applications on remote computer systems.[5] The primary benefit of Web services is that two computers with nothing in common architecturally can mutually invoke software routines and share the results. For example, today it is possible for an independent software engineer who chooses open-source systems like Linux to develop applications that make a Web services request for search results from Google.com,[6] or bestseller reports from Amazon.com.[7] For now, many of these applications appear to be mere novelties, but industry analysts predict that the Web services market will grow to $21 billion per year by 2007.[8] In the near future, companies will share or sell units of fundamental business operations, potentially making the global marketplace one of knowledge creation in addition to mere capital exchange.

The unit-operational properties of software objects I discussed earlier do not change; however, the unit operations of networked data communications extend the reach of these units, creating a network of networks. If the Internet has created a complex network of information through shared viewers, Web services strive to create a complex network of procedural systems through shared applications.

Web services offer an interesting object lesson for the problem of institutionalized education. The market forces of anytime-anywhere computing (sometimes called ubiquitous computing) have driven the growth of Web services. A significant force behind Web services adoption is the reduction of integration cost among disparate systems. However, a much larger force (and arguably the force driving the need for systems integration) is the public market's tenacity for application services in the first place. And in this context, "services" stand above any particular service; individual software developers want to take advantage of the existing systems that other individuals and corporations have already created. The transition from isolated object technology to Web services is a transition from unit operations in semi-static isolation to unit operations across a complex network.

Michel Serres conceives of an "ultimate parasite" who "produces disorder and who generates a different order."[9] In a reconfiguration of cyberneticist Claude

Shannon's conception of information as a relationship between organization and disorganization (signal/noise), Serres suggests a fundamentally creative force is at work in disorder. Reading Serres, Mark C. Taylor argues that knowledge emerges through a process of screening in which selected information is destroyed.[10] This practice is similar to Hayles's notion of a cybernetic dialectic, and another example of the production of meaning through a process of inclusion and exclusion.

No matter one's moral opinion about the value of ubiquitous computing and its impact on contemporary social practice, the process and infrastructure for the exchange of procedural unit operations now makes possible alternative models for production. Conceptually, extending this logic to the practice of research would yield a network of units of criticism, a kind of postdisciplinary critical network. *Critical* in every inflection of the word: for one part, it embraces criticism like the various forms of literary and philosophical inquiry. For another part, it underscores a kind of general analysis that relates to other fields. For another, it admits to a certain danger of collapse and the need to keep that possibility in mind. And for yet another part, it telegraphs an exigency of action.

Taylor has experience practicing this balance. In the early 1990s, he organized a joint seminar on media and philosophy with his students at Williams College in Massachusetts and those of Finnish philosopher Esa Saarinen at the University of Helsinki. The classes met together via videoconference. In *Imagologies,* an immaculately designed book on the preparation of the course and its subject matter, the authors include some of the email and telephone exchanges they produced in organizing the seminar in 1992.[11] At the time, merely setting up point-to-point videoconferencing was a significant task and investment, and the accounts of the process highlight the challenges of finding sponsorship, raising money, and accomplishing the technical achievement of connecting the two groups across the Atlantic. *Imagologies* is more about an infrastructure problem than a cultural or academic problem. While it posits many claims, in essence the thesis of the book is that a convergence of information technology and humanistic intellectualism is simply *thinkable.*

In 1998, Taylor and investment banker Herbert A. Allen began a new kind university based on an intersection of education and technology. The two founded the Global Education Network (GEN) in 1999, an electronic-education organization that delivers online coursework from top-tier universities. Underlying the founding principles of GEN is Taylor's claim that the values of the modern university, inherited directly from the Enlightenment, are outmoded and obsolete. Taylor's collaboration with the corporate world is important, and I will return to it in a moment.

Taylor traces the origins of the modern university to Kant's 1798 work *Conflict of the Faculties,* which served as the blueprint for the University of Berlin. Kant's model accounts for separate departments each with different responsibilities, fashions stable programs or curricula, and distinguishes between the "higher" and the "lower" faculties. The higher faculties, such as medicine, law, and theology, serve external ends. The lower faculties, such as philosophy and literature, include "historical" and "pure rational knowledge." Taylor marks this distinction as the fundamental principle in Kant's account of institutional knowledge and as the basis for our contemporary division between professional schools and liberal arts schools.[12]

The two fundamental assumptions of the modern university's low faculties are those adopted by Humboldt, *Wissenschaft* and *Bildung.* These concepts refer to the disinterested and intrinsic pursuit of knowledge, or "knowledge for its own sake." Taylor argues that this assumption drives contemporary satisfaction with a concept of the university that is now over two centuries old. The pursuit of knowledge is often likened to an economy of expenditure without return made famous by Bataille, Derrida, and Levinas. Bill Readings summarizes this ideology in his influential book on the emergence of the market university: "Thought is non-productive labor, and hence does not show up as such on balance sheets except as waste."[13]

The ostensible goal of such positioning is to protect the so-called low faculties from the high faculties' attempts to colonize, hold responsible, or otherwise capitalize on them. In times of need, it is often true that the humanities suffer more under the budget knife, but the isolation of the humanities from more professional programs and from industry at all costs has also contributed to a perception of unreality. Nevertheless, isolating the lower faculties for fear that the higher faculties will infect or destroy them only furthers the continued decline of the former. As Taylor points out, such a position is fundamentally inconsistent with many of the basic tenets of critical theory, including Derrida's many analyses of the undecidable ambiguity between risk and opportunity, poison and cure. A conceptual reorganization is in order.

Critical networks require an embodied study, a fusion of theory and practice. Badiou's name for this is a *thinking:*

I call thinking the non-dialectical or inseparable unity of a theory and a practice. To understand such a unity the simplest case is that of science; in physics there are theories, concepts and mathematical formulas and there are also technical apparatuses and experiments. But *physics* as a thinking does not separate the two. A text by Galileo or Einstein circulates between concepts, mathematics and experiments, and this circulation is the movement of a unique thinking.[14]

Badiou's other examples of domains that represent a thinking include politics and psychoanalysis; unlike science, the latter domains can't rely on the repetition of mathematical proof and laboratory experiment. These domains address singularities rather than repetitions; in Badiou's words, they "attempt to find a possibility which is *not* homogeneous with the state of things."[15] Thinking produces what Badiou calls *events,* disruptive restructurings of a situation. But Badiou takes thinking beyond the event, offering a special kind of fidelity that a thinking requires. Badiou encourages individuals faithful to an event to "then *show* other people the relation between the statements and or writings and the singular process. One must *rally* these others around a thinking, by referring to what does not repeat itself."[16] Successful comparative videogame criticism strikes me as another kind of thinking, one that musters the cultural critic as much as the programmer, the artist as much as the marketer.

This approach differs fundamentally from other postdisciplinary gestures that strive to fashion theory as a cement to fill the fissures between disciplines. Taylor argues that deconstruction has attempted to take this role in the modern institution, serving as a mercurial fixative that hopes to replace and converge the lower faculties of Kant, while holding that adhesion in characteristic deconstructive suspense.[17] This transformation purports to effect material institutional change, but as Taylor points out, that change is always limited *"within the precincts of the university. . . . Politics, in other words, is always academic politics."*[18]

In order to engage videogames as a horizontal field for literary or artistic production, the humanities must begin to interact with a wealth of intellectual and professional engagement, including engineering, architecture, computer science, biology and biotechnology, design, and the private sector. Industrial and fine arts like film, architecture, and painting have done this for years, as have engineering and the computer sciences, faculties which could be said to oscillate between both the higher and the lower registers. With the production of cultural meaning taking so many forms in so many industries, a feedback loop between the research practice and market practice can only accelerate the rate at which each understands and mediates the other. In objection to industrializing the humanities, some would claim is that the pursuit of intellectual capital must be free from the reigns of material capital. Taylor argues that the most important barrier to break is "the wall separating for-profit and nonprofit organizations and the wall separating different educational institutions."[19] It is indeed useful to hold the academy responsible for understanding and mediating between critical interrogation of material production and the material production of industry itself. In so doing, we should strive to return clear-thinking individuals back into the market. This goal can be accomplished partly through critical networks whose sole charge is to continuously reinvent themselves.

Some change is happening already at the microscopic level. Among the attempts to identify the trouble with the system university itself is *Virtual U,* "the world's first higher education simulation and learning tool,"[20] mentioned earlier in chapter 8. Funded by the Alfred P. Sloan Foundation, *Virtual U* is a videogame that teaches its users how to manage an American college or university. The player takes the role of the university president and manages resources in much the same way as the mayor of a *Sim City.* In *Virtual U,* software technology structures the player's experience, both educating him or her on aspects of university management and reinforcing the assumptions underlying such a structure. The game is an inspiring amalgam of software engineering, game design, management, and public policy, and in that sense it is a promising specimen of a critical network in practice. But ironically, by seeking to train Ed.D.'s in the practical art of perpetuating the University of Berlin and its progeny, *Virtual U* threatens to perpetuate the assumptions that prevent critical networks from coming into being in the first place. The simulation fever that reigns in *Virtual U* is its ability to represent and facilitate administrative change in academic institutions of all shapes and sizes. To take on areas like videogames, institutions need a facilitating infrastructure that will allow the structure of intellectual inquiry to change and expand.

A structural change in our thinking must take place for videogames to thrive, both commercially and culturally. The commercial videogame market has doubled in revenue since 1995.[21] The landscape is cutthroat for developers, who rely on publishers for funding, distribution, and marketing. The videogame publishing market has consolidated, and many publishers are publicly traded companies who are risk averse by nature. With game development budgets reaching tens of millions of dollars, developers must rely on publishers for financing, and to get that financing they have to present a game that the publisher believes can make money. Although privately funded projects akin to independent films are conceivable, continued industry and public support in the form of commercialization remains the industry's prime mover. Publishers typically take on games for which success is assured. This either means the game is by a well-known designer, of which there are only a few, or it follows the same model, genre, or tradition as previously successful games. This is neither a new story nor a surprising one.

Videogame criticism has a role to play in this cutthroat corporate ecosystem. The market does take the public's changing needs into account, but only visionaries who are able to understand the types of cultural texts that will prove successful will succeed themselves. It is here that a configurative relationship between criticism, production, marketing, and other fields can evolve industrial, humanistic, and artistic responses to videogames. For both the academy and the industry, this relationship requires a structural change that not only expands the boundaries of criticism and development but also fosters meaningful collaboration across these boundaries, collaboration that functions by creating new unit operations for literature, computer science, art, marketing, and other domains. Videogames ask the critic to ponder the unit operations of procedural systems. It is only appropriate that we also begin thinking of such criticism as a thinking, in Badiou's sense of the word: a set of relations between parts, not just in the text, but in the world as well.

Notes

Introduction

1. Kay originally conceived of SmallTalk as a language easy enough for kids to learn and use; he has often derided the realization of his approach in the industry, which he finds profane.

2. Jonathan Culler, *Literary Theory: A Very Short Introduction* (New York: Oxford University Press, 1997), 3.

3. Gonzalo Frasca, "Ludology Meets Narratology: Similitude and Differences between (Video)games and Narrative," *Parnasso* 3 (1999): 365–371.

4. See Roger Caillois, *Man, Play, and Games* (Chicago: University of Illinois Press, 2001); Johan Huizinga, *Homo ludens* (New York: Beacon, 1971); Brian Sutton-Smith, *The Ambiguity of Play* (Cambridge, Mass.: Harvard University Press, 1997); Stewart Culin, *Games of the North American Indians* (New York: Dover, 1975); Stewart Culin, *Korean Games, with Notes on the Corresponding Games of China and Japan* (New York: Dover, 1991).

5. Oskar Morgenstern and John von Neumann, *The Theory of Games and Economic Behavior* (Princeton: Princeton University Press, 1980).

6. Espen Aarseth et al., "What's in a Game?—Game Taxonomies, Typologies, and Frameworks," in *Proceedings of Level Up, Digital Games Research Conference,* ed. Marinka Copier and Joost Raessens (Utrecht: Universiteit Utrecht, 2003); Staffan Björk and Jussi Holopainen, *Patterns for Game Design* (Hingham, Mass.: Charles River Media, 2004).

7. Cf. Joseph Butler, "Of Personal Identity," in his *The Analogy of Religion* (New York: Everyman, 1906); Roderick Chisholm, "The Loose and Popular and the Strict and Philosophical Senses of Identity," in *Perception and Personal Identity: Proceedings of the 1967 Oberlin Colloquium in Philosophy,* ed. Norman Grimm and Robert Care (Cleveland: Press of Case Western Reserve University, 1969). Butler and Chisholm are among the many philosophers who have taken up the question of identity over time: how can one thing be both the same and different (i.e., go through changes) as time passes? Such a question is related obliquely to the formalist study of games as a medium. The "loose and popular sense" is Chisholm's way of explaining the way we skirt the philosophical issue of identity over time in normal parlance, for example, in speaking about a cup that has a handle at time$_0$ but breaks and loses its handle at time$_1$, while remaining the same cup.

Chapter 1

1. More on the history of software technology can be found in chapters 2 and 3.

2. For a clear discussion of this phenomenon, see Albert-László Barabasi, *Linked: The New Science of Networks* (Cambridge: Perseus, 2002), 179–183.

3. See Ludwig von Bertalanffy, *General Systems Theory: Foundations, Development, Applications* (New York: George Brazilier, 1976).

4. Graham Harman, *Tool-Being: Heidegger and the Metaphysics of Objects* (Chicago: Open Court, 2002), 217–296 *passim.*

5. Ibid., 24–35.

6. Ibid., 19.

7. Jonathan Lettvin, Humberto Maturana, Warner McCulloch, and W. H. Pitts, "What the Frog's Eye Tells the Frog's Brain," in *Proceedings IRE* 47 (1959); Francisco Varela and Humberto Maturana, "Autopoiesis: The Organization of a Living System, Its Characterization, and a Model," *Biosystems* 5 (1974).

8. Niklas Luhmann, *Social Systems* (Palo Alto: Stanford University Press, 1995), 16.

9. Mark C. Taylor, *The Moment of Complexity: Emerging Network Culture* (Chicago: University of Chicago Press, 2002), 51.

10. Martin Heidegger, "The Question Concerning Technology," in *The Question Concerning Technology and Other Essays* (New York: Harper, 1977), 17.

11. Ibid., 32.

12. Gilles Deleuze, *Spinoza: Practical Philosophy* (San Francisco: City Lights Books, 1988), 122.

13. Benedict de Spinoza, *The Ethics,* P1, Def 5, in *The Ethics and Other Works,* ed. and trans. Edwin Curley (Princeton: Princeton University Press, 1994).

14. Ibid., P18 Dem.

15. Ibid., P18, Schol 1.

16. Other aspects of Spinoza's thought, such as absolute causality, are less influential precursors to the contemporary modes of thought that concern us here.

17. See Georg Cantor, *Contributions to the Founding of the Theory of Transfinite Numbers* (New York: Dover, 1955).

18. Ibid., 85.

19. See Gottlob Frege, *Philosophical and Mathematical Correspondence* (Chicago: University of Chicago Press, 1980); Bertrand Russell, *The Principles of Mathematics* (New York: W. W. Norton, 1996).

20. Peter Hallward, *Badiou: A Subject to Truth* (Minneapolis: University of Minnesota Press, 2003), 333.

21. Alain Badiou, *Briefings on Existence: A Transitory Ontology,* trans. Norman Madarasz (Albany: State University of New York Press, 2003), 29.

22. Alain Badiou, "Politics and Philosophy," *Angelaki* 3, no. 3 (1998), 130.

23. Hallward, *Badiou: A Subject to Truth,* 63.

24. Alain Badiou, *L'etre et l'événement* (Paris: Seuil, 1988), 408–409.

25. Ibid., 35.

26. Ibid., 113.

27. Hallward, *Badiou: A Subject to Truth,* 96.

28. Badiou, *L'etre et l'événement,* 130–140.

29. Janet Murray, *Hamlet on the Holodeck: The Future of Narrative in Cyberspace* (Cambridge, Mass.: MIT Press, 1997), 71.

30. Ibid.

31. Joseph Weizenbaum, "ELIZA: A Computer Program for the Study of Natural Language Communication between Man and Machine," cited in Murray, *Hamlet on the Holodeck,* 69.

32. Grigoris Antoniou and Frank van Harmelen, *A Semantic Web Primer* (Cambridge, Mass.: MIT Press, 2003), 89, 110.

33. Espen Aarseth, *Cybertext: Perspectives on Ergodic Literature* (Baltimore: Johns Hopkins University Press, 1997), 62.

34. Murray, *Halmet on the Holodeck,* 93.

35. See Sir Alfred Mehran, *The Terminal Man* (London: Transworld, 2004).

36. *Guardian,* "The Man Who Lost His Past," September 6, 2004, http://film.guardian.co.uk/features/featurepages/0,4120,1298104,00.html/.

37. The review-aggregation Web site metacritic.com gives the film a metascore of 55 out of 100. See http://www.metacritic.com/video/titles/terminal/ for links to specific reviews.

38. The photo is known as "A Great Day in Harlem" and can be viewed at http://www.harlem.org/. For a numbered guide to all fifty-seven jazz artists see http://www.greatmodernpictures.com/pictures.htm/.

Chapter 2

1. David Hume, *An Enquiry Concerning Human Understanding* (New York: Hackett, 1993), section XII, part I.

2. Harman, *Tool-Being,* 270.

3. In "What Is a Sign?" Peirce articulates three different classes of signs: the *icon,* a representative sign, the *index,* a causal sign, and the *symbol,* an arbitrary sign. See Charles Sanders Peirce, "What Is a Sign?" in *The Essential Peirce: Selected Philosophical Writings 1893–1913,* ed. The Peirce Edition Project (Bloomington and Indianapolis: Indiana University Press, 1998), 4, 10–26.

4. See Ferdinand de Saussure, *Course in General Linguistics,* trans. Roy Harris (La Salle, Ill.: Open Court, 1983).

5. Although they evoke merely prosaic significance in the literary world, the terms *instances* and *instantiation* have fundamental technical meanings in the context of information technology, specifically object technology.

6. See Claude Lévi-Strauss, *The Raw and the Cooked* (New York: Harper Collins, 1969), 21.

7. See Roland Barthes, "The Death of the Author," in *Image, Music, Text,* trans. Stephen Heath (New York: Hill and Wang, 1978).

8. Taylor, *The Moment of Complexity,* 65.

9. Alain Badiou, *Infinite Thought,* trans. and ed. Oliver Feltham and Justin Clemens (New York: Continuum, 2003), 44–47.

10. Martin Davis, *Engines of Logic: Mathematicians and the Origin of the Computer* (New York: W. W. Norton, 2000), 181.

11. Martin Campbell-Kelly and William Asprey, *Computer: A History of the Information Machine* (New York: HarperCollins, 1997), 79–95 *passim.*

12. Ibid., 183.

13. Ibid., 189.

14. H. H. Goldstine, *The Computer from Pascal to von Neumann* (Princeton: Princeton University Press, 1972), 191–192.

15. Lev Manovich, *The Language of New Media* (Cambridge, Mass.: MIT Press, 2002), 48, 52–53.

16. Georges Ifrah, *The Universal History of Computing,* trans. E. F. Harding (New York: John Wiley, 2001), 161.

17. Walter Benjamin, "The Work of Art in the Age of Mechanical Reproduction," in *Illuminations,* trans. Harry Zohn, ed. Hannah Arendt (New York: Shocken, 1969), 222.

18. N. Katherine Hayles, *How We Became Posthuman* (Chicago: University of Chicago Press, 1999), 25. Another name for the same dialectic is *signal/noise.*

Chapter 3

1. Sigmund Freud, *The Interpretation of Dreams,* trans. and ed. James Strachey (New York: Avon, 1965), 311–439.

2. Michel Foucault, "What Is an Author?," trans. Josue V. Harari, in *Textual Strategies: Perspectives in Post-Structuralist Criticism,* ed. Josue V. Harari (New York: Cornell University Press), 141.

3. Lacanian *mathemes* are akin to the *mythemes* devised by Claude Lévi-Strauss to denote the basic units of myth.

4. Jacques Lacan, *Seminar XI: The Four Fundamental Concepts of Psychoanalysis,* trans. Alan Sheridan (New York: W. W. Norton, 1981), 29–30.

5. Slavoj Žižek, *Looking Awry: An Introduction to Jacques Lacan through Popular Culture* (Cambridge, Mass.: MIT Press, 1991), 92–93.

6. Http://www.amazon.com/exec/obidos/ASIN/026274015X/ref=ase_kensaiinternatio/002-0554595-1496032/. The review in question is titled "Title Awry," dated July 7, 2001.

7. Slavoj Žižek, *The Ticklish Subject* (London: Verso, 1999), 19.

8. Harman, *Tool-Being,* 208.

9. Peter Starr, *Logics of Failed Revolt: French Theory after May '68* (Palo Alto: Stanford University Press: 1995), 200.

10. Badiou, *L'etre et l'événement,* 214–215.

11. Hallward, *Badiou: A Subject to Truth,* 118.

12. Badiou does write about love and sexuality, and even borrows Lacan's assertion that the sexual relationship is impossible, albeit for greatly different ends. See Alain Badiou, *Conditions* (Paris: Seuil, 1992), 280–290.

13. In his work *Discourse Networks 1800/1900,* trans. Michael Metteer (Palo Alto: Stanford University Press, 1990), Kittler articulates the concept of a "discourse network" or *Aufschreibesystem,* a logic for the current manner in which cultural material is recorded, like a technological Weltanschauung focused specifically on historicity; see 9–15, 20.

14. Friedrich Kittler, "Gramophone, Film, Typewriter," in *Literature, Media, Information Systems,* ed. John Johnston (Amsterdam: G+B Arts, 1997), 32. Kittler's favorite example is the jumbo jet, in which crew members are connected to private frequencies, radar screens, and radio systems while passengers are connected to film media, muzak, and microwaved food.

15. Neil Postman, *Technopoly* (New York: Vintage, 1993), 113.

16. Ibid., 111.

17. Kittler, "Gramophone, Film, Typewriter," 25.

18. Kittler, "There Is No Software," in *Literature, Media, Information Systems.*

19. Kittler's example is WordPerfect. Today, in all fields save law, WordPerfect has been all but replaced by Microsoft Word, whose features (and failures) sometimes do define the way we write and read.

20. Friedrich Kittler, "Protected Mode," in *Literature, Media, Information Systems,* 156–160.

21. Matthew B. Griffin and S. M. Herrmann, "An Interview with Friedrich A. Kittler about Cultural Studies in Germany, Literature in the Age of Technology and the Blind Spot in Media Theory," *Auseinander* 1, no. 3 (1995). Kittler's response is as follows (see http://artematrix.org/kittler/kit1.htm/):

Have you ever had the experience that what you write on paper actually happens? When you program a computer something is constantly happening. It's almost like magic. You write something, strike "enter," and then what you just wrote, happens, assuming there are no errors in your program. It's a form of alphabetization on an entirely different field, which also entails other routines. You learn not only to create paragraphs and footnotes, but also what a regression is and how to solve problems. I see this as being positive for cultural studies. I can't imagine that students today would learn only to read and write using the twenty-six letters of the alphabet. They should at least know some arithmetic, the integral function, the sine function—everything about signs and functions. They should also know at least two software languages. Then they'll be able to say something about what "culture" is at the moment, in contrast to "society." Under "society" falls much more, such as "how to behave" or "what to wear," which are also part of "culture." I think, however, we understand "culture" in terms of a system of signs. Cultural studies refers to and examines the most important sign systems.

Based on this passage alone, Kittler could be said to encourage the same kind of *procedural literacy* training that more recent scholars such as Ken Perlin have called for.

22. In the past decade, Sun has expanded the Java language to allow the same flexibility, perhaps even more, without maintaining trade-secret security over the secrets on which the symbolic language is based.

23. This method of accessing subsets of on-chip instructions was predicated by Turing's ACE architecture.

24. Such instructions are also called *frameworks,* or aggregations of many components used for specific purposes.

25. The evolution of object technology in commercial operating systems is actually much more complicated than this simple statement makes clear. The origin Apple's Lisa and Macintosh OT-based operating systems actually predate those of Microsoft, who didn't really manage to make Windows useful for users or developers until the early 1990s, with the introduction of Windows 3 and later COM.

The original Mac OS was built on Object Pascal, an OT-modified version of the popular procedural language Pascal. When Steve Jobs was pushed out of Apple in 1985, he founded Next, whose operating system NextSTEP was built on a modified version of Alan Kay's SmallTalk. Upon his return to Apple, Jobs bought Next and built Mac OS X on NextSTEP; Mac OS X programs are low-level programmed in Objective C, which is more closely related to SmallTalk than it is to C++.

26. William S. Perlman, *No Bull Object Technology for Executives* (Cambridge: Cambridge University Press, 1999), 3.

27. Some computer scientists combine some of the criteria, but these four are textbook requirements of object-oriented systems.

28. One functional clarification to abstraction should be noted. In many object-oriented development languages, code can call methods directly through the object class, rather than through instances of that class. This architecture promotes efficiency, as programs need not allocate memory for multiple instances of common routines during execution.

29. Polymorphism is the most difficult OT property to understand. Consider this example: both a man and a cheetah have legs, but the material and functional properties of the leg in each vary greatly.

30. Manovich, *The Language of New Media*, 45.

31. Ibid., 46. The term *algorithm* is a transliteration and Latinization of the name of the ninth-century Arab mathematician Al Khuwarizmi.

32. Ibid., 223.

33. Ibid.

34. Ifrah, *The Universal History of Computing*, 74.

35. Ibid.

36. In an industrial context, these representations are called *business rules* or *business logic*, hinting at how the accumulation of capital is at the heart of OT representation.

37. I discuss this relationship in more detail in chapters 7–9.

38. Software engineers have created a common symbolic language for representing OT structures, much like structural engineers employ the common form of a blueprint. This graphical language is called UML, for unified modeling language. UML is a system of diagrammatic modeling techniques used to design object-oriented systems. Perhaps more so than in other disciplines, software engineers use computer systems to design the computer systems they want to build. These classes of applications are called computer-aided software engineering (CASE) tools. In the mid-1990s, UML was derived from the three major competing CASE systems, Booch, object-modeling technique (OMT), and object-oriented software engineering (OOSE). UML sits in a precarious space between natural language and symbolic language, allowing software engineers to share UML diagrams across national and language boundaries. As such, UML resides at a level above object technology, as an abstract and (theoretically) universal way to represent OT's representations of the material world. It is a set of unit operations for unit operations.

39. Perlman, *No Bull Object Technology,* 40–57 *passim.* It is worth noting that the same features of OT that facilitate IP rights also underwrite the rejection of the commercial and legal regulation of software, as is the case in the free software and open source software movements.

40. See Apollinaire, *Alcools,* trans. Donald Revell (Hanover: University Press of New England, 1995); Apollinaire, *Calligrames* (Paris: Gallimard, 1966).

41. Jay David Bolter and Richard Grusin, *Remediation: Understanding New Media* (Cambridge, Mass.: MIT Press, 1999), 68.

42. George Landow, *Hypertext: The Convergence of Contemporary Critical Theory and Technology* (Baltimore: Johns Hopkins University Press, 1992), 8.

43. This particular claim is attributed to Dr. Ari Patrinos, who worked on the project. See http://christianity.com/partner/Article_Display_Page/0,,PTID4859%7CCHID101267 %7CCIID204717,00.html/.

44. "Human Genome Project Information," at the DOE Human Genome Project Management Information System, http://www.ornl.gov/TechResources/Human_Genome/ home.html/.

45. Barabasi, *Linked,* 181.

46. Murray Gell-Mann, *The Quark and the Jaguar: Adventures in the Simple and the Complex* (New York: W. H. Friedman, 1994), 292, my emphasis.

47. Richard Dawkins, *The Selfish Gene* (Oxford: Oxford University Press, 1990), 192.

48. Richard Dawkins, *Unweaving the Rainbow: Science, Delusion, and the Appetite for Wonder* (New York: Houghton Mifflin, 1998), 306.

49. Ryan Mathews and Watts Wacker, *The Deviant's Advantage: How Fringe Ideas Create Mass Markets* (New York: Crown, 2002), 12.

50. Deviance in this case refers not to social or legal deviance, but to the notion that cultural units begin as marginalized units before becoming mass-market.

51. See http://www.mimeticsystems.com/.

52. QL2 Software. *WebQL,* http://www.webql.com/.

53. Murray, *Hamlet on the Holodeck,* 274.

Chapter 4

1. Claude Lévi-Strauss, *The Savage Mind* (Chicago: University of Chicago Press, 1968), 22.

2. Jacques Derrida, "Structure, Sign, and Play in the Discourse of the Human Sciences," in *Writing and Difference,* trans. Alan Bass (Chicago: University of Chicago Press, 1980), 285.

3. Gerard Genette, "Structuralisme et critique litteraire," *L'arc* 26 (1965), 34.

4. Norman K. Denzin and Yvonna S. Lincon, eds., *The Handbook of Qualitative Research* (Thousand Oaks, Calif.: Sage, 2005).

5. Ibid., 2.

6. Ibid., 3.

7. Http://www.acla.org/.

8. Tim Berners-Lee, *Weaving the Web: The Original Design and Ultimate Destiny of the World Wide Web* (New York: Harper, 2000), 28.

9. See Mike McShaffry, *Game Coding Complete* (Scottsdale, Ariz.: Paraglyph Press, 2003).

10. Aarseth, *Cybertext,* 22.

11. Ibid., 1.

12. Ibid., 9–13.

13. Aarseth, *Cybertext,* 16–17.

14. Ibid., 17.

15. Ibid.

16. Ibid., 14.

17. Ibid., 51.

18. See Frederic Jameson, *Postmodernism, or the Cultural Logic of Late Capitalism* (Durham: Duke University Press, 1991); Linda Hutcheon, *The Politics of Postmodernism* (New York: Routledge, 1989).

19. See Jay David Bolter, *The Writing Space: The Computer, Hypertext, and the History of Writing* (Hillsdale, N.J.: Lawrence Erlbaum, 1991); George Landow, *Hypertext: The Convergence of Contemporary Critical Theory and Technology* (Baltimore: Johns Hopkins University Press, 1992). Landow published a subsequent, "updated" version of this text, *Hypertext 2.0* (Baltimore: Johns Hopkins University Press), in 1996.

20. For example, the Center for Digital Humanities at UCLA (see http://www.cdh.ucla .edu/mission.html/) lists as its primary goal "The development of innovative technological solutions for research and instruction." No mention is made of digital artifacts as objects of humanistic inquiry. Electronic text sourcing tools like Project Gutenberg (see http://www.gutenberg.org/) belong in the domain of information science more than humanities.

21. Http://www.digra.org/.

22. Http://www.digra.org/hardcore/hcl/.

23. Ibid.

24. Frans Mäyrä, "The Quiet Revolution: Three Theses for the Future of Game Studies," *DiGRA Hard Core* 1, no. 3 (March 2005). Available at http://www.digra.org/hardcore/ hc4/.

25. Ibid.

26. Ibid.

27. Ibid.

28. Aarseth, *Cybertext,* 41.

Chapter 5

1. Aarseth, *Cybertext,* 100–101.

2. This figure for videogame budgets will quickly date itself. As I write this in spring 2005, the next generation of consoles from Microsoft, Sony, and Nintendo are poised for release within the next year. Among the early conjecture about the effect these new consoles will have on the marketplace, some developers worry that game budgets will increase to $40 million or more as the industry strives to mimic Hollywood. See http:// news.com.com/Developers+uneasy+about+new+game+consoles/2100-1043_3-5704069.html?tag=nefd.top/.

3. William Steig, *Shrek!* (New York: Farrar, Straus, and Giroux, 1993).

4. A 2003 study by Sue Clayton of the University of London actually sought to create "a generic blueprint for the perfect movie." The result: 8% music, 10% plot, 10% special effects, 12% love/sex/romance, 13% good vs. evil, 17% comedy, 30% action (sidebar, *Wired,* August 2003, 52). The obvious question: what do figures like "10% plot" really mean?

5. Peter Molyneux/Lionhead Studios's new game *The Movies,* due out in 2006, might very well challenge this claim with its procedural filmmaking technique.

6. The first table tennis game was *Tennis for Two,* created by William A. Higinbotham at Brookhaven National Laboratory in 1958. It was played on an oscilloscope. Ralph Baer adapted this design for television in 1966, and the resulting device was manufactured by Magnavox as the Odyssey.

7. Rusel Demaria and Johnny L. Wilson, *High Score! The Illustrated History of Electronic Games* (Berkeley: McGraw Hill, 2002), 23.

8. Ibid.

9. Bushnell's foresight in creating Chuck E. Cheese's deserves special mention. Before anyone else, Bushnell recognized that electronic games were part of a larger world of entertainment experience, the same kind of experience that propelled the success of theme parks and malls. Jeremy Rifkin has called this transition from property to experience the "age of access," which is also the title of his excellent book on the subject—Jeremy Rifkin, *The Age of Access: The New Culture of Hypercapitalism Where All of Life Is a Paid-For Experience* (New York: Tarcher, 2000).

For a brief history of the Chuck E. Cheese's Pizza Time Theater and its competitor, ShowBiz Pizza Place (created by initial franchisee Bob Brock), see http://users.pullman .com/fjstevens/tokens/cec/CECimages/CEChistory.html/.

10. Ben Sawyer, "The Next Ages of Game Development," *Adrenaline Vault,* September 30, 2002, http://www.avault.com/developer/getarticle.asp?name=bsawyer1/.

11. "10 Most Controversial Games of All Time," *PC Gamer,* May 2002, http://www .pcgamer.com/eyewitness/eyewitness_2003-06-05.html/.

12. Harold Bloom, *The Anxiety of Influence* (Oxford: Oxford University Press, 1997), 22–28.

13. Http://www.livejournal.com/users/ea_spouse/.

14. "EA Facing Possible Class Action Suit," *Game Daily,* November 12, 2004, http:// biz.gamedaily.com/features.asp?article_id=8323/.

15. "Lessons of the California Supermarket Strike," *Proletarian Revolution* 70 (spring 2004). Available at http://www.lrp-cofi.org/PR/strikePR70.html/.

16. Branded by espionage-auteur Tom Clancy, Ubisoft has released a good handful of games through these two franchises, both focusing on semirealistic espionage stealth gameplay.

17. Three sequels followed, two from original developers Looking Glass in 1999 and 2000, and one from Ion Storm in 2004, where many Looking Glass employees landed after the latter studio went out of business in 2000. Ion Storm closed its doors too in early 2005.

18. See http://www.interactivestory.net/ for more information and current project status.

19. See Michael Mateas and Andrew Stern, "Architecture, Authorial Idioms, and Early Observations of the Interactive Drama *Façade*" (Carnegie Mellon Technical Reports, December 2002); A. Loyall and J. Bates, "Real-Time Control of Animated Broad Agents," in *Proceedings of the 15th Annual Conference of the Cognitive Science Society* (Hillsdale, N.J.: Lawrence Erlbaum, 1993).

20. "Inside the Engine: Half-Life 2," *Maximum PC* (August 2003): 28–29.

21. Chris Crawford, *Chris Crawford on Game Design* (New York: New Riders, 2003), 51.

22. Bolter and Grusin, *Remediation,* 27.

23. Ibid., 53.

24. Ibid., 13.

25. More recently, Mateas has run a research project at the Georgia Institute of Technology to integrate ABL into the Unreal Engine. See http://egl.gatech.edu/inproduction/UTABLproj.html/.

26. Bolter and Grusin, *Remediation,* 100–101.

27. Markku Eskelinen, "Cybertext Theory and Literary Studies: A User's Manual," *Electronic Book Review,* http://www.altx.com/ebr/ebr12/eskel.htm/.

28. Jesper Juul, "Games Telling Stories? A Brief Note on Games and Narratives," *Game Studies* 1, no. 1 (2001), http://www.gamestudies.org/0101/juul-gts/.

29. Ibid.

30. Ibid.

31. Gonzalo Frasca, "Ludologists Love Stories Too: The Role of Narrative in Videogames," in *Proceedings of Level Up, Digital Games Research Conference,* ed. Marinka Copier and Joost Raessens (Utrecht: Universiteit Utrecht, 2003).

32. See Roland Barthes, *Mythologies; S/Z,* trans. Annette Lavers (New York: Hill and Wang, 1972); Vladimir Propp, *Morphology of the Folktale,* trans. Laurence Scott Austin: University of Texas Press, 1968).

33. Frasca, "Ludologists Love Stories Too."

34. Murray, *Hamlet on the Holodeck,* 188.

35. Ibid., 197.

36. Ibid., 206.

37. Ibid.

38. Henry Jenkins, "Game Design as Narrative Architecture," in *First Person: New Media as Performance, Story, and Game,* ed. Noah Wardrip-Fruin and Pat Harrigan (Cambridge, Mass.: MIT Press, 2004), 125.

39. Ibid.

40. Ibid.

41. Ibid., 126.

42. Roger Schank, *Tell Me a Story: Narrative and Intelligence* (Chicago: Northwestern University Press, 1995), 73.

43. Ibid., 148.

44. See Mark Turner, *The Literary Mind: The Origins of Thought and Language* (Oxford: Oxford University Press, 1998).

45. Giacomo Rizzolatti and Laila Craighero, "The Mirror-Neuron System," *Annual Review of Neuroscience* 27 (2004): 169–192.

46. See V. S. Ramachandran, *Phantoms in the Brain: Probing the Mysteries of the Human Mind* (New York: Perennial, 1999), 61, 193.

47. See, e.g., Giacomo Rizzolatti and Michael A. Arbib, "Language within Our Grasp," *Trends in Neuroscience* 21 (1998): 188–194.

48. Cf., e.g., James Hurford, "Language beyond Our Grasp: What Mirror Neurons Can, and Cannot, Do for the Evolution of Language," in *Evolution of Communication Systems: A Comparative Approach,* ed. Kimbrough Oller and Ulrike Griebel (Cambridge, Mass.: MIT Press, 2004), 298–300.

49. Murray, *Hamlet on the Holodeck,* 275.

Chapter 6

1. Murray, *Hamlet on the Holodeck,* 274.

2. Walter Benjamin, "On Some Motifs in Baudelaire," in *Illuminations,* 162.

3. Ibid., 172.

4. Aarseth, *Cybertext,* 3.

5. Ibid., 6.

6. Charles Baudelaire, *Œuvres complètes* (Paris: Gallimard, 1968), 101. My translation.

7. Benjamin, "On Some Motifs in Baudelaire," 156.

8. Jérôme Thélot, *Baudelaire violence et poésie* (Paris: Gallimard, 1992), 488–489.

9. Benjamin, "On Some Motifs in Baudelaire," 169.

10. Critic Leo Bersani referred to Baudelaire's subject as a "disseminated, scattered self" (Leo Bersani, *Baudelaire and Freud* [Berkeley: University of California Press, 1977], 3). I'd argue "poet" and "narrator" can be used interchangeably in both poets' work.

11. Benjamin, "On Some Motifs in Baudelaire," 170.

12. Ibid., 222.

13. Ibid., 188.

14. In general, Charles Bukowski, both the poet and his work, bears a striking similarity to Baudelaire.

15. Charles Bukowski, *Betting on the Muse* (Santa Rosa: Black Sparrow Press, 1996), 58. Reprinted by permission of HarperCollins.

16. Bukowski's crowd is twentieth-century Los Angeles.

17. Fred Thom, "*Amélie* (Review)," *La plume noire,* http://www.plume-noire.com/movies/reviews/amelie.html/.

18. For a more pointed characterization of these figures as an "American fantasy of Paris," see the review cited above in note 17.

19. Pierre-Auguste Renoir, *Dejeuner des canotiers,* 1881.

20. Guillaume Laurent (screenplay), *Le fableux destin d'Amélie Poulin.* My translation.

21. By March 2002, *The Sims* and its expansion packs had sold over 13 million copies. See http://thesims.ea.com/us/news/werenumber1.html/.

22. Note that this discussion refers to the original version of *The Sims,* not to its more complex 2004 sequel, *The Sims 2.*

23. Scott McCloud, *Understanding Comics* (New York: Perennial, 1994), 60–70.

24. Celia Pearce, "Sims, Battle Bots, Cellular Automata, God, and Go: An Interview with Will Wright," *Game Studies* 2, no. 1 (July 2002). Available at http://www.gamestudies .org/0201/pearce/.

25. Gonzalo Frasca, "The Sims: Grandmothers are Cooler than Trolls," *Game Studies* 2, no. 1 (July 2002). Available at http://www.gamestudies.org/0201/frasca/.

26. Jake Simpson, "Scripting and Sims 2: Coding the Psychology of Little People," in *Proceedings of the Game Developers Conference* (San Francisco: Computer Game Group, 2005). While Simpson's presentation refers to the sequel of the game discussed here, the Edith scripting engine also applies to the earlier game.

27. John MacLean-Foreman, "An Interview with Will Wright," *Gamasutra,* May 1, 2001. Available at http://www.gamasutra.com/features/20010501/wright_01.htm/.

Chapter 7

1. Stephen Wolfram, "Cellular Automata as Models of Complexity," *Nature* 311 (October 1984), 419.

2. This does not exclude the biological sciences from the scope of the theory either. Cellular automata theory has been applied liberally to biology, especially attempts to explain neurological phenomena and the broad function of living systems.

3. Stephen Wolfram, "Cellular Automata," *Los Alamos Science* 9 (fall 1983), 3.

4. Stephen Wolfram, *A New Kind of Science* (Champaign, Ill.: Wolfram Media, 2002), 23–60.

5. Wolfram, "Cellular Automata," 3.

6. Stephen Wolfram, "Cellular Automata as Models of Complexity," *Nature* 311 (October 1984), 424.

7. Ibid.

8. See Martin Gardener, "Mathematical Games: The Fantastic Combinations of John Conway's New Solitaire Game 'Life,'" *Scientific American* 233 (October 1970), 120.

9. Ibid.

10. Ted Friedman, "Semiotics of Sim City," *First Monday,* 4 (April 1999). Available at http://www.firstmonday.dk/issues/issue4_4/friedman/.

11. Paul Starr, "Policy as a Simulation Game," *American Prospect* 5, no. 17 (March 21, 1994), http://www.prospect.org/print/V5/17/starr-p.html/.

12. Pearce, "Sims, Battle Bots, Cellular Automata, God, and Go."

13. Paul Starr offers a more comprehensive overview of the mechanics of the game in his *American Prospect* article, cited above in note 11.

14. Starr, "Policy as a Simulation Game."

15. Friedman, "Semiotics of Sim City."

16. It is important to note that Wolfram recognizes that "comprehensive" modeling is a long-term goal, and not one achieved through *A New Kind of Science.* To this end, Wolfram continues to publish a series of "Open Problems and Projects" directed at all levels of researchers, from high school through postgraduate.

17. Paul Callahan, "What Is the Game of Life?," Math.com: Wonders of Math, http://www.math.com/students/wonders/life/life.html/.

18. Gonzalo Frasca, "Simulation 101: Simulation versus Representation," http://www.ludology.org/articles/sim1/simulation101.html/.

19. Gonzalo Frasca, "Simulation versus Narrative: Introduction to Ludology," in *Game Theory Reader,* ed. Mark J. P. Wolf and Bernard Perron (New York: Routledge, 2003), 223.

20. Frasca, "Simulation 101."

21. Murray, *Hamlet on the Holodeck,* 110–112.

22. Http://www.3dpipelinesim.com/biochem_fx.html/.

23. Gonzalo Frasca, "Videogames of the Oppressed: Videogames as a Means for Critical Thinking and Debate" (master's thesis, the Georgia Institute of Technology, 2001).

24. Murray, *Hamlet on the Holodeck,* 143–144.

25. Eskelinen may be referring to Celia Pearce's interpretation of chess, in which she compares the game to *Macbeth.* See Celia Pearce, "Towards a Game Theory of Games," in *First Person: New Media as Story, Performance, and Game,* ed. Noah Wardrip-Fruin and Pat Harrigan (Cambridge, Mass.: MIT Press, 2004), 143–153; also available at http://cpandfriends.com/writing/first-person.html/. This essay was written over a year after Eskelinen's article, but it is possible that he was familiar with an earlier draft presented at a conference or symposium (the article is dated 2001 on Pearce's Web site).

26. Markku Eskelinen, "The Gaming Situation," *Game Studies* 1, no. 1 (July 2001), http://www.gamestudies.org/0101eskelinen/.

27. Frasca, "Videogames of the Oppressed."

28. Pearce, "Sims, Battle Bots, Cellular Automata, God, and Go."

29. Ibid.

30. Friedman, "The Semiotics of Sim City."

31. Ibid.

32. Julian Bleeker, "Urban Crisis: Past, Present, and Virtual," *Socialist Review* 25 (1995): 189–221.

33. Starr, "Policy as a Simulation Game."

34. Ibid.

35. 3D Pipeline is a military and government-oriented simulation consultancy that focuses on real-time three-dimensional physics.

36. Another less related but equally interesting property of this particular simulation is the mechanism by which biological agents are introduced into the scenario. The user selects a predefined agent (such as sarin gas) or sets the physical properties of a "custom" agent. Then, the user manually "releases" the agent into the environment by clicking and dragging the mouse. This mode of interaction is interesting because it implicates the user in the role of the terrorist (for more on this subject, see my discussion of *September 12* in the next chapter).

37. This limitation could be overcome with a broader understanding of cognitive mapping in the spatial-theoretical sense. For example, Janet Murray's interpretation of *Tetris* could be said to construct a cognitive map of the contemporary workplace, or by extension the postindustrial world economy. However, I'm inclined to agree with Frasca that the more generic HCI model for mental modeling is more fungible than cognitive mapping for the purposes of understanding and interpreting games and simulations.

38. See Ferdinand de Saussure, *Course in General Linguistics*.

39. Jacques Derrida, "Difference," in *Writing and Difference*. I recommend writing *différance* in its Anglicized form, *differance*, since part of Derrida's use of *difference* calls into question the primacy of writing over speech. In French, the words *différence* and *différance* sound identical, and it is generally desirable to maintain this property in English, rather than pronouncing the neologism as a foreign word.

40. Derrida musters many other terms that perform similar work, including *hymen* (both inside and outside), *pharmakon* (both poison and cure), and *supplement* (both surplus and necessity).

41. Starr, "Policy as a Simulation Game."

42. Ibid.

43. Sherry Turkle, "Seeing through Computers," *American Prospect* 8, no. 31 (March 1997), my emphasis. Available at http://www.prospect.org/print/V8/31/turkle-s.html/.

44. Jacques Derrida, *Archive Fever: A Freudian Impression,* trans. Eric Prenowitz (Chicago: University of Chicago Press, 1996), 91.

45. Turkle, "Seeing through Computers."

46. Ibid.

47. Ibid.

48. Eskelinen, "The Gaming Situation."

49. Derrida, *Archive Fever,* 12. Derrida relates the archive drive with the death drive. Archive fever is a way of *working through* the archive drive, in the psychoanalytic sense.

50. Although it is not the subject of this book, I have committed myself to this goal in my research and professional work, especially as it relates to politics. In 2003, Gonzalo Frasca and I designed the first official game for a U.S. presidential candidate (*The Howard Dean for Iowa Game,* http://www.deanforamericagame.com/), and in 2004 I designed two other games about public policy decision making, *Activism* (http://www.activismgame .com/) and *Take Back Illinois* (http://www.takebackillinoisgame.com/). As this book goes to press, I am in the early stages of the development process for a U.S. federal budget game, directed by the Woodrow Wilson Foundation and sponsored by the GAO. This last game that circles back serendipitously to Paul Starr's experience with the CBO.

51. Badiou, *L'etre et l'événement,* 38.

Chapter 8

1. Cooper's Leatherstocking Tales are a series of early nineteenth-century novels (*The Deerslayer, The Last of the Mohicans, The Pathfinder, The Pioneers,* and *The Prairie*) that detail the adventures of early American hero Natty Bumppo. They are widely held to be the first major American novels, although the books are often criticized for terrible dialogue and overly complex plots. Fritz Lang's 1927 *Metropolis* is an early film adaptation of German expressionism and is generally acknowledged as the precursor of film noir.

2. Benjamin, "The Work of Art in the Age of Mechanical Reproduction," 220.

3. Ibid., 224.

4. Ibid., 234.

5. Ibid., 236.

6. Ibid.

7. See Walter Benjamin, *The Arcades Project,* trans. Rolf Tiedemann, Howard Eiland, and Kevin McLaughlin (New York: Belknap Press, 1999).

8. Susan Buck-Morss, *The Dialectics of Seeing: Walter Benjamin and the Arcades Project* (Cambridge, Mass.: MIT Press, 1990), 336.

9. Ibid., 221.

10. See Benjamin, "On Some Motifs in Baudelaire," 155–200.

11. Buck-Morss, *The Dialectics of Seeing,* 47.

12. Benjamin, "The Work of Art in the Age of Mechanical Reproduction," 231.

13. Http://www.theesa.com/archives/2005/05/e3_2005_state_o_1.php/. For more industry data, see http://www.theesa.com/facts/top_10_facts.php/.

14. Http://www.theesa.com/about/related_links.php/.

15. Johan Huizinga, *Homo ludens* (New York: Beacon, 1971), 13.

16. Katie Salen and Eric Zimmerman, *Rules of Play: Game Design Fundamentals* (Cambridge, Mass.: MIT Press, 2004), 75.

17. Roger Callois, *Man, Play, and Games,* trans. Meyer Barash (Chicago: University of Illinois Press, 2001), 10, my emphasis.

18. See Emile Durkheim, *Elementary Forms of the Religious Life,* trans. Karen E. Fields (New York: Free Press, 1995), 34–38.

19. See Rudolf Otto, *The Idea of the Holy* (Oxford: Oxford University Press, 1958), 14.

20. Hans Georg Gadamer, *Truth and Method,* trans. Joel Weinsheimer and Donald G. Marshall (New York: Continuum, 1989), 112–113.

21. The ESA itself has been quite progressive about expanding the role of videogames. ESA president Doug Lowenstein's 2005 Electronic Entertainment Expo (E3) State of the Industry address serves as an especially poignant call to expand the role and purpose of videogames: see http://www.theesa.com/archives/2005/05/e3_2005_state_o_1 .php/. The ESA also aggregates research on the uses of games in non-entertainment contexts, such as education and health. See http://www.theesa.com/facts/third_party .php/.

22. Neil Postman, *Amusing Ourselves to Death: Public Discourse in the Age of Show Business* (New York: Penguin, 1986), 16.

23. Ibid., 74.

24. Ibid., 80.

25. Huizinga, *Homo ludens,* 3.

26. Raph Koster, *A Theory of Fun for Game Design* (Scottsdale, Ariz.: Paraglyph Press, 2005), 40.

27. Ibid., 50.

28. Ibid.

29. Ibid., 96.

30. Ibid., 152.

31. Ibid., 181.

32. Ibid., 148.

33. Ibid., 152.

34. I am indebted to William Huber for suggesting the term fun'.

35. Crawford, *Chris Crawford on Game Design,* 35.

36. See http://www.opensorcery.net/velvet-strike/.

37. See the artist statement at http://www.netarts.org/mcmogatk/2003/works/harger/antiwargame.html/.

38. Crawford, *Chris Crawford on Game Design,* 383.

39. Frasca, "Videogames of the Oppressed."

40. See Jesper Juul's weblog meditation on "didactic games," http://www.jesperjuul.dk/ludologist/index.php?p=33&c=1/.

41. Jesper Juul, "The Open and the Closed: Games of Emergence and Games of Progression," *Computer Games and Digital Cultures*, http://www.jesperjuul.dk/text/openandtheclosed.html/.

42. Gonzalo Frasca, "Ideological Videogames: Press Left Button to Dissent," *IGDA The Ivory Tower* (November 2003), http://www.igda.org/columns/ivorytower/ivory_Nov03.php/.

43. Ben Sawyer, weblog comment (September 30, 2003), http://www.gamegirladvance.com/archives/2003/09/29/newsgaming_september_12.html/.

44. Chris Crawford makes this distinction in his 1984 book *The Art of Computer Game Design* (New York: Osborne, 1984), which is unfortunately out of print. Much of the material found its way into Crawford's 2003 book *Chris Crawford on Game Design,* but the original insight about objective and subjective representation can be found in chapter 1 of the 1984 book (available online at http://www.vancouver.wsu.edu/fac/peabody/game-book/Coverpage.html/). Crawford reiterated this sentiment during the first Serious Games Summit at the 2004 Game Developers Conference (March 2004).

45. Alain Badiou, "Que pense le poème?" in *L'art est-il une connaissance?,* ed. Roger Pol Droit (Paris: Le Monde Editions, 1993), 221.

46. Http://books.slashdot.org/comments.pl?sid=138365&cid=11577246/.

47. Nicolas Ducheneaut, Robert J. Moore, and Eric Nickell, "Designing for Sociability in Massively Multiplayer Games: An Examination of the 'Third Places' of SWG," in *Other Players,* ed. Jonas Heide Smith and Miguel Sicart (Copenhagen: IT University of Copenhagen, 2004), available at http://www.itu.dk/op/papers/ducheneaut_moore_nickell.pdf/. I am indebted to the authors for introducing me to the connection between bazaar sales and commuting discussed below.

48. Ibid., 2.

49. Http://www.legendmud.org/raph/gaming/index.html/.

50. Ducheneaut, Moore, and Nickell, "Designing for Sociability," 11–12.

51. Http://www.sprawlcity.org/hbis/index.html/.

52. Http://www.dailynews.com/Stories/0,1413,200~20950~2854247,00.html/.

53. Http://www.transact.orglca/congestion5.htm/.

54. Http://www.calmis.ca.gov/FILE/OCCPROJ/laF&G.htm/.

55. Http://www.legendmud.org/raph/whatsnew.html/.

Chapter 9

1. Aarseth, *Cybertext*, 1.

2. Ibid., 3.

3. See Barthes, "The Death of the Author," in *Image, Music, Text,* 142–148.

4. Aarseth, *Cybertext*, 1.

5. Compare Barthes's notion of *writerly texts,* which also accounts for openness of experience in terms of a property of the work, rather than a property of the reader. Barthes, *S/Z,* 4–5.

6. Aarseth, *Cybertext,* 22.

7. Ibid., 19.

8. Ibid., 18.

9. Ibid., 55.

10. N. Katherine Hayles, "What Cybertext Theory Can't Do," *Electronic Book Review,* http://www.altx.com/ebr/riposte/rip12/rip12hay.htm/.

11. The only substantive subtlety current game criticism offers is genre distinction; game critics wouldn't review a puzzle game like *Tetris* from the perspective of a first-person shooter like *Halo.* However, this distinction stands a level above the criticism itself; it is more about the player's subjective preconceptions before the game, rather than her assumptions within it. It is also true that film is largely a commercial medium measured by a similar kind of popular criticism. However, the subtleties of film criticism far outweigh those of game criticism, owing largely to the homogeneity of commercial game content and the game industry's enormous aversion to risk.

12. Http://www.costik.com/weblog/2003_10_01_blogchive.html#1065487259088 17670/.

13. Ibid.

14. Ibid.

15. Http://www.gamegirladvance.com/archives/2003/09/29/newsgaming_september_ 12.html/.

16. Huizinga, *Homo ludens,* 10.

17. Crawford, *The Art of Computer Game Design,* chapter 1.

18. Ibid.

19. Huizinga, *Homo ludens,* 10.

20. Game designer and researcher Eric Zimmerman made both of these characterizations in a 1999 interview with Jenelle Porter, available at http://www.artistsspace.org/ exhibitions/1999/searchers99/sept99.html/.

21. Huizinga, *Homo ludens,* 28.

22. Ibid., 8, my emphasis.

23. See Michel de Certeau, *The Practice of Everyday Life,* trans. Steven Rendall (Berkeley: University of California Press, 2002).

24. Crawford, *The Art of Computer Game Design.*

25. "Haitians Protest Game at Wal-Mart," *Miami Herald,* December 15, 2003, http:// www.miami.com/mld/miamiherald/7492312.htm/.

Chapter 10

1. See Leonhard Euler, *Introduction to Analysis of the Infinite,* books I and II, trans. John D. Blanton (New York: Springer, 1988).

2. See Paul Erdős, Ronald L. Graham, and Jaroslav Nesetril, eds., *The Mathematics of Paul Erdős* (New York: Springer, 1996).

3. See Stanley Milgram, "The Small World Problem," *Physiology Today* 2 (1967): 60–67.

4. See Mark Granovetter, "The Strength of Weak Ties," *American Journal of Sociology* 78 (1973): 1360–1380.

5. Gilles Deleuze and Félix Guattari, *A Thousand Plateaus,* trans. Brian Massumi (Minneapolis: University of Minnesota Press, 1987), 3–10, 351–400.

6. See, e.g., Stuart Moulthrop, "Rhizomes and Resistance: Hypertext and the Dreams of a New Culture," in *Hyper/Text/Theory,* ed. George Landow (Baltimore: Johns Hopkins University Press, 1994).

7. Of related interest is the self-referential Rhizomat. See http://www.bleb.net/rhizomat/.

8. Deleuze and Guattari actually offer a multitude of semi-interchangeable epithets for their theoretical practice, including nomadism, schizoanalysis, the body without organs, the desiring-machine, the war machine, and so forth. For simplicity's sake, and because I think it is the most telegraphic of all their terms, I will focus on nomadism in the subsequent discussion.

9. Deleuze and Guattari, *A Thousand Plateaus,* 158.

10. Ibid., 54.

11. Brian Massumi, *A User's Guide to Capitalism and Schizophrenia: Deviations from Deleuze and Guattari* (Cambridge, Mass.: MIT Press, 1992), 57.

12. Ibid., 6.

13. Alain Badiou, *Gilles Deleuze: The Clamor of Being,* trans. Louise Burchill (Minneapolis: University of Minnesota Press, 2000), 79, 122.

14. Ibid., 11.

15. Gilles Deleuze and Claire Parnet, *Dialogues* (New York: Columbia University Press, 1977), 69.

16. Deleuze and Guattari, *A Thousand Plateaus,* 399.

17. Ibid., 399.

18. Ibid., 383.

19. Deleuze and Parnet, *Dialogues,* 145.

20. Ibid.

21. Ibid., 500.

22. Both the play and screenplay of *Six Degrees of Separation* were written by John Guare.

23. There was a software program called Six Degrees that helped business users manage the complex relationships between contacts, emails, and files on their personal computers. The product has since been sold and renamed Clarity. See http://www.ralstontech.com/.

24. See http://en.wikipedia.org/wiki/Six_Degrees_of_Kevin_Bacon/.

25. Milgram, "The Small World Problem," 61–63.

26. For a longer explication of Milgram's experiment, see Barabasi, *Linked,* 27–39.

27. Granovetter, "The Strength of Weak Ties," 1360, 1365.

28. See Barabasi, *Linked,* 86–88.

29. See, e.g., Stefan Wuchty, "Scale-Free Behavior in Protein Domain Networks," *Molecular Biology and Evolution* 18 (2001): 1694–1702.

30. Http://www.friendster.com/.

31. Http://www.ryze.com/.

32. Http://www.linkedin.com/.

33. Http://www.ecademy.com/.

34. Ross Mayfield, "Social Network Models," March 30, 2003, http://radio.weblogs .com/0114726/2003/03/30.html/. Mayfield refers to two types of social network systems I did not discuss above. Meetup is a service that facilitates in-person meetings between disparate people (famously put to use by the Howard Dean presidential campaign in 2003); weblogs like Moveable Type and LiveJournal are web-based diary-like tools that often form close-knit communities of readers interested in similar subject matter.

35. Ibid.

36. Although there are innumerable successful applications of psychoanalysis, a careful search of the literature will yield only a few attempts to actually *use* schizoanalysis as a technique. This is partly because, unlike most practitioners of psychoanalysis, Deleuze and Guattari never articulate an iterable schizoanalytic praxis for any specific area of cultural activity. Among the works that do take on the challenge are Eugene Holland, *Baudelaire and Schizoanalysis* (Cambridge: Cambridge University Press, 1993) and Rolando Perez, *On Anarchy and Schizoanalysis* (Brooklyn, N.Y.: Autonomedia, 1990). Holland's book is measured and traditional, an admirable attempt at a difficult task. Perez cites innumerable passages from Deleuze and Guattari's lurid, provocative language with little productive analysis or explication.

37. Jesper Juul, "The Open and the Closed."

38. Ibid.

Chapter 11

1. In November 2002 and 2004, respectively, Rockstar released sequels *Grand Theft Auto: Vice City,* and *Grand Theft Auto: San Andreas.*

2. Http://www.freerepublic.com/focus/f-news/1373357/posts/.

3. The ESRB (Electronic Software Rating Board) is the game industry equivalent of the MPAA.

4. Http://www.theregister.co.uk/content/54/32765.html/.

5. Http://www.nbc6.net/entertainment/2706043/detail.html/.

6. Gonzalo Frasca, "Sim Sin City: Some Thoughts about Grand Theft Auto 3," *Game Studies* 3, no. 2 (2003). Available at http://www.gamestudies.org/0302/frasca/.

7. See, e.g., Gilles Deleuze, *Kant's Critical Philosophy,* trans. High Tomlinson and Barbara Habberjam (Minneapolis: University of Minnesota Press, 1984).

8. Deleuze and Guattari, *A Thousand Plateaus,* 160.

9. Ibid., 503.

10. Deleuze and Guattari, *A Thousand Plateaus,* 149–166; Gilles Deleuze and Félix Guattari, *Anti-Oedipus: Capitalism and Schizophrenia,* trans. Robert Hurley, Mark Seem, and Helen R. Lane (Minneapolis: University of Minnesota Press, 1983), 325–329.

11. Spinoza, *Ethics,* part III.

12. Massumi, *A User's Guide to Capitalism and Schizophrenia,* 70.

13. Http://www.gamegirladvance.com/archives/2002/09/26/playlife_in_gta3.html/.

14. Machinima is a variety of video art produced from recorded gameplay performances.

15. Howard Rheingold, *Smart Mobs: The Next Social Revolution* (New York: Perseus, 2002).

16. Howard Rheingold, "View: Is Friendster Changing Our Friendships?," *Wired* 12, no. 1 (January 2004): 64.

17. See Barry Wellman, ed., *Networks in the Global Village: Life in Contemporary Communities* (New York: Westview Press, 1999).

18. Http://www.dojomediaserver.com/specials/Famicom/timeline.html/.

19. GTA was built on the popular RenderWare engine, whereas *Wind Waker* was largely built from the ground up.

20. Gustave Flaubert, *Madame Bovary* (Paris: Flammarion, 1986), 208; *Madame Bovary,* trans. and ed. Paul de Man (New York: W. W. Norton, 1965), 102. In all subsequent references, the first page number refers to the Flammarion French edition, the second to the Norton English edition. While I have not altered the translation in these citations, I have modified the typography of the English edition to match that of the French.

21. Ibid.

22. Ibid., 210; 103.

23. Ibid., 209; 102.

24. Ibid., 210–211; 103–104.

25. Ibid., 215; 107.

26. Ibid., 216; 108.

27. James Joyce, *Ulysses* (New York: Vintage, 1990), 221.

28. Ibid., 225.

29. Ibid., 225–226.

30. Ibid., 234.

31. Ibid., 225.

32. Ibid., 230.

33. Ibid., 231.

34. Ibid., 226.

35. Ibid., 224.

36. Ibid., 233.

37. Frasca, "Sim Sin City."

38. Immanuel Kant, "Perpetual Peace: A Philosophical Sketch," in *Perpetual Peace and Other Essays,* 110.

39. See Michel Foucault, *Discipline and Punish* (New York: Vintage, 1995).

Chapter 12

1. Katie Dean, "Gaming: Too Cool for School?" *Wired News,* January 15, 2001, http://www.wired.com/news/culture/0,1284,40967,00.html/.

2. Http://www.gamestudies.org/.

3. Espen Aarseth, "Computer Game Studies, Year One," *Game Studies* 1, no. 1 (2001). Available at http://www.gamestudies.org/0101/editorial.html/.

4. Susanne Lohmann, "Darwinian Medicine for the University," in *Governing Academia,* ed. Ronald G. Ehrenberg (Ithaca: Cornell University Press, 2003), 77.

5. Interestingly, Microsoft Corp was a primary evangelist and architect of SOAP, a non-proprietary standard.

6. Http://www.google.com/apis/index.html/.

7. Http://www.amazon.com/gp/browse.html/ref=sd_allcat_ws/103-7007929-2315857 ?node=3435361/.

8. Anthony C. Picardi and Laurie A. Seymore, "U.S. Web Services Market Anaysis, 2002," *IDC Research* (Decmber 2002).

9. Michel Serres, *The Parasite,* trans. Lawrence R. Schehr (Baltimore: Johns Hopkins University Press, 1982), 3.

10. Taylor, *The Moment of Complexity,* 204.

11. Mark C. Taylor and Esa Saarinen, *Imagologies: Media Philosophy* (New York: Routledge, 1994).

12. Taylor, *The Moment of Complexity,* 241.

13. Bill Readings, *The University in Ruins* (Cambridge, Mass.: Harvard University Press, 1996), 175.

14. Badiou, *Infinite Thought,* 79.

15. Ibid., 82.

16. Ibid.

17. Taylor, *The Moment of Complexity,* 254.

18. Ibid.

19. Ibid., 260.

20. Despite the objections I raise below, *Virtual U* is a not-for-profit endeavor that distributes the source code for its engine for free, inviting experimentation, improvement, or alteration.

21. Http://www.theesa.com/facts/top_10_facts.php/.

Bibliography

Written Works

Aarseth, Espen. *Cybertext: Perspectives on Ergodic Literature.* Baltimore: Johns Hopkins University Press, 1997.

———. "Computer Game Studies, Year One." *Game Studies* 1, no. 1 (2001). Http://www.gamestudies.org/0101/editorial.html/.

Aarseth, Espen, Staffan Björk, Jan Klabbers, Solveig Marie Smedstad, and Lise Sunnana. "What's in a Game?—Game Taxonomies, Typologies, and Frameworks." In *Proceedings of Level Up, Digital Games Research Conference,* ed. Marinka Copier and Joost Raessens. Utrecht: Universiteit Utrecht, 2003.

Antoniou, Grigoris, and Frank van Harmelen. *A Semantic Web Primer.* Cambridge, Mass.: MIT Press, 2003.

Apollinaire, Guillaume. *Alcools.* Trans. Donald Revell. Hanover: University Press of New England, 1995.

———. *Calligrames.* Paris: Gallimard, 1966.

Aristotle. *Metaphysics.* Trans. Joe Sachs. New York: Green Lion Press, 1999.

Arnold, Ken, and James Gosling. *The Java Programming Language.* Reading, Mass.: Addison-Wesley, 1998.

Badiou, Alain. *Briefings on Existence: A Transitory Ontology.* Trans. Norman Madarasz. Albany: State University of New York Press, 2003.

———. *Conditions.* Paris: Seuil, 1992.

———. *L'etre et l'événement.* Paris: Seuil, 1988.

———. *Gilles Deleuze: The Clamor of Being.* Trans. Louise Burchill. Minneapolis: University of Minnesota Press, 2000.

———. *Infinite Thought.* Trans. and ed. Oliver Feltham and Justin Clemens. New York: Continuum, 2003.

———. "Politics and Philosophy." *Angelaki* 3, no. 3 (1998): 113–133.

———. "Que pense le poème?" In *L'art est-il une connaissance?* Ed. Roger Pol Droit. Paris: Le Monde Editions, 1993.

Barabasi, Albert-László. *Linked: The New Science of Networks.* Cambridge: Perseus, 2002.

Bardini, Thierry. *Bootstrapping: Douglas Engelbart, Coevolution, and the Origins of Personal Computing.* Palo Alto: Stanford University Press, 2000.

Barthes, Roland. *Image, Music, Text.* Trans. Stephen Heath. New York: Hill and Wang, 1978.

———. *Mythologies.* Trans. Annette Lavers. New York: Hill and Wang, 1972.

———. *The Pleasure of the Text.* Trans. Richard Miller. New York: Hill and Wang, 1975.

———. *S/Z.* Trans. Richard Miller. New York: Hill and Wang, 1974.

Bateson, Gregory. *Steps to an Ecology of Mind.* New York: Ballentine, 1972.

Baudelaire, Charles. *Œuvres Complètes.* Paris: Gallimard, 1968.

Benjamin, Walter. *The Arcades Project.* Trans. Rolf Tiedemann, Howard Eiland, and Kevin McLaughlin. New York: Belknap Press, 1999.

———. *Illuminations.* Trans. Harry Zohn. Ed Hannah Arendt. New York: Shocken, 1969.

Bergson, Henri. *Matter and Memory.* Trans. N. M. Paul. New York: Zone Books, 1990.

Berners-Lee, Tim. *Weaving the Web: The Original Design and Ultimate Destiny of the World Wide Web.* New York: Harper, 2000.

Bersani, Leo. *Baudelaire and Freud.* Berkeley: University of California Press, 1977.

Bittanti, Matteo, ed. *Doom: Giocare in prima persona.* Milan: Costa and Nolan, 2005.

Björk, Staffan, and Jussi Holopainen. *Patterns in Game Design.* Hingham, Mass.: Charles River Media, 2004.

Bleeker, Julian. "Urban Crisis: Past, Present, and Virtual." *Socialist Review* 25 (1995): 189–221.

Bloom, Harold. *The Anxiety of Influence.* Oxford: Oxford University Press, 1997.

Bogost, Ian. "Estetiche col marchio di fabbrica: alcune implicazioni dl design dei First-Person Shooters." In *Doom: Giocare in prima persona,* ed. Matteo Bittanti. Milan: Costa and Nolan, 2005.

———, Michael Mateas, Janet Murray, and Michael Nitsche. "Asking What Is Possible: The Georgia Tech Approach to Game Research and Education." *International Digital Media and Arts Association Journal* 1, no. 2 (spring 2005): 59–68.

Bolter, Jay David. *Writing Space: The Computer, Hypertext, and the History of Writing.* Hillsdale, N.J.: Lawrence Erlbaum, 1991.

———, and Richard Grusin. *Remediation: Understanding New Media.* Cambridge, Mass.: MIT Press, 1999.

Booch, Grady. *Object-Oriented Design with Applications.* Redwood City: Benjamin/Cummings, 1991.

Brown, Stephen. *Postmodern Marketing.* New York: Routledge, 1995.

Buchanan, Mark. *Nexus: Small Worlds and the Groundbreaking Science of Networks.* New York: W. W. Norton, 2002.

Buck-Morss, Susan. *The Dialectics of Seeing: Walter Benjamin and the Arcades Project.* Cambridge, Mass.: MIT Press, 1990.

Bukowski, Charles. *Betting on the Muse*. Santa Rosa: Black Sparrow Press, 1996.

Burnham, Van. *Supercade: A Visual History of the Videogame age, 1971–1984*. Cambridge, Mass.: MIT Press, 2001.

Butler, Joseph. *The Analogy of Religion*. New York: Everyman, 1906.

Butters, G. R. "Equilibrium Distributions of Sales and Advertising Prices." *Review of Economic Studies* 44, no. 3 (October 1977): 465–491.

Callahan, Paul. "What Is the Game of Life?" Math.com: Wonders of Math. Http://www .math.com/students/wonders/life/life.html/.

Callois, Roger. *Les jeux et les hommes. Le masque et le vertige*. Cher: Gallimard, 1967.

———. *Man, Play, and Games*. Trans. Meyer Barash. Chicago: University of Illinois Press, 2001.

Cantor, Georg. *Contributions to the Founding of the Theory of Transfinite Numbers*. New York: Dover, 1955.

Chisholm, Roderick. "The Loose and Popular and the Strict and Philosophical Senses of Identity." In *Perception and Personal Identity: Proceedings of the 1967 Oberlin Colloquium in Philosophy*, ed. Norman Grimm and Robert Care, 82–106. Cleveland: Press of Case Western Reserve University, 1969.

Cialdini, R., and D. Schroeder. "Increasing Compliance by Legitimizing Paltry Contributions: When Even a Penny Helps." *Journal of Personality and Social Psychology* 34 (1976): 590–598.

Clayton, Sue. "Cracking the Box Office Genome." *Wired* (August 2003): 52.

Cohen, Abraham. *Everyman's Talmud: The Major Teachings of the Rabbinic Sages*. New York: Schocken, 1995.

Cooper, James Fenimore. *The Deerslayer*. New York: Bantam, 1991.

———. *The Last of the Mohicans*. New York: Penguin, 1986.

———. *The Pathfinder*. New York: Signet, 1993.

————. *The Pioneers.* New York: Signet, 1996.

————. *The Prairie.* New York: Penguin, 1987.

Crawford, Chris. *The Art of Computer Game Design.* New York: Osborne, 1984.

————. *Chris Crawford on Game Design.* New York: New Riders, 2003.

Culin, Stewart. *Games of the North American Indians.* New York: Dover, 1975.

————. *Korean Games, with Notes on the Corresponding Games of China and Japan.* New York: Dover, 1991.

Culler, Jonathan. *Literary Theory: A Very Short Introduction.* New York: Oxford University Press, 1997.

Darwin, Charles. *The Origin of Species.* New York: Grammercy, 1995.

Davis, Martin. *Engines of Logic: Mathematicians and the Origin of the Computer.* New York: W. W. Norton, 2000.

Dawkins, Richard. *The Selfish Gene.* Oxford: Oxford University Press, 1990.

————. *Unweaving the Rainbow: Science, Delusion, and the Appetite for Wonder.* New York: Houghton Mifflin, 1998.

Dean, Katie. "Gaming: Too Cool for School?" *Wired News,* January 15, 2001. Http://www.wired.com/news/culture/0,1284,40967,00.html/.

de Certau, Michel. *The Practice of Everyday Life.* Trans. Steven Rendall. Berkeley: University of California Press, 2002.

Debord, Guy. *Society of the Spectacle.* Detroit: Black and Red, 1983.

Deleuze, Gilles. *Expressionism in Philosophy: Spinoza.* Trans. Martin Joughlin. New York: Zone Books, 1992.

————. *Kant's Critical Philosophy.* Trans. High Tomlinson and Barbara Habberjam. Minneapolis: University of Minnesota Press, 1984.

————. *The Logic of Sense.* Trans. Mark Lester. Ed. Constantin V. Boundas. New York: Columbia University Press, 1990.

————. *Spinoza: Practical Philosophy.* Trans. Robert Hurley. San Francisco: City Lights Books, 1988.

————, and Félix Guattari. *Anti-Oedipus.* Trans. Robert Hurley, Mark Seem, and Helen R. Lane. Minneapolis: University of Minnesota Press, 1983.

————. *A Thousand Plateaus.* Trans. Brian Massumi. Minneapolis: University of Minnesota Press, 1987.

Deleuze, Gilles, and Claire Parnet. *Dialogues.* New York: Columbia University Press, 1977.

DeMaria, Rusel, and Johnny L. Wilson. *High Score! The Illustrated History of Electronic Games.* Berkeley: McGraw Hill, 2002.

Denzin, Norman K., and Yvonna S. Lincoln, eds. *The Handbook of Qualitative Research.* Thousand Oaks, Calif.: Sage, 2005.

Derrida, Jacques. *Archive Fever: A Freudian Impression.* Trans. Eric Prenowitz. Chicago: University of Chicago Press, 1996.

————. *Limited, Inc.* Trans. Samuel Weber et al. Evanston: Northwestern University Press, 1972.

————. *Margins of Philosophy.* Trans. Alan Bass. Chicago: University of Chicago Press, 1984.

————. *Of Grammatology.* Trans. Gayatri Chakravorty Spivak. Baltimore: Johns Hopkins University Press, 1976.

————. *Writing and Difference.* Trans. Alan Bass. Chicago: University of Chicago Press, 1980.

Ducheneaut, Nicolas, Robert J. Moore, and Eric Nickell. "Designing for Sociability in Massively Multiplayer Games: An Examination of the 'Third Places' of SWG." In *Other Players,* ed. Jonas Heide Smith and Miguel Sicart. Copenhagen: IT University of Copenhagen, 2004. Available at http://www.itu.dk/op/papers/ducheneaut_moore_nickell.pdf/.

Durkheim, Emile. *Elementary Forms of the Religious Life.* Trans. Karen E. Fields. New York: Free Press, 1995.

"EA Facing Possible Class Action Suit." *Game Daily,* November 12, 2004. Http:// biz.gamedaily.com/features.asp?article_id=8323/.

Eco, Umberto. *The Role of the Reader.* Bloomington: Indiana University Press, 1979.

———. *A Theory of Semiotics.* Bloomington: Indiana University Press, 1976.

Ehrenberg, Ronald G., ed. *Governing Academia.* Ithaca: Cornell University Press, 2003.

Eliot, T. S. *The Waste Land and Other Poems.* New York: Harcourt Brace, 1934.

Erdős, Paul, Ronald L. Graham, and Jaroslav Nesetril, eds. *The Mathematics of Paul Erdős.* New York: Springer, 1996.

Eskelinen, Markku. "Cybertext Theory and Literary Studies: A User's Manual." *Electronic Book Review.* Http://www.altx.com/ebr/ebr12/eskel.htm/.

———. "The Gaming Situation." *Game Studies* 1, no. 1 (July 2001). Http://www .gamestudies.org/0101eskelinen/.

Euler, Leonhard. *Introduction to the Analysis of the Infinite,* book I. Trans. John D. Blanton. New York: Springer, 1988.

———. *Introduction to the Analysis of the Infinite,* book II. Trans. John D. Blanton. New York: Springer, 1989.

Flaubert, Gustave. *Madame Bovary.* Paris: Flammarion, 1986.

———. *Madame Bovary.* Trans. and ed. Paul de Man. New York: W. W. Norton, 1965.

Forrester, Jay W. *Urban Dynamics.* New York: Wright Allen, 1969.

Foucault, Michel. *Discipline and Punish.* New York: Vintage, 1995.

———. "What Is an Author?" Trans. Josue V. Harari. In *Textual Strategies: Perspectives in Post-Structuralist Criticism,* ed. Josue V. Harari, 141–160. New York: Cornell University Press, 1980.

Frasca, Gonzalo. "Ideological Videogames: Press Left Button to Dissent." *IGDA The Ivory Tower* (November 2003). Http://www.igda.org/columns/ivorytower/ivory_Nov03 .php/.

———. "Ludologists Love Stories Too: The Role of Narrative in Videogames." In *Proceedings of Level Up, Digital Games Research Conference,* ed. Marinka Copier and Joost Raessens. Utrecht: Universiteit Utrecht, 2003.

———. "Ludology Meets Narratology: Similitude and Differences between (Video)-games and Narrative." *Parnasso* 3 (1999): 365–371.

———. "The Sims: Grandmothers Are Cooler than Trolls." *Game Studies* 2, no. 1 (July 2002). Http://www.gamestudies.org/0201/frasca/.

———. "Sim Sin City: Some Thoughts about Grand Theft Auto 3." *Game Studies* 3, no. 2 (2003). Http://www.gamestudies.org/0302/frasca/.

———. "Simulation 101: Simulation versus Representation." Http://www.ludology .org/articles/sim1/simulation101.html/.

———. "Simulation versus Narrative: Introduction to Ludology." In *Game Theory Reader,* ed. Mark Wolf and Bernard Perron. New York: Routledge, 2003.

———. "Videogames of the Oppressed: Videogames as a Means for Critical Thinking and Debate." Master's thesis, The Georgia Institute of Technology, 2001.

Frege, Gottlob. *Philosophical and Mathematical Correspondence.* Chicago: University of Chicago Press, 1980.

Freud, Sigmund. *The Interpretation of Dreams.* Trans. and ed. James Strachey. New York: Avon, 1965.

Friedman, Ted. "Semiotics of Sim City." *First Monday* 4 (April 1999). Http://www .firstmonday.dk/issues/issue4_4/friedman/.

Gadamer, Hans Georg. *Truth and Method.* Trans. Joel Weinsheimer and Donald G. Marshall. New York: Continuum, 1989.

Gardener, Martin. "Mathematical Games: The Fantastic Combinations of John Conway's New Solitaire Game 'Life.'" *Scientific American* 233 (October 1970): 120–123.

Garfinkel, Simson. *Database Nation: The Death of Privacy in the 21st Century.* Cambridge: O'Reilly, 2001.

Gell-Mann, Murray. *The Quark and the Jaguar: Adventures in the Simple and the Complex.* New York: W. H. Friedman, 1994.

Genette, Gerard. "Structuralisme et critique litteraire." *L'arc* 26 (1965): 30–44.

Gibson, William. *Neuromancer.* New York: Ace Books, 2003.

Gladwell, Malcolm. *The Tipping Point.* Boston: Little, Brown, 2000.

Gleik, James. *Chaos: Making a New Science.* New York: Viking Penguin, 1987.

———. *What Just Happened: A Chronicle from the Information Frontier.* New York: Knopf, 2002.

Goldstine, H. H. *The Computer from Pascal to von Neumann.* Princeton: Princeton University Press, 1972.

Grannovetter, Mark. "The Strength of Weak Ties." *American Journal of Sociology* 78 (1973): 1360–1380.

———. "The Strength of Weak Ties: A Network Theory Revisited." *Sociological Theory* 1 (1983): 203–233.

Griffin, Matthew B., and S. M. Herrmann. "An Interview with Friedrich A. Kittler about Cultural Studies in Germany, Literature in the Age of Technology, and the Blind Spot in Media Theory." Auseinander 1, no. 3 (1995). Http://www.artematrix.org/kittler/kit1.htm/.

Guardian. "The Man Who Lost His Past." September 6, 2004. Http://film.guardian.co.uk/features/featurepages/0,4120,1298104,00.html/.

Guare, John. *Six Degrees of Separation.* New York: Vintage, 1990.

Guattari, Félix. *Chaosmosis.* Trans. Paul Bains and Julian Pefanis. Indianapolis: Indiana University Press, 1995.

"Haitians Protest Game at Wal-Mart." *Miami Herald.* December 15, 2003. Http://www.miami.com/mld/miamiherald/7492312.htm/.

Halasz, Gabor, ed. *Paul Erdıs and His Mathematics.* New York: Springer-Verlag, 2002.

Hallward, Peter. *Badiou: A Subject to Truth.* Minneapolis: University of Minnesota Press, 2003.

Harman, Graham. *Tool-Being: Heidegger and the Metaphysics of Objects.* Chicago: Open Court, 2002.

Hayles, N. Katherine. *How We Became Posthuman.* Chicago: University of Chicago Press, 1999.

———. "What Cybertext Theory Can't Do." *Electronic Book Review.* Http://www.altx .com/ebr/riposte/rip12/rip12hay.htm/.

Heidegger, Martin. *Being and Time.* Trans. Richard Polt and Gregory Fried. Albany: State University of New York Press, 1996.

———. *The Question Concerning Technology and Other Essays.* Trans. William Lovitt. New York: Harper, 1977.

Holland, Eugene. *Baudelaire and Schizoanalysis.* Cambridge: Cambridge University Press, 1993.

Huizinga, Johan. *Homo ludens.* New York: Beacon, 1971.

Hume, David. *An Enquiry Concerning Human Understanding.* New York: Hackett, 1993.

Hunt, John. *Smalltalk and Object Orientation: An Introduction.* London: Springer-Verlag, 1997.

Hurford, James. "Language beyond Our Grasp: What Mirror Neurons Can, and Cannot, Do for the Evolution of Language." In *Evolution of Communication Systems: A Comparative Approach,* ed. Kimbrough Oller and Ulrike Griebel, 297–313. Cambridge, Mass.: MIT Press, 2004.

Hutcheon, Linda. *The Politics of Postmodernism.* New York: Routledge, 1989.

Ifrah, Georges. *The Universal History of Computing.* Trans. E. F. Harding. New York: John Wiley, 2001.

"Inside the Engine: Half-Life 2." *Maximum PC* (August 2003): 28–29.

Jakobson, Roman. *On Language.* Ed. Linda R. Waugh. New York: Belknap, 1995.

Jameson, Fredric. *Postmodernism, or the Cultural Logic of Late Capitalism.* Durham: Duke University Press, 1991.

Jenkins, Henry. "Game Design as Narrative Architecture." In *First Person: New Media as Performance, Story, and Game,* ed. Noah Wardrip-Fruin and Pat Harrigan, 118–130. Cambridge, Mass.: MIT Press, 2004.

Johnson, Stephen. *Interface Culture: How New Technology Transforms the Way We Create and Communicate.* San Francisco: HarperEdge, 1997.

Joyce, James. *Ulysses.* New York: Vintage, 1990. (First published 1922.)

Juul, Jesper. "Games Telling Stories? A Brief Note on Games and Narratives." *Game Studies* 1(1) (2001). Http://www.gamestudies.org/0101/juul-gts/.

———. "The Open and the Closed: Games of Emergence and Games of Progression." *Computer Games and Digital Cultures.* Http://www.jesperjuul.dk/text/openandtheclosed .html/.

Kermode, Frank. *The Sense of an Ending.* New York: Oxford University Press, 1967.

Kant, Immanuel. *Critique of Judgment.* Trans. Werner S. Pluhar. Indianapolis: Hackett, 1987. (First published 1790.)

———. *Perpetual Peace and Other Essays.* Trans. Ted Humphrey. Cambridge: Hackett, 1983.

Kauffman, Stuart. *The Origins of Order: Self-Organization and Selection in Evolution.* Oxford: Oxford University Press, 1993.

Kellner, Douglas. *Media Culture.* New York: Routledge, 1995.

Kittler, Friedrich. *Discourse Networks 1800/1900.* Trans. Michael Metteer. Palo Alto: Stanford University Press, 1990.

———. *Gramophone, Film, Typewriter.* Trans. Geoffrey Winthrop-Young and Michael Wutz. Palo Alto: Stanford University Press, 1986.

———. *Literature, Media, Information Systems.* Ed. John Johnston. Amsterdam: G+B Arts, 1997.

Kochen, Manfred, and Brenda Dervin, eds. *The Small World: A Volume of Recent Research Advances Commemorating Ithiel de Sola Pool, Stanley Milgram, Theodore Newcomb.* Westport, Conn.: Greenwood Publishing, 1989.

Koster, Raph. *A Theory of Fun for Game Design.* Scottsdale, Ariz.: Paraglyph Press, 2005.

Kreps, David M. *Game Theory and Economic Modeling.* Oxford: Clarendon, 1990.

Kuhn, Thomas. *The Structure of Scientific Revolutions.* Chicago: University of Chicago Press, 1970.

Lacan, Jacques. *Ecrits.* Trans. Alan Sheridan. New York: W. W. Norton, 1977.

————. *The Four Fundamental Concepts of Psycho-Analysis.* Trans. Alan Sheridan. New York: W. W. Norton, 1978.

————. *Seminar XI: The Four Fundamental Concepts of Psychoanalysis.* Trans. Alan Sheridan. New York: W. W. Norton, 1981.

Landow, George. *Hypertext: The Convergence of Contemporary Critical Theory and Technology.* Baltimore: Johns Hopkins University Press, 1992.

————. *Hypertext 2.0.* Baltimore: Johns Hopkins University Press, 1996.

————, ed. *Hyper/Text/Theory.* Baltimore: Johns Hopkins University Press, 1994.

Leibniz, Gottfried Willhelm Freidrich. *Philosophical Essays.* Ed. D. Garber and R. Areiw. New York: Hackett, 1989.

"Lessons of the California Supermarket Strike." *Proletarian Revolution* 70 (spring 2004). Http://www.lrp-cofi.org/PR/strikePR70.html/.

Lettvin, Jonathan, Humberto Maturana, Warren McCulloch, and W. H. Pitts. "What the Frog's Eye Tells the Frog's Brain." *Proceedings of the IRE* 47 (1959).

Lévi-Strauss, Claude. *The Raw and the Cooked.* New York: Harper Collins, 1969.

————. *The Savage Mind.* Chicago: University of Chicago Press, 1968.

Lohmann, Susanne. "Darwinian Medicine for the University." In *Governing Academia,* ed. Ronald G. Ehrenberg, 71–90. Ithaca: Cornell University Press, 2003.

Loyall, A. Bryan, and Joseph Bates. "Real-time Control of Animated Broad Agents." In *Proceedings of the 15th Annual Conference of the Cognitive Science Society.* Hillsdale, N.J.: Lawrence Erlbaum, 1993.

Luhmann, Niklas. *Social Systems.* Trans. John Bednarz, Jr., and Dick Baecker. Palo Alto: Stanford University Press, 1995.

Lundgren, Sus, and Staffan Björk. "Game Mechanics: Describing Computer-Augmented Games in Terms of Interaction." In *Proceedings of TIDSE 2003 Technologies for Interactive Storytelling and Digital Entertainment.* Darmstadt: Springer-Verlag, 2003.

Lyotard, Jean François. *The Postmodern Condition: A Report on Knowledge.* Trans. Geoff Bennington and Brian Massumi. Minneapolis: University of Minnesota Press, 1984.

MacLean-Foreman, John. "An Interview with Will Wright." *Gamasutra,* May 1, 2001. Http://www.gamasutra.com/features/20010501/wright_01.htm/.

Mandelbrot, Benoit. *Fractals: Form, Chance, and Dimension.* San Francisco: Freeman, 1977.

Manovich, Lev. *The Language of New Media.* Cambridge, Mass.: MIT Press, 2002.

Markley, Robert, ed. *Virtual Realities and Their Discontents.* Baltimore: Johns Hopkins University Press, 1996.

Massumi, Brian. *A User's Guide to Capitalism and Schizophrenia: Deviations from Deleuze and Guattari.* Cambridge, Mass.: MIT Press, 1992.

Mateas, Michael, and Andrew Stern. "Architecture, Authorial Idioms, and Early Observations of the Interactive Drama *Façade.*" Carnegie Mellon Technical Reports, December 2002.

Mathews, Ryan, and Watts Wacker. *The Deviant's Advantage: How Fringe Ideas Create Mass Markets.* New York: Crown, 2002.

Mayfield, Ross. "Social Network Models." March 30, 2003. Http://radio.weblogs.com/0114726/2003/03/30.html/.

Mäyrä, Frans. "The Quiet Revolution: Three Theses for the Future of Game Studies." *DiGRA Hard Core* 1, no. 3 (March 2005). Http://www.digra.org/article.php?story=20050327082956955/.

McCloud, Scott. *Understanding Comics.* New York: Perennial, 1994.

McLuhan, Marshall. *Understanding Media.* New York: Times Mirror, 1963.

McShaffry, Mike. *Game Coding Complete.* Scottsdale, Ariz.: Paraglyph Press, 2003.

Mehran, Sir Alfred. *The Terminal Man.* London: Transworld, 2004.

Milgram, Stanley. *Obedience to Authority.* London: Tavistock, 1974.

———. "The Small World Problem." *Physiology Today* 2 (1967): 60–67.

Moravec, Hans. *Mind Children: The Future of Robot and Human Intelligence.* Cambridge, Mass.: Harvard University Press, 1988.

Morgenstern, Oskar, and John von Neumann. *The Theory of Games and Economic Behavior.* Princeton: Princeton University Press, 1980.

Moulthrop, Stuart. "Rhizomes and Resistance: Hypertext and the Dreams of a New Culture." In *Hyper/Text/Theory,* ed. George P. Landow, 299–319. Baltimore: Johns Hopkins University Press, 1994.

Muller, Pierre-Alain. *Instant UML.* Birmingham, U.K.: Wrox Press, 1997.

Murray, Janet H. *Hamlet on the Holodeck: The Future of Narrative in Cyberspace.* Cambridge, Mass.: MIT Press, 1997.

Nakhimovsky, Alexander, and Tom Myers. *Google, Amazon, and Beyond: Creating and Consuming Web Services.* Berkeley: Apress, 2004.

Negroponte, Nicholas. *Being Digital.* New York: Knopf, 1995.

Nelson, Theodore. *Literary Machines.* Sausalito: Mindfull Press, 1992.

Nicholls, Peter. *Modernisms: A Literary Guide.* Berkeley: University of California Press, 1995.

Nyce, James, ed. *From Memex to Hypertext: Vannevar Bush and the Mind's Machine.* Burlington: Academic Press, 1992.

Oller, Kimbrough, and Ulrike Griebel, eds. *Evolution of Communication Systems: A Comparative Approach.* Cambridge, Mass.: MIT Press, 2004.

Otto, Rudolf. *The Idea of the Holy.* Oxford: Oxford University Press, 1958.

Pearce, Celia. "Sims, Battle Bots, Cellular Automata, God, and Go: An Interview with Will Wright." *Game Studies* 2, no. 1 (July 2002). Http://www.gamestudies.org/0201/pearce/.

————. "Towards a Game Theory of Games, in First Person." In *First Person: New Media as Story, Performance, and Game,* ed. Noah Wardrip-Fruin and Pat Harrigan, 143–153. Cambridge, Mass.: MIT Press, 2004.

Peirce, Charles Sanders. "What Is a Sign?" In *The Essential Peirce: Selected Philosophical Writings 1893–1913,* ed. The Peirce Edition Project, 4–10. Bloomington and Indianapolis: Indiana University Press, 1998.

The Peirce Edition Project, ed. *The Essential Peirce: Selected Philosophical Writings 1893–1913.* Bloomington and Indianapolis: Indiana University Press, 1998.

Penny, Simon, ed. *Critical Issues in Electronic Media.* Albany: State University of New York Press, 1995.

Perez, Rolando. *On Anarchy and Schizoanalysis.* Brooklyn, N.Y.: Autonomedia, 1990.

Perlman, William S. *No Bull Object Technology for Executives.* Cambridge: Cambridge University Press, 1999.

Picardi, Anthony C., and Laurie A. Seymore. "U.S. Web Services Market Anaysis, 2002." *IDC Research* (December 2002).

Plato. *Complete Works.* Ed. J. Cooper and D. S. Hutchison. New York: Hackett, 1997.

Poster, Mark. *The Mode of Information: Poststructuralism and Social Context.* Cambridge: Polity Press, 1990.

Postman, Neil. *Amusing Ourselves to Death: Public Discourse in the Age of Show Business.* New York: Penguin, 1986.

————. *Technopoly.* New York: Vintage, 1993.

Powers, Richard. *Galatea 2.2.* New York: Picador, 2004.

Propp, Vladimir. *Morphology of the Folktale.* Trans. Laurence Scott. Austin: University of Texas Press, 1968.

Pynchon, Thomas. *The Crying of Lot 49.* New York: Perennial, 1999.

Queneau, Raymond. *Cent mille milliards de poèmes.* Paris: Gallimard, 1961.

Ramachandran, V. S. *Phantoms in the Brain: Probing the Mysteries of the Human Mind.* New York: Perennial, 1999.

Readings, Bill. *The University in Ruins.* Cambridge, Mass.: Harvard University Press, 1996.

Rheingold, Howard. *Smart Mobs: The Next Social Revolution.* New York: Perseus, 2002.

———. "View: Is Friendster Changing Our Friendships?" *Wired* 12, no. 1 (January 2004).

Rifkin, Jeremy. *The Age of Access: The New Culture of Hypercapitalism Where All of Life Is a Paid-For Experience.* New York: Tarcher, 2000.

Rizzolatti, Giacomo, and Michael A. Arbib. "Language within Our Grasp." *Trends in Neuroscience* 21 (1998): 188–194.

Rizzolatti, Giacomo, and Laila Craighero. "The Mirror-Neuron System." *Annual Review of Neuroscience* 27 (2004): 169–192.

Russell, Bertrand. *The Principles of Mathematics.* New York: W. W. Norton, 1996. (First published 1903.)

Ryan, Marie-Laure. *Possible Worlds: Artificial Intelligence and Narrative Theory.* Bloomington: Indiana University Press, 1991.

Salen, Katie, and Eric Zimmerman. *Rules of Play.* Cambridge, Mass.: MIT Press, 2004.

Saussure, Ferdinand de. *Course in General Linguistics.* Trans. Roy Harris. La Salle, Ill.: Open Court, 1983.

Sawyer, Ben. "The Next Ages of Game Development." *Adrenaline Vault,* September 30, 2002. Http://www.avault.com/developer/getarticle.asp?name=bsawyer1/.

Schank, Roger. *Tell Me a Story: Narrative and Intelligence.* Chicago: Northwestern University Press, 1995.

Schechter, Bruce. *My Brain Is Open: The Mathematical Journeys of Paul Erdős.* New York: Simon and Schuster, 2000.

Serres, Michel. *The Parasite.* Trans. Lawrence R. Schehr. Baltimore: Johns Hopkins University Press, 1982.

Simpson, Jake. "Scripting and Sims 2: Coding the Psychology of Little People." In *Proceedings of the Game Developers Conference.* San Francisco: Gomputer Game Group, 2005.

Spinoza, Benedict de. *The Ethics and Other Works.* Ed. and trans. Edwin Curley. Princeton: Princeton University Press, 1994.

Starr, Paul. "Policy as a Simulation Game." *American Prospect* 5, no. 17 (March 21, 1994). Http://www.prospect.org/print/V5/17/starr-p.html/.

Starr, Peter. *Logics of Failed Revolt: French Theory after May '68.* Palo Alto: Stanford University Press, 1995.

Steig, William. *Shrek!* New York: Farrar, Straus, and Giroux, 1993.

Sutton-Smith, Brian. *The Ambiguity of Play.* Cambridge, Mass.: Harvard University Press, 1997.

Taylor, David A. *Object-Oriented Technology: A Manager's Guide.* Reading, Mass.: Addison-Wesley, 1990.

Taylor, Mark C. *The Moment of Complexity: Emerging Network Culture.* Chicago: University of Chicago Press, 2002.

————, and Esa Saarinen. *Imagologies: Media Philosophy.* New York: Routledge, 1994.

Thélot, Jérôme. *Baudelaire violence et poésie.* Paris: Gallimard, 1992.

Thom, Fred. "*Amélie* (Review)." *La plume noire.* Http://www.plume-noire.com/movies/reviews/amelie.html/.

Tsu, Sun. *The Art of War.* New York: Dover, 2002.

Turing, Alan M. "Computing Machinery and Intelligence." In *Computers and Thought,* ed. E. A. Feigenbaum and Julian Feigenbaum. New York: McGraw Hill, 1963.

Turkle, Sherry. *Life on the Screen.* New York: Simon and Schuster, 1995.

———. "Seeing through Computers." *American Prospect* 8, no. 31 (March 1997). Http://www.prospect.org/print/V8/31/turkle-s.html/.

Turner, Mark. *The Literary Mind: The Origins of Thought and Language.* Oxford: Oxford University Press, 1998.

Varela, Francisco, and Humberto Maturana. "Autopoiesis: The Organization of a Living System, Its Characterization, and a Model." *Biosystems* 5 (1974): 187–196.

Von Bertalanffy, Ludwig. *General Systems Theory: Foundations, Development, Applications.* New York: George Brazilier, 1976.

von Neumann, John. *Theory of Self-Reproducing Automata.* Champaign: University of Illinois Press, 1966.

Waldrop, M. Mitchell. *Complexity: The Emerging Science at the Edge of Order and Chaos.* New York: Simon and Schuster, 1992.

Wardrip-Fruin, Noah, and Pat Harrigan, eds. *First Person: New Media as Performance, Story, and Game.* Cambridge, Mass.: MIT Press, 2004.

Wellman, Barry, ed. *Networks in the Global Village: Life in Contemporary Communities.* New York: Westview Press, 1999.

Wiener, Norbert. *Cybernetics, or Control and Communication in the Animal and the Machine.* Cambridge, Mass.: MIT Press, 1948.

Wolf, Mark J. P., and Bernard Perron, eds. *Game Theory Reader.* New York: Routledge, 2003.

Wolfram, Stephen. "Cellular Automata." *Los Alamos Science* 9 (fall 1983): 2–21.

———. *Cellular Automata and Complexity: Collected Papers.* Cambridge: Perseus, 1993.

———. "Cellular Automata as Models of Complexity." *Nature* 311 (October 1984): 419–424.

————. *A New Kind of Science.* Champaign, Ill.: Wolfram Media, 2002.

Wuchty, Stefan. "Scale-Free Behavior in Protein Domain Networks." *Molecular Biology and Evolution* 18 (2001): 1694–1702.

Žižek, Slavoj. *Looking Awry: An Introduction to Jacques Lacan through Popular Culture.* Cambridge, Mass.: MIT Press, 1991.

————. *The Ticklish Subject.* London: Verso, 1999.

Film and Television

The A-Team. Created by Stephen J. Cannell. 1983.

Battleship Potemkin. Dir. Sergei Eisenstein. Mosfilm, 1925.

A Beautiful Mind. Dir. Ron Howard. Universal, 2001.

Casablanca. Dir. Michael Curtiz. Warner Bros., 1942.

Charlie's Angels. Dir. Joseph "McG" Nichol. Columbia Tri-Star, 2000.

The Godfather. Dir. Martin Scorsese. Paramount, 1972.

Harry Potter and the Chamber of Secrets. Dir. Chris Columbus. Warner Bros., 2002.

Harry Potter and the Goblet of Fire. Dir. Mike Newell. Warner Bros., 2005.

Harry Potter and the Prisoner of Azkaban. Dir. Alfonso Cuarón. Warner Bros., 2004.

Harry Potter and the Sorcerer's Stone. Dir. Chris Columbus. Warner Bros., 2001.

Indiana Jones and the Last Crusade. Dir. Steven Spielberg. Paramount, 1989.

Indiana Jones and the Temple of Doom. Dir. Steven Spielberg. Paramount, 1984.

Le fableux destin d'Amélie Poulin (English title: *Amélie*). Dir. Jean-Pierre Jeunet. Miramax, 2001.

The Lord of the Rings (trilogy). Dir. Peter Jackson. New Line, 2001–2003.

Macgyver. Created by Lee David Zlotoff. 1985.

The Matrix. Dir. Andy Wachowski and Larry Wachowski. Warner Bros., 1999.

Metropolis. Dir. Fritz Lang. 1927.

My Trip to Liberty City. Written and dir. Jim Munroe. Http://www.nomediakings.org/mytrip.htm/.

Raiders of the Lost Ark. Dir. Steven Spielberg. Paramount, 1981.

Shrek. Dir. Andrew Adamson, Vicky Jenson. DreamWorks SKG, 2001.

Six Degrees of Separation. Dir. Fred Schepisi. MGM, 1993.

Spider-Man. Dir. Sam Raimi. Columbia Tristar, 2002.

Star Wars. Dir. George Lucas. Twentieth Century Fox, 1977.

The Terminal. Dir. Steven Spielberg. DreamWorks SKG, 2004.

Titanic. Dir. James Cameron. Paramount, 1997.

Tombés du ciel (English title: *Lost in Transit*). Dir. Philippe Loiret. 1993.

Toy Story. Dir. John Lasseter. Pixar/Disney, 1995.

Waterworld. Dir. Kevin Reynolds. Universal, 1995.

When Harry Met Sally. Dir. Rob Reiner. MGM, 1989.

Videogames, Software, and Other Digital Works

Acclaim. *Crazy Taxi.* SEGA, 1999.

Alias Systems. *Maya.* 2000.

Atari. *Combat.* 1978.

———. *E.T.* 1982.

———. *Pong.* 1972.

———. *Star Wars.* 1983.

Avid Technology. *SoftImage.* 2002–.

Baer, Ralph. *Odyssey.* Magnavox, 1972.

Bally/Midway. *Tron.* 1982.

Bioware. *Aurora Editor.* Infogrames, 2002.

———. *Neverwinter Nights.* Infogrames, 2002.

Blank, Mark, and Dave Lebling. *Zork.* Infocom, 1981.

Creo. *Six Degrees.* 2002–2004.

Criterion Software. *RenderWare.* 1993–2004.

Crowther, Willie, and Don Woods. *Adventure.* 1976.

Digitalmill. *Virtual U.* Alfred P. Sloan Foundation, 2002–2003.

Discreet. *3D Studio MAX.* Autodesk, 1992.

The Ecademy, Ltd. *Ecademy USA.* Http://www.ecademy.com/.

Epic Megagames. *Unreal Tournament.* Infogrames, 2000.

Friendster, Inc. *Friendster.* 2002–2004. Http://www.friendster.com/.

Havok.com, Inc. *Havok Physics.* 1998–.

Higinbotham, William A. *Tennis for Two.* 1958.

iD Software. *Doom.* iD Software, 1993.

———. *Quake.* Activision, 1996.

———. *Quake 2.* Activision, 1998.

———. *Quake 2 Engine.* 2001.

Ion Storm. *Deus Ex.* Eidos Interactive, 2000.

Kee Games. *Tank.* 1974.

Kinematic. *9/11 Survivor.* 2003. Http://www.kinematic.org/.

Konami. *Metal Gear.* Konami, 1987.

———. *Metal Gear Solid.* Konami, 1998.

LinkedIn, Ltd. *LinkedIn.* 2003–2005. Http://www.linkedin.com/.

Looking Glass Studios. *Thief.* Eidos Interactive, 1998.

Mateas, Michael, and Andrew Stern. *Façade.* InteractiveStory.net, 2005. Http://www
.interactivestory.net/.

Maxis. *Sim Ant.* Electronic Arts, 1993.

———. *Sim City.* Electronic Arts, 1989.

———. *Sim Health.* Electronic Arts, 1994.

———. *The Sims.* Electronic Arts, 2000.

———. *The Sims: Hot Date.* Electronic Arts, 2001.

———. *The Sims 2.* Electronic Arts, 2004.

Meetup, Inc. *Meetup local interest groups.* 2002–. Http://www.meetup.com/.

Microsoft Corp. Microsoft Windows. 1985–.

———. Microsoft Word. 1983–.

Newsgaming.com. *September 12.* 2003. Http://www.newsgaming.com/games/index12
.htm/.

Nintendo. *Donkey Kong.* Nintendo, 1981.

———. *The Legend of Zelda.* Nintendo, 1984.

———. *The Legend of Zelda: The Wind Waker.* Nintendo, 2003.

———. *The Legend of Zelda II: Adventure of Link.* Nintendo, 1989.

———. *Mario Bros.* Nintendo, 1983.

———. *Super Mario Bros.* Nintendo, 1985.

On, Josh. *Antiwargame.* 2001. Http://www.antiwargame.org/.

Origin Systems. *Ultima Online.* Electronic Arts, 1997.

Pandemic Studios. *Full Spectrum Warrior.* THQ, 2004.

Persuasive Games. *Activism.* 2004. Http://www.activismgame.com/.

———. *The Howard Dean for Iowa Game.* Dean for America, 2003. Http://www .deanforamericagame.com/.

———. *Take Back Illinois.* 2004. Http://www.takebackillinoisgame.com/.

Pazhintov, Alexey. *Tetris.* Spectrum Holobyte, 1986.

QL2 Software. *WebQL.* QL2, 2001–.

Raven Software. *HeXen 2.* Activision, 1997.

Red Storm Entertainment. *Tom Clancy's Rainbow Six.* Majesco, 1998.

Rockstar Games. *Grand Theft Auto: San Andreas.* Take Two Interactive, 2004.

———. *Grand Theft Auto: Vice City.* Take Two Interactive, 2002.

———. *Grand Theft Auto III.* Take Two Interactive, 1999.

Ryze, Ltd. *Ryze business networking.* 2002–. Http://www.ryze.com/.

Schleiner, Anne-Marie, et al. *Velvet-Strike,* 2002. Http://www.opensorcery.net/velvet-strike/.

Sony Online Entertainment. *Star Wars Galaxies: An Empire Divided.* LucasArts, 2003.

Taito. *Space Invaders.* Taito, 1977.

3D Pipeline. *BioChemFX.* 2001–.

Ubi Soft. *Tom Clancy's Splinter Cell.* Ubi Soft, 2002.

U.S. Army. *America's Army.* 2002–. Http://www.americasarmy.com/.

Valve Software. *Half-Life.* Sierra Online Entertainment, 1998.

———. *Half-Life Counter Strike.* Vivendi Universal, 2001.

———. *Half-Life 2.* Vivendi Universal, 2004.

Verant Interactive. *EverQuest.* 989 Studios, 1999.

Wolfram Research. Mathematica. 1985–.

Index

Index

Index